Computers in Architecture

Computers in Architecture
Tools for design

Edited by François Penz

Longman

Longman Group UK Ltd,
Longman House, Burnt Mill, Harlow,
Essex CM20 2JE, England
and Associated Companies throughout the world.

ISBN 0 582 09386 4

First published 1992

British Library Cataloguing in Publication Data
A CIP record for this book is available from the British Library

Designed and typeset by JBD, London

Typeset in Garamond 3 and BC Folio Condensed

Set in Linotronic: Alphabet Set, London

Produced by Longman Group (FE) Limited
Printed in Hong Kong

Contents

Acknowledgements

The papers which appear in this book were presented at the International Symposium on Computers in Architecture, held at Jesus College on 11th and 12th September 1990.

Invited representatives of most schools of Architecture in the UK as well as a number of practices constituted the bulk of the audience apart from the speakers themselves.

The main theme of the Symposium was 'Tools for Design' investigating the impact of computers on the design process in Architecture.

This is a very broad topic which was of interest both to academics and to practitioners who were for once assembled together.

There was also a session on research highlighting future developments in this area.

This Symposium was sponsored by Apple UK to whom I am very grateful for their generosity and I would like to thank Melanie Baxter in particular for being at the origin of this project.

I would also like to thank Philippa Clements from Longman for her diligence and thoroughness as well as Jill Bennett for her patience in handling the design of the book.

Finally I would like to thank Sue, Emma and Nicolas for their help, love and encouragement.

François Penz

Contributors

Robert Aish
YRM Architects and Planners, London
Matthew Bourne
Department of Architecture, University of Cambridge
André G. P. Brown
School of Architecture and Building Engineering, University of Liverpool
Alan H. Bridges
Department of Architecture and Building Science, University of Strathclyde
Albert Gassull
Universitat Politéchnica de Catalunya, Barcelona
John Hare
Arup Associates, London
David Harriss
Nicholas Grimshaw & Partners, London
Frank Horton
School of Architecture and Building Engineering, University of Liverpool
Mark Leslie
Leslie Fox Albin, London
M. Locatelli
University of Milan
Earl Mark
School of Architecture and Planning, Massachusetts Institute of Technology
G. Mazzochi
University of Milan
William J. Mitchell
Harvard University Graduate School of Design
R. Morandi
University of Milan
Helen Mulligan
Cambridge Architectural Research Limited, Cambridge
François Penz
Department of Architecture, University of Cambridge
John Pringle
Michael Hopkins & Partners, London
Patrick Purcell
MIT Media Laboratory, Cambridge, Massachusetts
Antony Radford
The University of Adelaide
Paul Richens
The Martin Centre, Department of Architecture, University of Cambridge
Simon Ruffle
Cambridge Architectural Research Limited, Cambridge
Juan Carlos Sabater
Universitat Politéchnica de Catalunya, Barcelona
Jean-Louis Schulmann
Image Digitale, Paris
Philip Steadman
Centre for Configurational Studies, Faculty of Technology, The Open University, Milton Keynes
Patricia Wright
Medical Research Council, Applied Psychology Unit, Cambridge

Section 1: Computers in Education

Introduction

François Penz

The Department of Architecture at Cambridge together with the Martin Centre has been involved with CAD research for over 20 years, in particular with the creation of Applied Research Cambridge. The University itself pioneered some of the early work in computers in the 1950s and 1960s. Given this glorious past it therefore seemed fitting that our Department should organize a conference on 'Computers in Architecture', although CAD teaching in the Department of Architecture has only recently been introduced as part of our undergraduate course. It is within this educational context that we were first associated with Apple UK as users of their products. And it is this so-called 'user friendly' environment which allowed us to introduce computers in our life-drawing classes, that illustrated trying to mix 'the poetic with the science' which is very much part of the philosophy of our school. This way of teaching illustrates an almost 'Darwinian' view of teaching which fits within its immediate context; in other words CAD teaching evolves very much as part of a wider context and to mix computers and art is no accident within our Department; but it would be unthinkable in other schools because their particular context would be very different. This point is obviously very important because it highlights the fact that CAD teaching is not an isolated topic which could follow an international or even national curriculum and that it is ultimately about architecture – hence the title of the book *Computers in Architecture*.

The original aim of the symposium was to explore CAD as a design tool and this is very well covered in the educational section, possibly because of the nature of the work in schools where the emphasis is with the early part of the design process and not so much with the production phase. Experiments about the impact of computers on the creativity process are illustrated by the chapters from Cambridge and Liverpool. Typological work of architectural precedents is illustrated by Sabater and Gassull and by Bridges whereas Mitchell and Steadman concentrate on the range of computer applications in architectural and design education. On the practical side Hare, Harriss and Pringle illustrate CAD in the working environment and its productivity aspect very clearly. Leslie and Aish, in contrast, demonstrate an approach which involves the computer at an earlier stage in the design process.

Purcell from the MIT Media Laboratory gives a long-term account of 'future developments', whilst Ruffle and Mulligan, Mazzochi and Schulmann show the way to use computers and programming with simple tools such as HyperCard, but always with designers in mind. Richens stands back and highlights the future with great enthusiasm for neural network research and integrated CAD systems. Mark from MIT leads the way in the field of computer animation and video within the educational context of project design.

But whichever way we may want to plan the future, and it always turns out to be different from what was expected, we shall have to keep the designer in mind; and above all we shall have to remind ourselves that ultimately all this work is about architecture and presumably about providing ourselves and future generations with a better environment. But will it?

Tools For Design: A Controlled Experiment Comparing Computer Work With Traditional Hand Drawings

François Penz & Matthew Bourne, Department of Architecture, University of Cambridge
Patricia Wright, Medical Research Council, Applied Psychology Unit, Cambridge

Background

Computers were recently introduced in the Department of Architecture at the University of Cambridge. The CAD teaching is organized through lecture courses for both first and second year undergraduates as well as a series of workshops.

Originally the Department had acquired in 1985 a powerful computer system which proved too complicated for students to use profitably. Given this background and in reaction to the mainframe – like mentality Apple Macintosh computers were introduced in our Department in 1989. One of the first exercises carried out with our new 'Macs' was to bring together the life-drawing classes and the computers, which was originally an attempt to bring together the 'arts and the sciences', very much in the spirit of the current philosophy of the Department. It was also a way of introducing computers at undergraduate level in a 'non-threatening' way, simply making the point that it was 'another pencil', another medium.

The life-drawing classes

The life–drawing classes have been running in our Department for a number of years and are set up as a vertical studio (open to all students within the Department) organized by Brenda Mayo, a Cambridge-based artist.

The life class aims to promote the idea of drawing as a physical activity. The activity of drawing is as important as the end product. To begin the class, numerous drawings are made with chunks of charcoal on A1 paper. The students work standing at tables or squatting on the floor and several computer screens are dotted around in the life room (Figure 1.1) forming nodules of activity which generate their own energy. Certainly if traditional drawing technique is fairly physical, by contrast the computing activity is very 'sedentary' and the energy which it may generate in the room is entirely concentrated on the screen. Emphasis is placed on mark making when working with traditional tools, whereas when working with computers there is no way of applying various degrees of pressure. On the other hand the software allows variation in the contrast and intensity of the 'electronic charcoal' as a function of the speed at which the cursor moves. The images are built through an accumulation of marks made in direct response to the figure in space.

Each drawing aims to reflect the essence of the pose, to match the vitality of the figure in space and to communicate something of the model's personality. The drawings are pinned up at the end of the session and discussed by everyone. The screens are then simply turned back and become part of the general display. There are no facilities for printing on the spot and this was found to be the best way of operating. To be noted also is the fact that the computer drawings on the screen are only a fraction of the size of the traditional charcoal ones, which makes comparisons rather difficult. It is only at the printing stage that the computer pictures can then be enlarged and presented side by side (Figure 1.3).

Working with a different medium (the computer) probably means developing new techniques, although to start with the students try simply to reproduce existing skills. They produce drawings which often could have been done by pencil (Figure 1.4) but later on may try to take advantage of exploring this new tool in a more adventurous way. Although we would work in black and white or 'grey scale' most of the time there were some attempts to use colour.

The students involved in this experiment are mostly

Figure 1.1
The Life-drawing class with the Macintoshes dotted around

Figure 1.2
Photograph showing an occasion when the computer was brought down as part of a crit

Figures 1.4
Example of life drawings on the Macintosh using simple techniques, not unlike the traditional line drawings

Figure 1.3
A printed and enlarged computer drawing next to a hand drawn one - same pose and same angle of vision but different students

first and second year undergraduates and attend the classes on a voluntary basis. Most of them attend the life drawing classes to practice and enhance their traditional drawing skills and are not particularly interested in using computers, certainly to start with. Many of them have never used computers before and are then given five to ten minutes of tuition to start with. Towards the end of the sessions some students are quite happy to start with traditional techniques and then swap over onto the computer for a while, but it is by no means a 'mainstream activity' and is probably regarded as mildly eccentric.

The drawings were all done with the mouse, using Macintoshes (SEs and one Mac II) using various paint programs.

Comments

This activity is seen really as a way to introduce students to using the computers in a non-threatening environment. To be drawing a life model is in itself something special which helps students to concentrate. It is certainly very different from a 'nature morte' exercise. Consequently most students would quickly forget that they are drawing with a computer and concentrate on the task at hand and in doing so get over the first hurdle in coming to grips with the technology. The educational benefit is certainly the most interesting aspect of this work, probably far more than the results themselves.

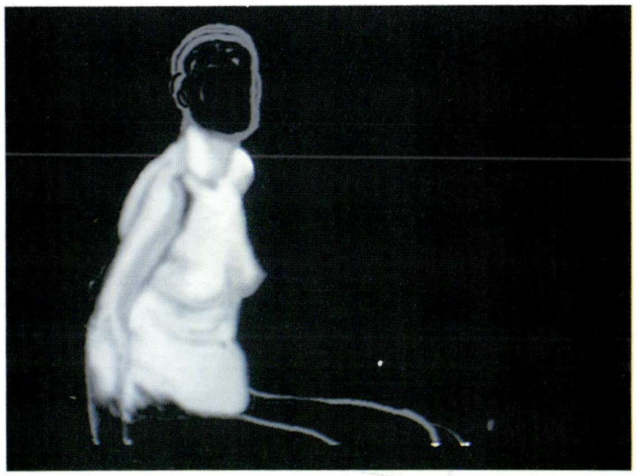

Figures 1.5-1.7
Examples of drawings which start to show a more adventurous use of the medium

Figures 1.8 and 1.9
Drawing using a 24 bit colour program, drawing executed in a single pose of 40 minutes

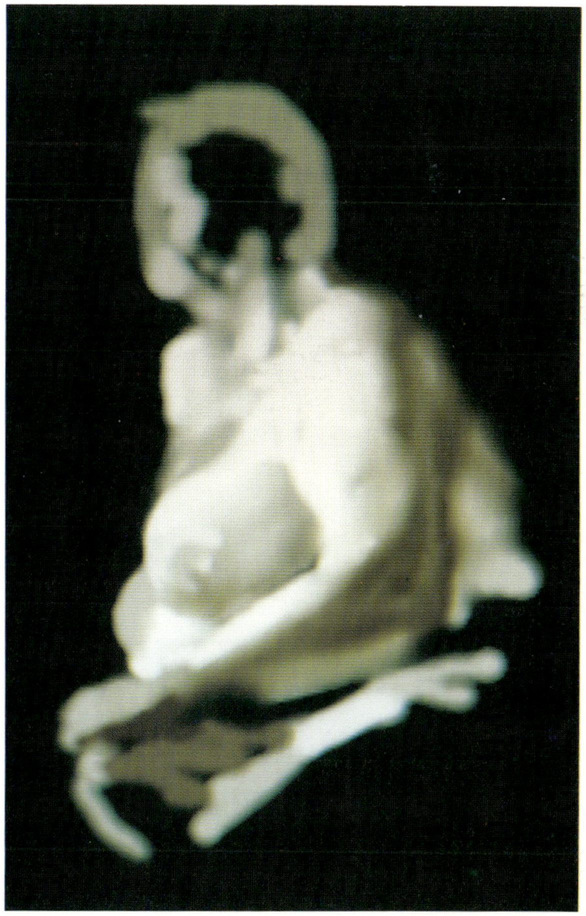

Figures 1.10 and 1.12
In the images shown here I have deliberately avoided the use of such sterile techniques as ray-tracing (the bane of creative architectural representation, whose soul-destroying call for 5-figure pseudo-reality constructs a universe out of painstakingly-lit and exquisitely-rendered blocks of plastic) instead, developing in the earlier pieces a complicated sequence of mechanically/hand rendered stages that result in an image that captures much of the expressive power of traditional painted renderings. The tautology of these digitally processed images that seem to rely on their sympathy with water colour, or gauche effects to find their expressive potential does not escape me now; and throughout my experiments I have sought to establish a more appropriate mode of stylization, one that evolves from the computers position in and contribution to the history of imaging technology. In many of the pictures, you will see the creation of exaggerated depths of field, sharp-focusing and broad blurring of ranges to create a dynamic sense of interest and attention within the traditionally very isotropic perspective of computer renderings

Figures 1.11 & 1.13
Part of M J Bourne 1st year portfolio - internal spaces for a house in Hampstead. The perspectives were produced in ModelShop and rendered in PixelPaint

Figure 1.12

Studio work

Part of the background of the teaching takes place in the studio as well as in the out space (Figure 1.2) and is best described by Matthew Bourne, a third year undergraduate.

"A year of thought on the topic of CAD has forced me to admit my original unalloyed enthusiasm, and my absorption in the techniques of image-creation failed to directly engage what I have come to consider the central questions focused around the use of CAD as a component of Architectural education. In this respect, I was perhaps inevitably falling into the broader conceptual malaise endemic to the thinking of software-developers and increasingly the software users, characterised by the mismatch between the intentions of architectural education and CAD methodologies. Whilst the former seeks to invest sensibilities of thought and intention, through formal and conceptual experimentation, the latter's aim – as it is presently conceived – is to facilitate straightforward design 'production' – operating from the logical (and flawed) assumption that the 'user' knows exactly what they want to create and how they wish to do it. Thence the adoption of the 'neutral' toolbox, which is specifically non-architectural in its application to the problems of formal generation around an architectural brief. As such, its neutrality as a tool of production is subverted, being instead methodologically-rigged by the software designers highly limited approach to 'problem' recognition. All subsequent 'solutions' depend upon the initial phrasing of intention – and when that intention regardless of the specific merits of any ultimate purpose is invariably to knock-out a minimalist stand-alone 500k application that operates as neatly and anonymously as possible behind the Apple façade to allow maximum 'flexibility' of end use, one develops the situation we are now familiar with, where two such radically different projects as three-dimensional modelling and flat-draughting are reduced to the same operation +/- a notional dimension. The whole potential of architectural design within the 'virtual' environment, is being systematically telescoped into a highly circumscribed set of formal options.

Thus arises the ill-favoured spectre of the CAD-tool as a 'tool without qualities' – a software conception with no instinct for its own direction or possible contribution, other than a bargain-basement mimesis of traditional hand draughting techniques (lacking most of the intuitive advantages of those techniques due to the catastrophic failure of a sense of scale). This notion of computer-aided Architectural design found its currency as a minimum requirements brief in the face of the severely limiting technologies of the 1960s, subsequently proving to be a winning formula in the territories of engineering design – where design of course consists of a straight formal manipulation and analysis – and for reasons of laziness or lack of imagination, has lagged over into present day conceptions of computer-aided architectural design, despite the radically different hardware environment around us.

Whilst latterday sophistications of this reductive notion of CAD produce ever more powerful tools for information production, the critically *creative* areas of the design 'process' (rather than the *productive*) are being ignored or dismissed as topical interests for modern IT innovations. The worlds of semantics, associations and exploration during the design stage are not benefiting from the new 'multi-media' technologies, whose serious application at the early phases of a design, would offer the designer a vast range of resources – from interactive

Figure 1.13

Figure 1.14

Figures 1.14 & 1.15
Examples which show the evolution from Figures 1.11 & 1.13. Here the images are heavily remdered and look less like computer pictures

background video footage to the site, to ambient and directional acoustic feedback, to the visualisation of the metaphoric or generative themes dominating the projects evolution – combining to define a purely original conception of the rôle of a computer-aided design 'tool' within a world increasingly shaped by these dynamic representational media. However, we can see the huge potential of multimedia similarly facing the risk of creative impoverishment at the hands of the Reductivists. Multimedia has been firmly conceived as a tool of presentation (production), as an automation within the digital domain of conventional hand-worked animation techniques, or of film-editing techniques: and even at its most avant-garde and progressive edge, of interactive presentations and educational material, multi-media implementation risks being a closely scripted documentary over which the user might exert a degree of editorial control, but little true freedom for experimentation and genuine creative 'discovery'.

Of course being a student, the issues of creative exploration within a design are of greater importance to me than those of production information. For us, to a very real degree, the perspective image – that seed of *intent* – is the critical information expressed.

It is of sadness and frustration to me that modelling tools are of such limited breadth of conception – so ill-suited to the requirements of a non-formally oriented mode of thought, and that the raw power of the new multimedia resources might still be diverted away from their potentially inspirational contribution to the growing sensibility of the 'design-culture', and squandered on the 'Victorian' clockwork charade of laboriously prepared presentations, which make use of these new techniques as ends in themselves and as slick demonstrations of empty graphic style.

The selection of images from my portfolio collected in the pages of this article are a demonstration of the techniques I have employed and continue to develop, during the design conception stages of a project to harness the communicative power of the Macintosh.

The quality of image is emerging despite, or in defiance of, the methodologies insisted upon by the programs' implementations – as such, the nature of the image is a fiction: a persuasive vision of the support CAD could offer in terms of communication and a qualitative expression.

With similar experiments in animation through my designs, I hope to formulate and explore the possibilities of a much more subjective and volatile notion of a computer design space. One which is rooted in the continuity and vocabulary of experimentation in the photographic arts, and which possesses the flexibility to fuse with many of the other aspects of modern media technology not as a demonstration of technique, but as an ongoing exploration of itself within its subject."

Figure 1.15

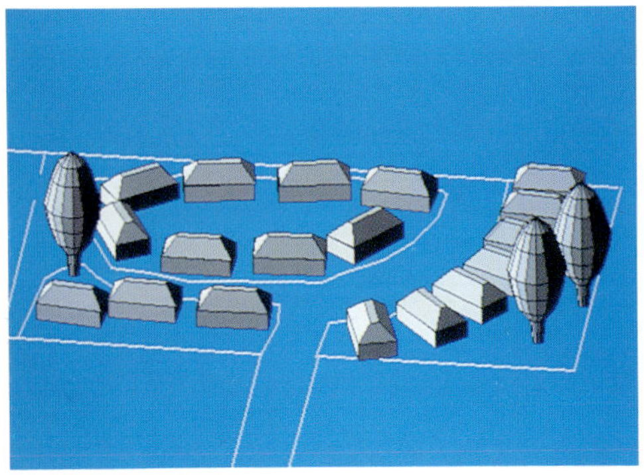

Figure 1.16
Housing layout: a basic unit is simply replicated

Figure 1.17
Line plot also at a large scale

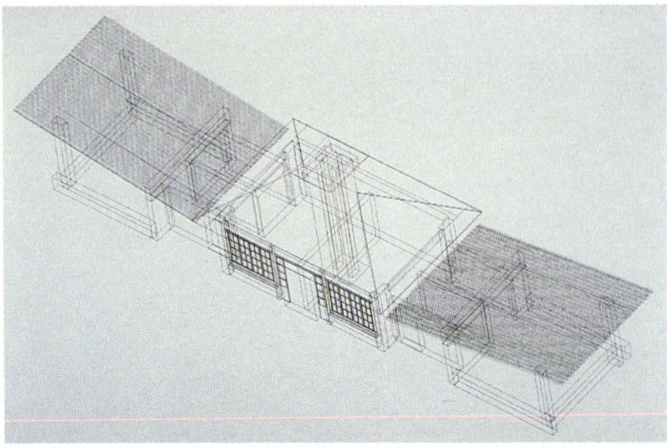

Figure 1.18
Example of a layout which takes into account half of the neighbourhood!

Figure 1.19
This image originally produced in ModelShop and was then pasted in a paint program as part of a collage

The controlled experiment

This background and the life-drawing classes in particular were our first attempt at the exploration of a much wider concern into 'the influence of computers on the design process'. This interest became formalised into a research project jointly set up between the Department of Architecture and the Medical Research Council, Applied Psychology Unit, Cambridge.

The aim of the project was to compare the effect of responding to a design brief by hand drawings and by computer work. To increase the generality of our findings it was decided to involve the entire second year undergraduate teaching in the Department of Architecture for a whole week. The exercise was introduced as a normal studio project where the material produced during the week was to be included in students' portfolios for assessment at the end of the academic year.

During that week all the lectures were cancelled and the students spent half of their time working with the computers and the other half at their drawing boards located in the Department. These locations were all close to the classroom where the computers had been set up, and it was possible for those supervising the exercise to circulate easily among the students.

The brief

All students responded to two design briefs: one brief (Pavilions) concerned the adaptation of some existing buildings[1] for a new use by the physically handicapped; the other (Field) concerned a housing development on an adjacent field intended to finance the adaptation. It was intended that the work should be on some housing aspect as it was the chosen theme of the studio for that term. It was also intentional to introduce new elements for the students such as working with existing structures and also thinking about accommodation for the disabled. In other words it was presented as a project of architectural and design interest and not simply as a 'computer' exercise. The point about two briefs was to compare very different types of design work operating at different scales. Finally all students displayed their work at the end of the week at a 'crit' class.

Hardware and software

The main classroom in the Architecture Department was rearranged to accommodate 18 Mac II computers with 13 inch screens. These were loaned for the exercise by Apple UK and were installed and maintained by the local Apple Centre. The machines were arranged in clusters of four or five machines in an attempt to break the 'computer room' feel. This gave each student a reasonably sized working area to which he/she could return while working on the CAD phase of the exercise. All machines were networked to LaserWriters and Plotters which were in the same room.

The software chosen for the computer-based design was ModelShop. Students had been previously introduced to this three-dimensional drawing package during the lecture course and workshops. However general tuition about the Macs and ModelShop in particular were found to be essential throughout the week. Four tutors were on hand during that week and it was found to be extremely labour intensive!

The pavilion to be adapted was already modelled in ModelShop, as was the site for the housing layout exercise.

Design of the experiment

The contribution of the Applied Psychology Unit to this week-long CAD exercise was to devise the means of

[1] The Pavilions are part of the Roger Ascham site in Cambridge, perhaps one of the few remaining open-air movement school buildings in the country.

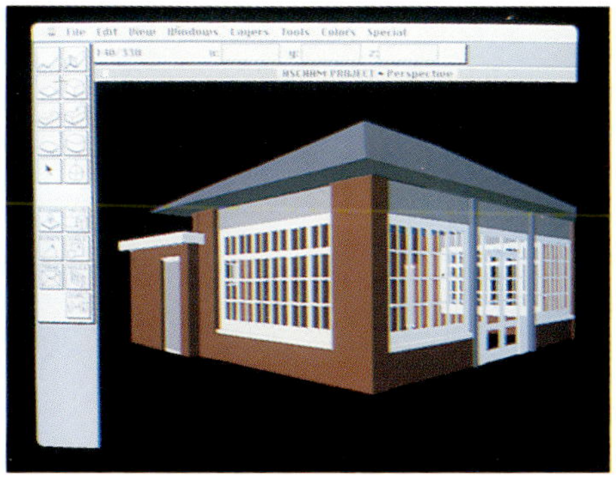

Figure 1.20
Original ModelShop model of the Pavilion

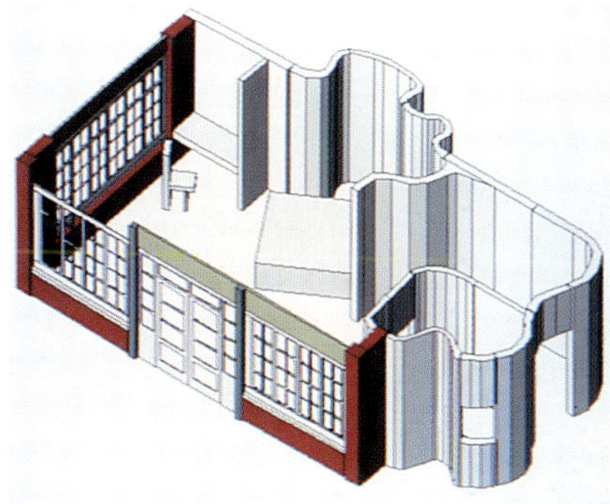

Figure 1.21
The original Pavilion being adapted: note the chair to give a sense of scale

measuring students' skills, attitudes and performance before during and after the exercise. Students' skills were assessed in several ways. Before the project started the students took part in a series of very short tests which enabled estimates of the following:

- copy drawing ability. A map of Florence had to be copied by hand and using MacPaint;
- ability to manipulate shapes mentally.
- general intellectual ability
- attitudes to CAD in architecture, assessed by a short questionnaire;
- skill at mousing, measured using a purpose-built HyperCard stack.

The purpose of these preliminary tests was to provide data that could be related to students' performance on the design briefs. These data would allow questions to be asked such as the following. Does skill in drawing matter for using CAD tools? Is the exercise measuring anything other than skill in learning new techniques? Does skill with CAD depend on the student's attitude?

During the week all students were allocated two briefs and were asked to create three designs for each. One brief dealt with redesigning the Pavilions and the other with the development of the adjacent Field. Half the students started with the Pavilions and half of this group used CAD while the others used traditional drawing techniques. Similarly for those who began with the Field brief, half used CAD and half used hand drawing. After the allotted two working days for the first brief, students changed to the other design brief and the other drawing medium. This counterbalancing ensured that when the data were pooled for the class as a whole the findings could not be due to artefacts e.g. that the first design was done with more care or one of the briefs was easier than the other. Throughout the week students recorded how long they spent working on each brief and any problems they encountered or other comments they wished to make.

After finishing the second brief, students completed two short questionnaires. One covered their attitude to the exercise and how much they had learned; the other dealt with characteristics of the software and hardware used. The designs produced by the students were independently graded by two of the teaching staff in the Department of Architecture. Any differences between them were discussed and a final mark out of 10 was allocated to each design. These marks, particularly those given for the brief done using CAD, were related to the measures obtained from the preliminary tests. Some of the questions which could be answered on the basis of these data are summarised below.

Figure 1.22
Bird's eye perspective printed in colour at a large scale

Figure 1.23
Colours were important to some students who enjoyed experimenting with it

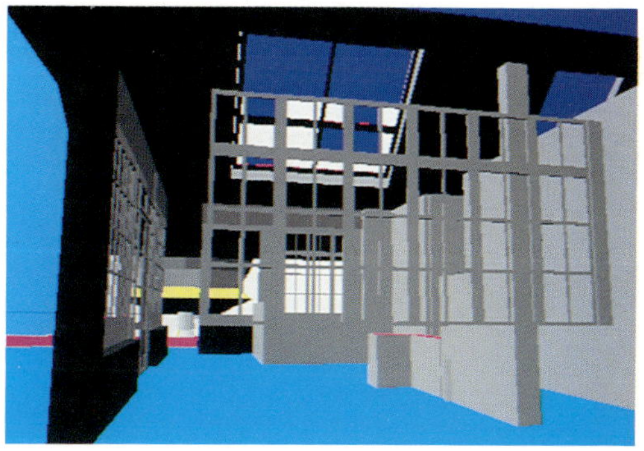

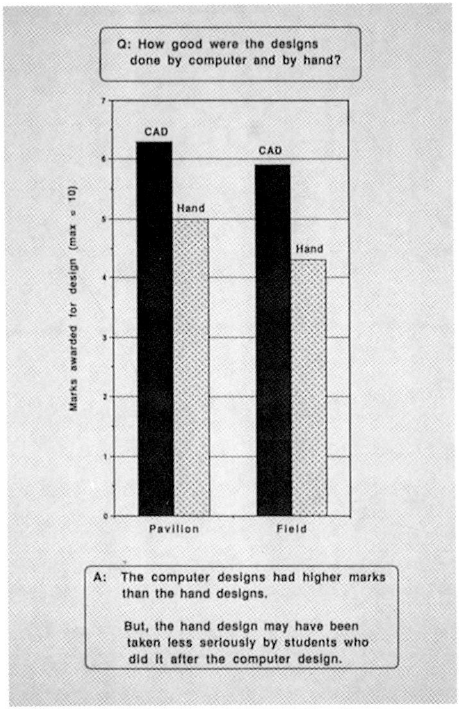

Figure 1.24
Summary of marks for designs by CAD and by hand

Figure 1.25
Creativity and CAD

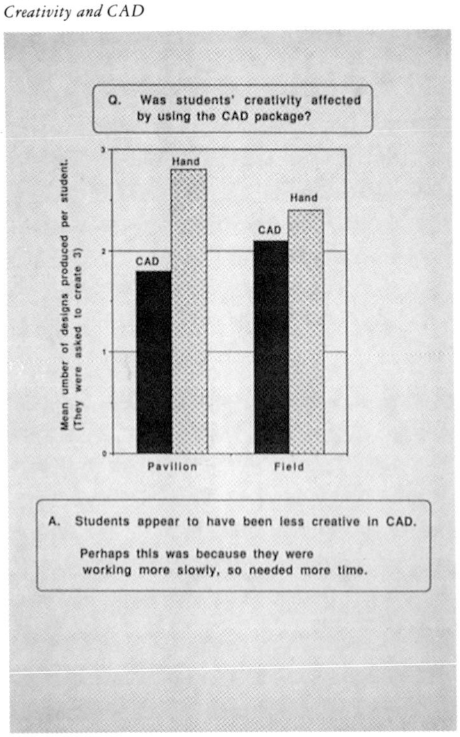

Results

Which skills were important for using CAD?

Figure 1.26 summarises the relation between the pre-test scores and the marks awarded for the CAD designs. It was found that copy drawing skill was indeed important. Those who could draw well tended to have

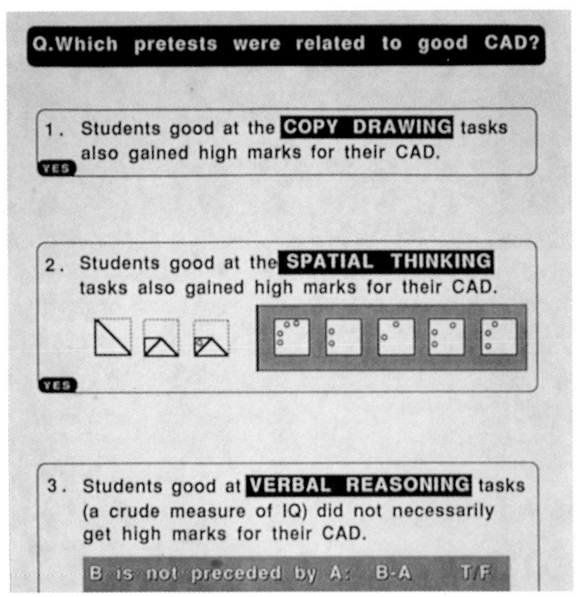

Figure 1.26
Pretests and CAD designs

high marks for their CAD design. Also important was the ability mentally to represent shapes, rotate them and think about them. However, the IQ measure used did not correlate with the quality of students' CAD designs. These data are encouraging because they suggest that the exercise is picking up factors which may be of long-term importance in the use of CAD rather than just being characteristic of the early learning of complex software.

How good were the designs done by hand and by computer?

Figure 1.24 shows that for both design briefs the marks awarded tended to be higher when the drawing was done on the computer rather than by hand. It must be borne in mind that the marking could not be done 'blind' to the drawing medium. Nevertheless these data give no reason for thinking that using the computer has impaired students' design skills. The value of the counterbalancing within the experiment becomes evident at this stage. It might have been possible that the higher marks gained by those redesigning the Pavilions on the computer could be the result of this group by chance being all the really bright students in the second year; yet these are the same students who did the Field by hand. So the replication of the higher CAD marks across the two design briefs makes it very unlikely that this is due to particular students being in one of the groups. However, there may have been an uncontrolled factor contributing to the lower marks for the hand designs. It was noticeable among those who started with CAD that some of the students felt a sense of anticlimax when they moved the hand drawn brief. Although the Department had made it clear that both briefs would be treated as part of their portfolio, some students may have put less effort into their designs done by hand.

Comments on the two briefs

The housing layout did not appear to produce very interesting solutions (Figure 1.16); indeed most students were satisfied to produce a basic unit which would then be copied as many times as necessary although there were some exceptions to that (Figures 1.18 and 1.19). The pavilion project did appear to be more inspired, however, also perhaps because it is more closely related to 'architecture' as opposed to a 'planning' exercise. Although the Pavilion exercise was found more 'satisfying' to the students, the housing layout was acknowledged as being 'easier'.

Comments on the hand-drawn brief

In general the hand-drawn part of the exercise was not taken as seriously as it should have been, mostly because the students were immersed into 'computer week' and somehow found it difficult to switch quickly from one to the other. Curiously it was also noted that most hand drawings looked very much like the computer-generated ones.

Was students' creativity affected by the design medium?

Work done at the Department of Typography at the University of Reading (Black, 1990) has suggested that students explore fewer alternative ideas, and in that sense are less creative, when working with computers than when working with pencils. One of the reasons for designing this experiment had been to see whether such restrictions would be found in another field of visual design. This is why students had been asked to submit three designs for each brief. The intention had been to see how divergent an individual's solutions were within each medium. Figure 1.25 shows that for both briefs students submitted more designs when drawing by hand than when using CAD. This does not necessarily mean that the students were less creative in their computer work. They may just have been working a little more slowly. However, because many students only submitted one CAD design, the intended examination of creativity was not possible.

Was the students' pattern of work affected by the design medium?

Figure 1.27 shows that the total amount of time spent working on CAD design was a little longer than that spent when working by hand. Indeed, while most students said they had enough time for the hand design work, several commented that they would have liked more time for the CAD work. Figure 1.28 shows that students claimed they spent much longer in a single work session when working on the computer than when working by hand. For hand drawing the average working period was about two hours, a little more for the Pavilions and a little less for the Field. However, when using CAD the claimed work period had lengthened to over three hours for the Pavilions. This may well have implications for creativity. If students take a break, they may return to their work with sharpened critical faculties or with new ideas. If students extend their working period they may persevere in chasing the same idea.

Did students learn much from the exercise?

In the debriefing questionnaire students were asked to give marks out of 10 for the amount they felt they had learned. Averaging across the entire class the mean rating was 7.9. It is possible to have a high average in spite of a minority who feel they learned little, but that was not the case with this exercise. Figure 1.31 shows the number of students who thought they learned a lot (rating of 7 or above) or learned only a little (rating of 4 or below). Clearly most students felt that they learned a lot. It may be of interest to note that a higher proportion of the women felt that they had learned a lot. 75% of the women gave ratings of 9 or 10 whereas only 40% of the men did. Of course, a reason for feeling

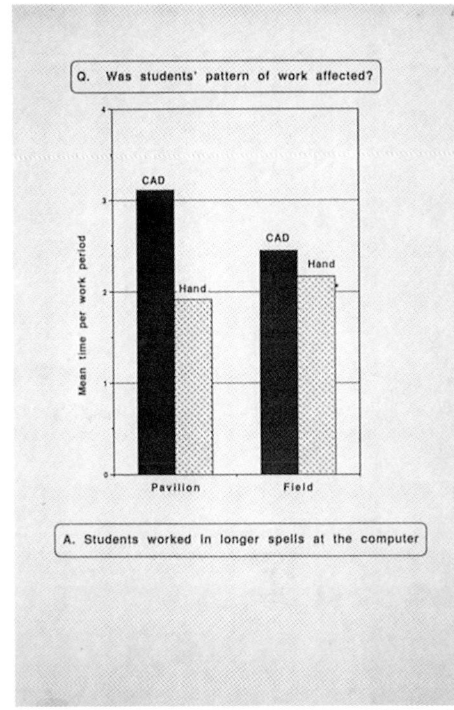

Figure 1.27
Pattern of Work (1)

Figure 1.28
Pattern of Work (2)

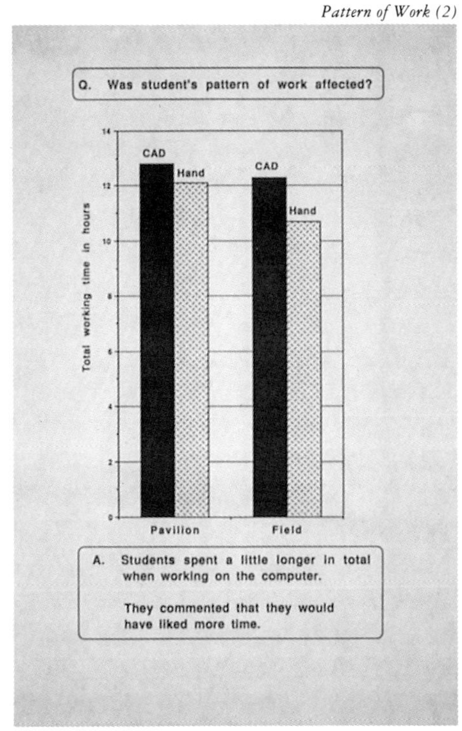

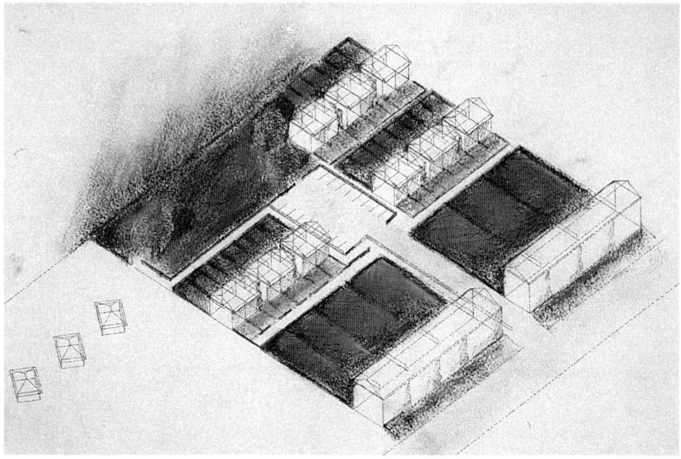

Figures 1.29 and 1.32
Two examples of computer plots being coloured and rendered by hand

that one did not learn a lot could be that one already knew a lot. This was undoubtedly the case for a few of the men.

Did men and women respond in similar ways to the exercise?

A comparison of men and women was not built into the counterbalancing of the experimental design. However, it was noticed on the pre-tests that the women had significantly slower speeds on the mousing tests. This suggested that they may have had less hands-on experience at using computers than the men. Therefore a post hoc analysis of their performance on the design briefs was undertaken. It was found that in the faculty assessment of quality of the CAD design (which was done with the full knowledge of who the designer was) ten students were given high marks of 7 or above. Of these ten students, nine were men. There could be many reasons for this but it should be noted that most of the women did the Field brief using CAD. Figure 1.24 has shown that the Field brief tended to receive lower scores than the Pavilion, irrespective of drawing medium.

What attitudes did students start and end with?

Before the exercise students thought that computer design would save time (the data shown in Figure 1.27 suggest that this was not the case), assist major changes, help create different views, require less drawing skill (but the data showed a positive correlation with drawing skill) and curtail their freedom. The latter expectation turned out to be correct. In the debriefing questionnaire 24 students reported that when using CAD they changed their working method and 23 said that they compromised their design decisions.

A different way of assessing student attitude to CAD was to ask them to rate how happy they would be to tackle specific design briefs by hand and by CAD. Figure 1.30 shows that most students were happy to tackle the proposed briefs by hand, but for each brief there was a group of students who felt that they would be very unhappy if they had to do it using CAD. Only for a brief concerned with redesigning an airport was the division of happy and unhappy students broadly similar for the two design media. This difference among the design topics raises questions about what sorts of briefs are most appropriate for introducing CAD to students.

In spite of the appearance of some unhappiness at using CAD on specific briefs, most students reported that their attitudes had become more favourable towards CAD as a result of the exercise (Figure 1.33).

Figure 1.30
Design briefs and CAD

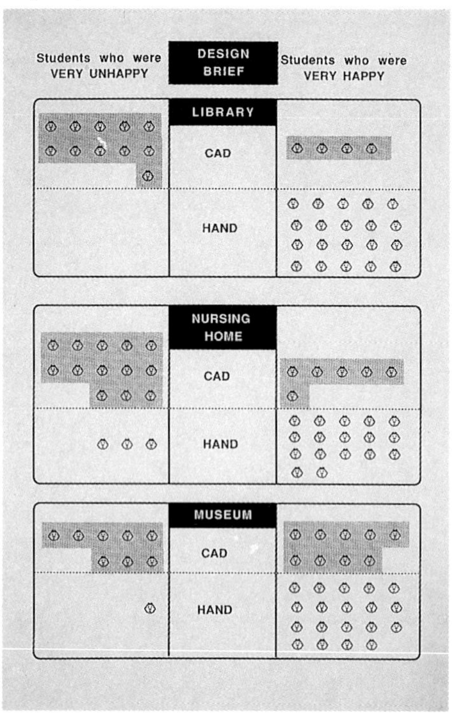

Figure 1.31

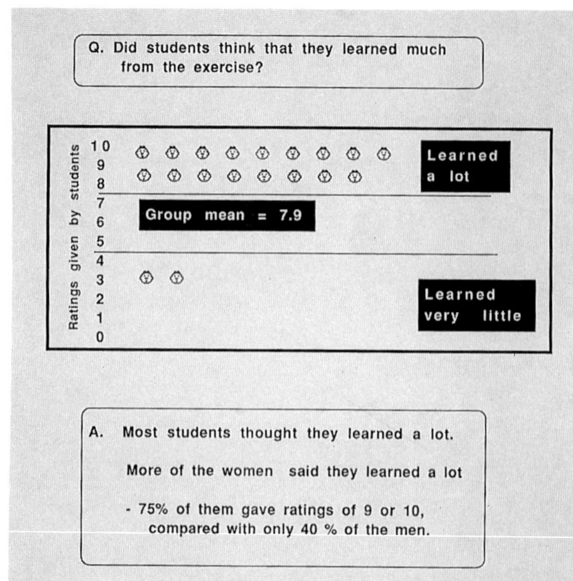

Figure 1.32

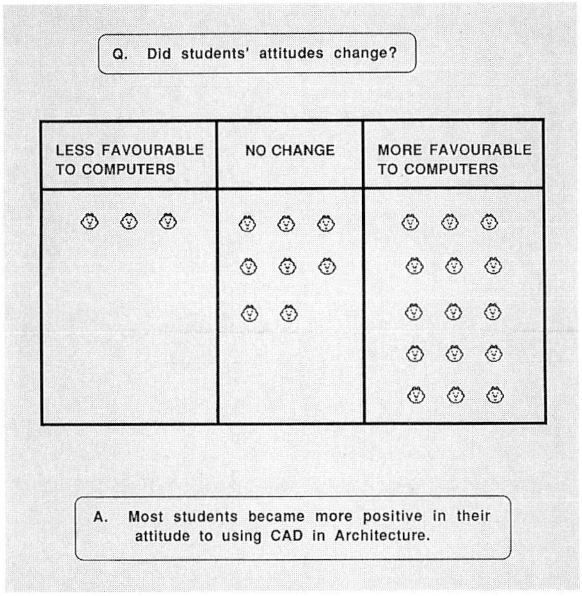

Figure 1.33
Student's attitude

Conclusions

The present study was a class exercise of only one week's duration, and used Macintosh computers not mainframe CAD packages. These characteristics need to be borne in mind when drawing conclusions from the study. Never-the-less four categories of conclusions seem warranted.

1 CAD and Creativity

Although it had been a major motivation behind this study, we still do not know what kind of influence CAD has on design creativity. The present data show that the pattern of students' work changes with the drawing medium used. So the possibility that this will influence design creativity cannot be lightly dismissed.

2 Teaching CAD

The experience gained from this exercise has raised several questions about the ways of teaching CAD to students.

- Some design briefs may be more suitable then others, e.g. larger-scale drawing may be easier for students;
- CAD might be introduced for part of the design process, rather than for all of it as it was here (see 4 below);
- Some kinds of skills appear to be prerequisites for developing good CAD design (e.g. drawing ability, spatial thinking). Whether these skills should be developed outside the CAD environment remains an open question at the moment.

The answers to such questions must await the results of further controlled studies.

3 Immersion Training

The week long exercise was undoubtedly of great benefit to the students. They learned a lot. They did things they would otherwise have avoided. Their attitudes towards the use of computers in architecture became more favourable. Apple's far-sightedness in supporting this exercise appeared fully justified.

4 Mixed Media

In terms of the output it was obvious that the students were finding the plotted output unsatisfactory and experimented with plotting on card which would allow them to use water colour and other techniques (see Figures 1.29 and 1.32). This gave rise to a lot of interest in the year and the students and a studio tutor organised a special session to show and explore ways in which to 'humanize' those plots. Some of the examples shown here are in fact quite encouraging and were suddenly found to be acceptable by most of the students. This mixed-media approach is of great interest and shows how computer work can be a part of a larger design process.

Reference

Black, A (1990) Visible planning on paper and screen. The impact of working media on decision-making by novice graphic designers. Behaviour and Information Technology, 9 (4), 283-296.

Computer Aids For Design Development

André G.P. Brown and Frank Horton
School of Architecture and Building Engineering,
University of Liverpool

Introduction

In this chapter we are concerned with the development of appropriate computer-based tools to assist in the development of design ideas. The work which we describe falls into two clearly identifiable areas and this chapter is divided into two main sections to recognize this. In the first we consider the function of drawing at the conceptual stage of the design process. We are responding to the observations of writers such as McKim (1972) who identify the detrimental effect on the design process, resulting from lack of competence and confidence when sketch designing. He makes observations such as the following:

> a clumsy sketch usually evokes judgemental processes that restrict or stop idea-flow ... ideas that cannot be adequately recorded in sketch form are often lost.

Having looked at design development from the standpoint of sketch drawing we then go on, in the second part, to look at the potential for computers to augment the development of design ideas by giving feedback about the technological performance of the building in a particular area. The area dealt with in this case is sunlight penetration into buildings.

Drawing design and computers

Negroponte's (1970, 1975) original work on the architecture machine began with a model of the designer at work. Negroponte's imaginary architect begins work with a pad of paper and sketches her way through the design process towards a finished design. This is a common, almost a lay, view of design: architecture begins with the near-mythical back of an envelope and progresses by stages to a blueprint. The fact that this perspective is commonplace does not make it correct, but a view so widely held is worthy of attention. Negroponte (and others) have used the model to specify a way of integrating the computer into the design process. The 'architecture machine' must acknowledge and fit into this way of working and this has initiated a search for hardware and software devices which would 'seamlessly integrate' the machine with other, more traditional, aspects of CAAD.

In practice the world of CAAD has grown away from this model. The machine is used predominantly not as an aid to design, but as one of the specialized instruments of office practice: an instrument used to produce hard-edged, dimensioned and annotated production drawings. This is acknowledged when 'CAAD' is translated as computer-aided architectural draughting. Eastman's (1989) recent review of the state of the art goes so far as to suggest that the idea of 'integrated' CAD was misplaced.

All this suggests that there are two diametrically opposite approaches to CAD in architecture. The first stresses the central role that computing could play: it promotes a search for computing ways of doing the whole job and will be fully satisfied only when computer and design are inseparable. We call this the 'strong' approach to CAD. The second, or 'weak' approach is more pragmatic and seeks to automate only those parts of the design process which can be readily and naturally helped by computing. Both the strong and the weak positions pose empirical questions about the designer (the human agent) and how that agent does her work. In computer terms these are questions about the user interface, about how user and machine interact. In

Figure 2.1
Le Corbusier's Chapel at Ronchamp

the strong CAD programme they interact all the time from the first to the last point in the design sequence. In the weak model there are points where what is done by hand is to be presented to the machine and vice versa. The strong and weak approaches to CAD share a common set of problems to do with the way that designing and computing relate.

In the remainder of this chapter we shall look at some experimental work which asks questions about the nature of these relationships. We look first at the design approach of one of the acknowledged 'great' architects Le Corbusier. In 1950 Le Corbusier was commissioned to design the Chapel at Ronchamp. The Chapel was dedicated in 1955. The building was on the drawing board for a long time and was a significant commission for Le Corbusier (Le Corbusier, 1957).

He wanted to use the Chapel as an illustration of his own design method and took care to see that the creative process was well documented. This provides us with a case study of a building of acknowledged high quality and with the bare bones of its creation and development lovingly preserved.

TABLE 2.1 THE STAGES OF ARCHITECTURAL DESIGN

RIBA plan of work[1]	DOE[2]	DHSS[3]	Large London practice[4]	Small London practice[5]	Broad summary
A Inception B Feasibility	1. Pre-design 2. Design	1. Outline project Intentions	Outline scheme	Feasibility studies	Feasibility/outline
C Outline proposals	2.1 Outline design	2. Planning project and first scheme			
D Scheme design	2.2 Final sketch design	3. Design and cost planning Cost plan, sketch plan, equipment schedule	Sketch design	Sketch design	Sketch design
E Detail design	2.3 Detail design	Detailed design	Preliminary working drawings	Detail design	Detail design
F Production information		Production material	Final working drawings	Final drawings	Working drawings drawings
G Bills of quantities		Bills of quantities pre-tender estimate			
H Tender action	2.4 Contract preparation	4. Contract and construction	Contract supervision	Revision	
J Project planning	3. Construction 3.1 Construction pre-planning				
K Site operations	3.2 Construction control				
L Completion	3.3 Construction completion 3.4 Contractural completion				
	4. Post-construction	5. Commissioning and evaluation			

[1]*RIBA, Architectural practice and management, RIBA Publications, London, 1965.*
[2]*PSA, Plan of Work A.C. construction and works circular 60/73, 1973.*
[3]*Capricode, Hospital building procedure, note number 1, 1974.*
[4]*GTDWB internal document standard terms, 1975.*
[5]*Leslie, Fox, Albin, internal document standard terms, 1987.*

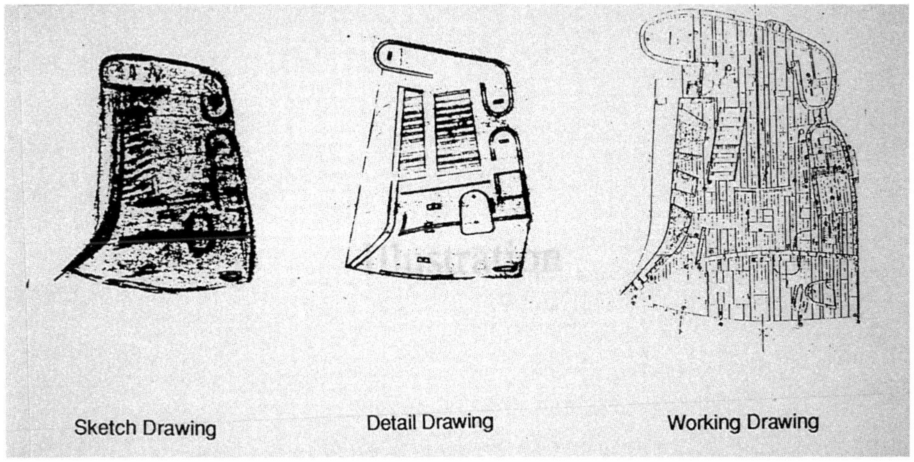

Figure 2.2
Typical examples of sketch drawing, detail drawing and working drawing

The *Le Corbusier Archive* (Brooks, 1985) includes all the Ronchamp drawings, from the earliest sketch to the working drawings. We analysed a sample (40) of these in different ways to find out what this set of drawings told us about the way that the act of drawing is used in design. This analysis supports the conventional wisdom on design: sketching, re-sketching, drawing and tracing were used by Le Corbusier as *the* way of investigating a design. Moreover, in accord with the modernist principle 'the plan is the generator' the majority of all the drawings of Ronchamp are plans. In time series the reworked plans show that the outline idea for Ronchamp was fixed very early in the process and that this early idea was a fixed point around which much of the later work revolved. The way that the scheme developed largely conformed to the outline given by the *RIBA Plan of Work* (1965): the drawings progress from rough charcoal sketches through detail drawings to working drawings in a rough sequence corresponding to the sequence A to F in the plan. This same sequence is used by other organizations with slight differences in nomenclature (see Table 2.1) and suggests working definitions of the major types of drawing used by Le Corbusier.

1 *The sketch:* the drawn equivalent of a personal reminder, drawn to capture an idea and to communicate it to oneself. Such drawings are rarely to scale, and they are freely drawn using soft media: charcoal, felt-tip pen, soft pencil.
2 *The detail drawing:* usually drawn to scale to aid the design process by communicating to fellow professionals what is going on.
3 *The working drawing:* the formal drawn communication between architect and contractor. Inspection of the archive revealed that drawings

a) Total drawings;

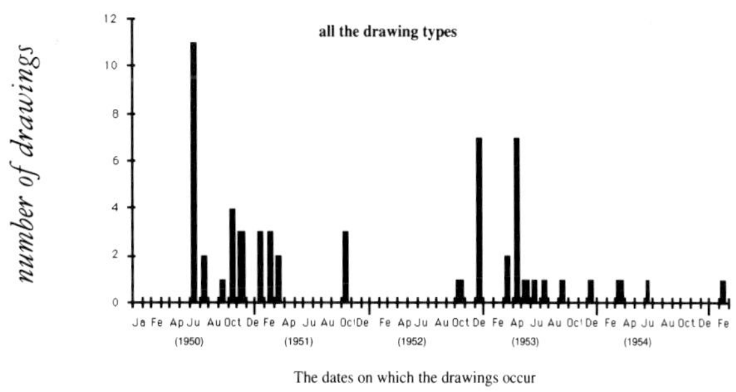

b) Detail drawings;

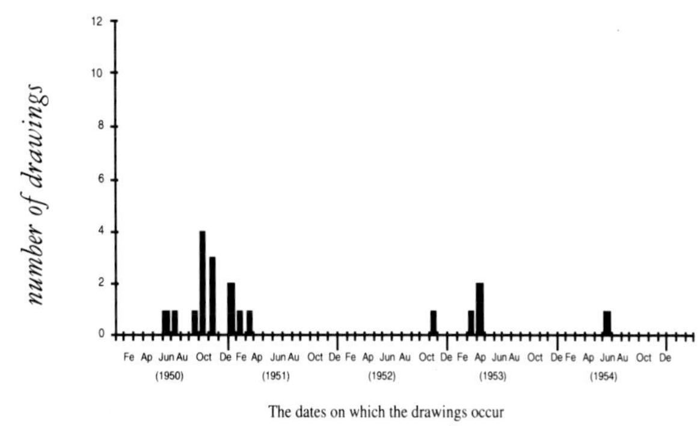

c) Working drawings;

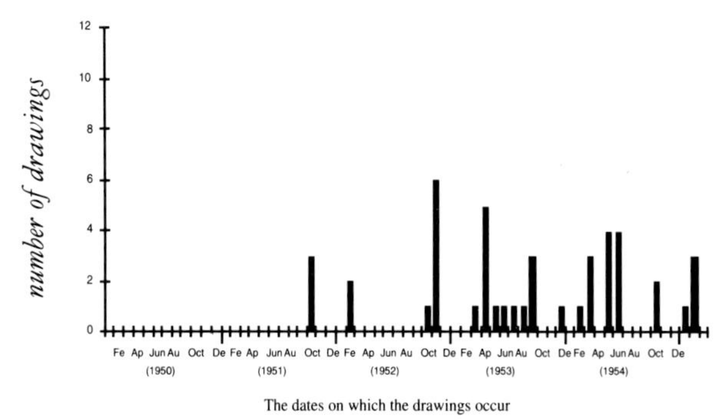

Figure 2.3 (left)
Histograms showing the numbers of each type of drawing produced during the design process: (a) total drawings; (b) detail drawings; (c) working drawings; (d) sketch drawings

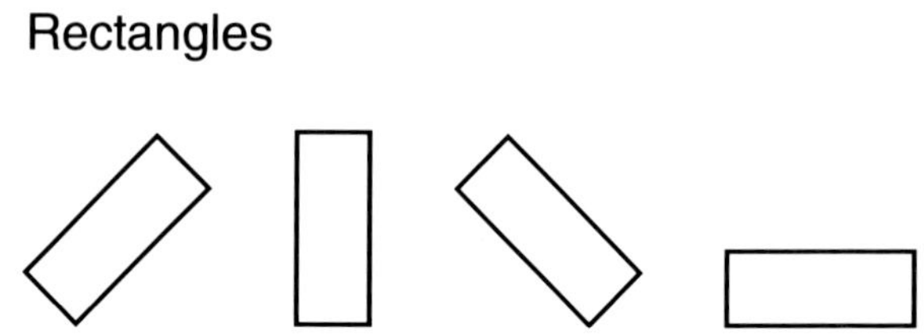

Figure 2.4
Simple shapes and staring points (after Van Sommers, 1984)

d) Sketch drawings.

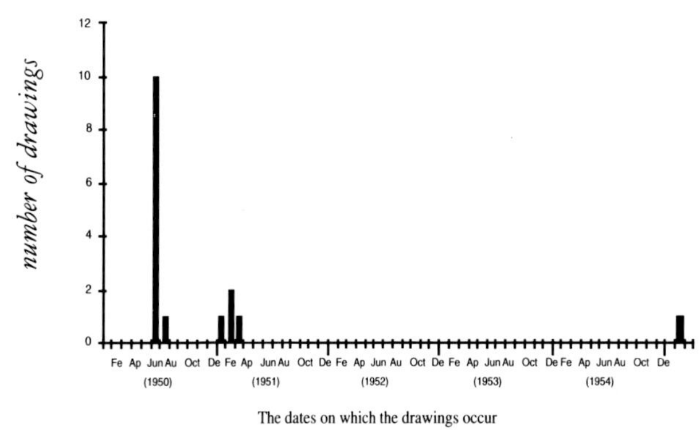

could be confidently and unambiguously allocated to each category (see Figure 2.2 for examples). When this is done the pattern of drawing production can be shown over time (with minor exceptions all the drawings are dated) (Figure 2.3). The patterns that these figures reveal are generally surprise free. The type of drawings produced varies with the progress of the project.

The exceptions occur in sketching. Figure 2.3(d) shows not one but two periods of intense sketching, the first (beginning around June 1950) exactly where it might be expected, and the second (beginning January 1951) some seven months later. This second sketch phase actually occurs after the scheme had been accepted by the Commission for Holy Art. It signifies a renowned period of creative endeavour born out of the recognition that the project will be built. The second observation arises from the data but does not show clearly in the histograms. Throughout the whole project Le Corbusier continually produces sketches; the histograms are based on the development of the plan, the predominant drawing type. The whole archive reveals a number of other sketches which deal with elements, fragments of the design, the bell towers, the main entrance and so on. This suggests that within the whole design there are problems which are difficult and need to be worked at continually. Indeed Le Corbusier (Le Corbusier, 1957) reports that he was still working on one of these details *after* the building was completed:

> The positioning of the essential elements of worship in the Chapel of Notre-Dame-du-Haut was temporarily settled for the dedication ceremony on the 25th of June 1955. Since then the great wooden cross fixed at the back of the altar has appeared awkward to me. I felt an increasing uneasiness about it, I concentrated on it and today, two years later I began to draw …

The second piece of work we report looks at the nature of the drawing task. Here, we rest heavily on the observational studies of Van Sommers (1984) supported by a pilot study of our own.

Van Sommers asks very simple questions: how do people tackle drawing, where do they start, what physical motions are used? Under laboratory conditions he asked subjects to perform simple drawing tasks and recorded the results. From this work we can extract some very simple drawing principles and develop these into a hierarchy. In no particular order, the graphic primitives underlying hand drawing are as follows:

1 Drawing begins at 11 o'clock: this assertion is spatial not temporal (though it might be true that little is done in design offices until coffee time, and certainly architectural students rarely start drawing before the eleventh hour). Most right-handed drawers begin to draw with pen or pencil at the 11 o'clock position (as in handwriting).

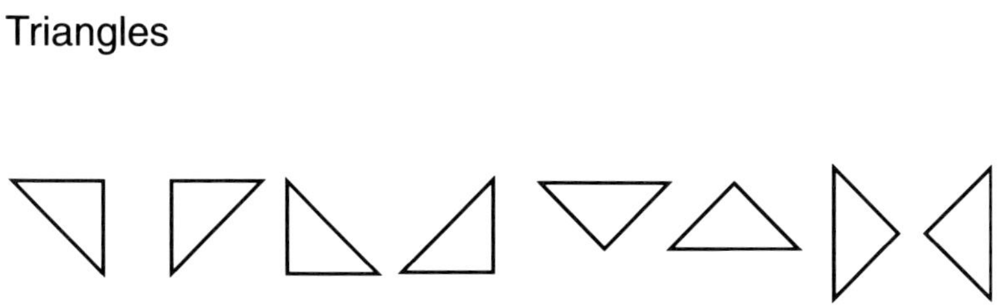

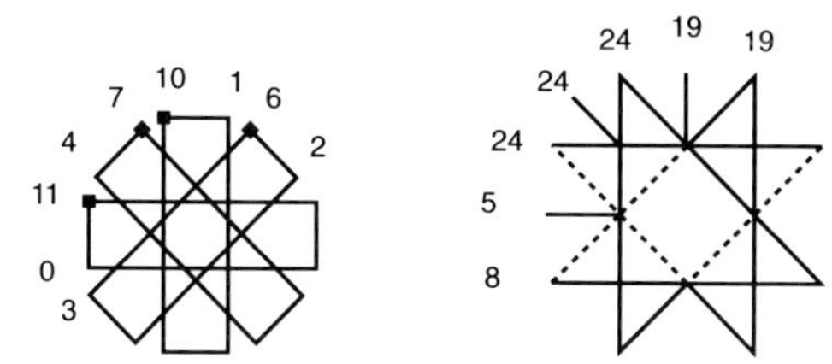

Figure 2.4
Simple shapes and starting points (after Van Sommers, 1984)

We shall use this assertion to illustrate the way that Van Sommers' work was done. Subjects were asked to copy the simple shapes shown in Figure 2.4, which also shows the starting points chosen. This also worked with more complex shapes (Figure 2.5)

2 We cannot draw from back to front or find it very difficult to do so. We do not generally create a drawing by working from the background to the foreground; we can if pushed, but we try to avoid the problem. What we are avoiding is an*ticipated embedding* – the anticipation that the boundary of one drawn object will interrupt the boundary of another. Anticipated embedding involves drawing the interrupted object first, which most drawers find difficult.
3 Drawing is adding: drawings are built up gradually by adding to what has already been drawn. Van Sommers refers to this as *accretion*. This build-up tends to take place by locating new elements in some relation to what is already there – *anchoring*.
4 Salience: one of the governing, yet idiosyncratic, principles of all perception. We 'see' what we value: we draw what we see.

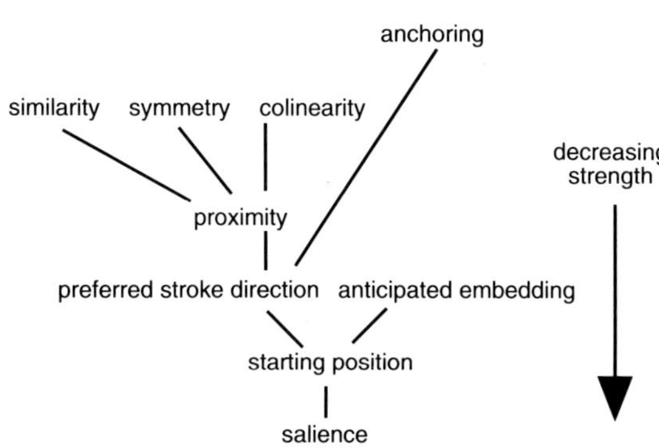

Figure 2.6
Relative strength of the drawing principles (after Van Sommers, 1984)

These major principles are supplemented by some simple geometric ideas – similarity, symmetry, proximity and collinearity – and Van Sommers shows how these elements combine to form an ordered hierarchy of drawing principles (Figure 2.6).

Van Sommers' used children as the principal subjects and this is open to the charge that he deals only with the naive or inexperienced drawer. It can be argued that drawing is a learned skill and that the most experienced and knowledgeable draughter will have in her repertoire a number of routines and habits which transcend or supersede the 'natural' habits identified by Van Sommers. A partial check on this idea was provided by a pilot study which compared the drawing skills of experienced and naive drawers (Jenkinson, 1990). Here subjects were asked to do four different drawings and the performance was video-taped.

Subjects were asked to draw a potted plant from life, to draw from imagination, to design a chair and to design anything. The pilot study was small (four subjects) and will not bear too much inferential weight. However, since two of the four were professional artists, the results are worth discussing as a complement to Van Sommers' study of lay drawers.

Generally Van Sommers' principles seem to hold, but the Jenkinson studies reveal that the different tasks set encouraged differing approaches to drawing. Design was seen to be a separate kind of activity to life drawing although each type of drawing was built up from similar primitive actions.

> It is a progression from working in broad outline to work in detail and then ... adding ornamental details. (Jenkinson, 1990).

It is also worth noting that two other drawing habits not mentioned by Van Sommers are seen in this

Figure 2.5
Starting points for more complex shapes (after Van Sommers, 1984)

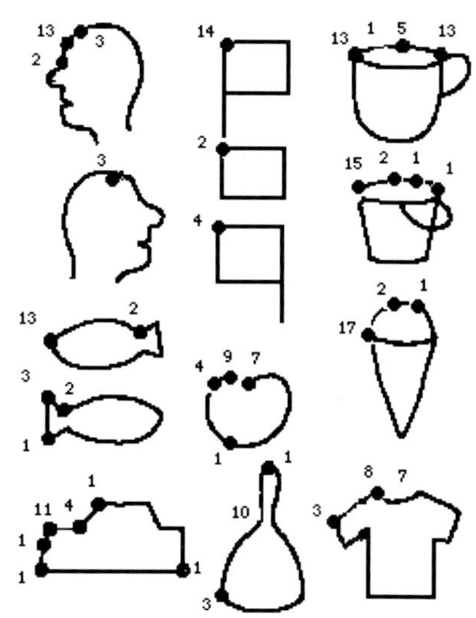

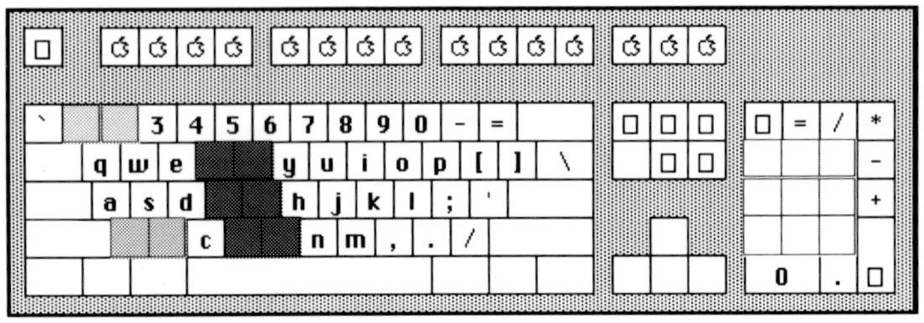

(a)

= The 9 keys chosen to each represent a shape tool

= The keys which the index finger has to cover in touch typing

= Very rarely used keys to the bottom left

= Rarely used keys to the top left

Figure 2.8 a and b
(a) the conventional keyboard;
(b) the allocation of keys according to user preference in terms of finger action (density of shading indicates level of accessibility)

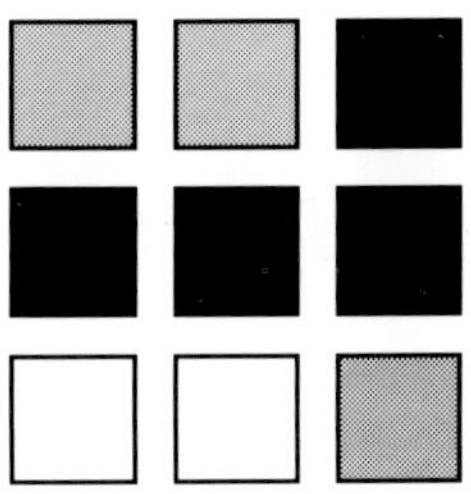

(b)

Figure 2.7
The customized configuration

circle	curved cornered rectangle	rectangle
pointer	text	straight line
freehand line	eliptical arc	polygon

small group. The first is the tendency to build up a drawing by overdrawing – drawing faintly and gradually building on this foundation. Second, we observed the constant use of non-mark-making actions: the pencil moves across paper as if drawing but no mark is made. We call this 'ghosting'.

Discussion

These two pieces of work are interesting in themselves but also suggest directions to look in investigating the interface between drawer and machine.

Mitchell (Chapter 7) suggests that drawing with a standard computer mouse is like attempting to draw with a brick. This is appealing and commonsensical but could be misleading. Despite the Van Sommers constraints drawers do seem able to adopt different techniques for different tasks; indeed the 'brick' could serve as a tactile reminder of the nature of the medium being used. However, the interface might be ergonomically better designed for ease of use. We explored a primitive redesign of the Macintosh interface which used the mouse to draw but configured the numeric keypad to call the various tools. The pattern we used is shown in Figure 2.7 and was derived from the ergonomics of the keyboard (Figure 2.8).

The efficiency of this change was tested by drawing a standard figure, the wheelbarrow (Figure 2.9), which is simple but requires the fundamental tools and constraints which we have identified, following our own investigations and those of Van Sommers. Compare part (c) with the same drawing (d) done using MacDraw II with the modified keyboard and a clear ergonomic benefit is seen.

How far does this get us? It is a long way from the kind of drawing done by Le Corbusier. Here, the hand-crafted quality of the concept sketches seems to be an intrinsic part of the drawing. This is supported by the observation of experienced drawers. Drawing faint lines first and 'ghosting' movements suggest that the tactile or proprioceptive element in drawing is an important part of the experience. Repeating this pattern whilst drawing to screen would be possible in simple paint type programs but would result in a number of extraneous and confusing objects in a more sophisticated vector-based package. Furthermore, we question the utility of improved ergonomics. This might be an important and useful advance if we talk of the gains to be made by making the work of a tracer quicker and more productive. For the designer or architect such gains are likely to be less important since any time savings made will be swamped by thinking time: intellectual work is not easily improved by time and motion study. However, there may be real gains to the user in such an improved interface since it can speed up the way that ideas are transferred from mind to machine. For the experienced draughter sketching is a fast process which could be impeded by a clumsy machine interface. Work of the kind reported here is valuable if it leads to a more 'natural' use of the machine, to the design of a better 'brick'.

Computer-based technical aids

Technical applications (programs) like those used by the environmental engineer and the structural engineer have traditionally been aimed towards the latter end of the design process. In the case of the environmental engineer the data to be fed into a program have often come from a largely completed design, when the problem is simply to calculate the performance requirements of servicing plant. In short, only in the

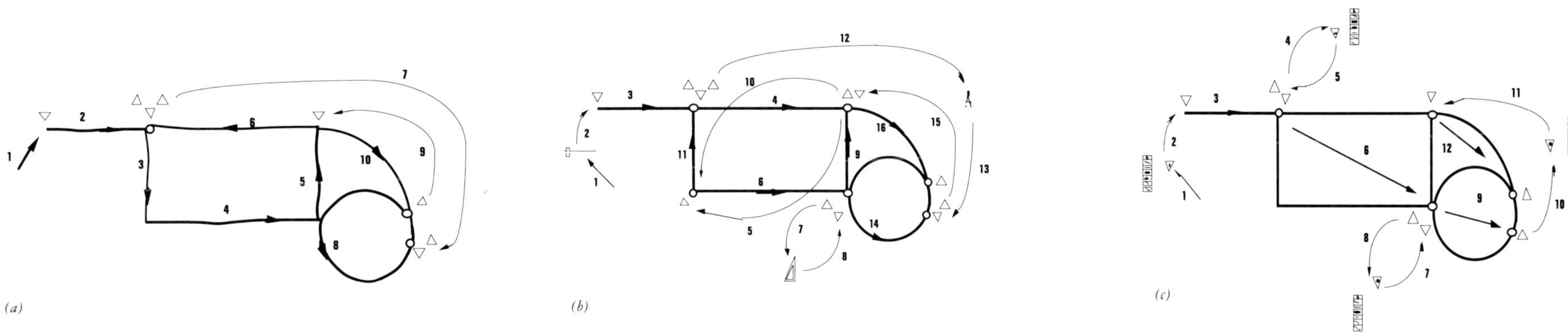

broadest of senses has the computer been used as part of the design process. If we are to produce buildings which do perform well from a technical standpoint then surely a key part of the answer is to have the computer act as a technical assistant right through the design process. In this era of green awareness it is wholly appropriate to look to computers to help to fine-tune designs and aid us in producing buildings which have optimal technical characteristics.

Archipak, the integrated program and database for environmental design devised by Sockolay (1990), is one of a small number of programs which try to address the problem of giving advice on environmental technology early in the design process: it provides the user with a 'what if?' scenario. The user can, for instance, try the effects of different forms of construction on the thermal characteristics of the building and obtain advice on optimal orientation and grouping of buildings. Perhaps where the program is lacking is in the interface: the program is driven by typing in text and numbers.

A suite of programs which tackles similar problems with a similar philosophy about the virtue of the 'what if?' analysis has been developed under the direction of G.Z. Brown at the University of Oregon. Where this suite differs from Sockolay's in an important way is that the interface is friendlier to the user (it is graphical) and data input is 'softer': the mouse is used to sketch items such as windows or to point to items such as a type of construction. The suite is written for the Macintosh and thereby takes advantage of other standard user-friendly features which are described well elsewhere (eg Witte, 1988).

The suite of programs was recently described in some detail by Brown (1990). In short it consists of three major elements, all of which are intended to be aids to the designer at the early stages of the design process. Two are tools for environmental design and one is a design ideas generator. The first tool is a *Preliminary Energy Design Tool* and has as its aim the optimization of mechanical and electrical systems in a building, or, more accurately, the optimization of energy conservation potential. The second environmental design package is referred to as a *Sunlight Design Tool*. The thrust of this tool is towards investigating and modifying sunlight penetration into a building. We shall look at this tool in more detail shortly. Finally, the ideas generator is entitled *Metaphors Prototype*. This application uses metaphors and analogies to evoke images of two- or three-dimensional forms as a way of starting down the road to the creation of a building.

The Sunlight Design Tool was developed (in Pascal and using the Macintosh toolbox) at the University of Oregon and an experiment was conducted at Liverpool University to give an idea of its success. A first report on the results of these experiments was given by Wood *et al.* (1989).

The Sunlight Design Tool interface is shown in Figure 2.10. The sunlit room under investigation is presented to the user as five rectangular black areas, representing the floor and four walls folded flat into the plane of the computer screen. Building orientation, latitude and times of day and year are selected using familiar Macintosh techniques such as the scroll bar and click-dragging. All these variables are easily accessed and are visible on the interface to facilitate modification at any time. The final element of the interface is the simple graphical toolbox which allows the user to draw on the walls or floor of the room.

The tool can be used in two principal ways. The user

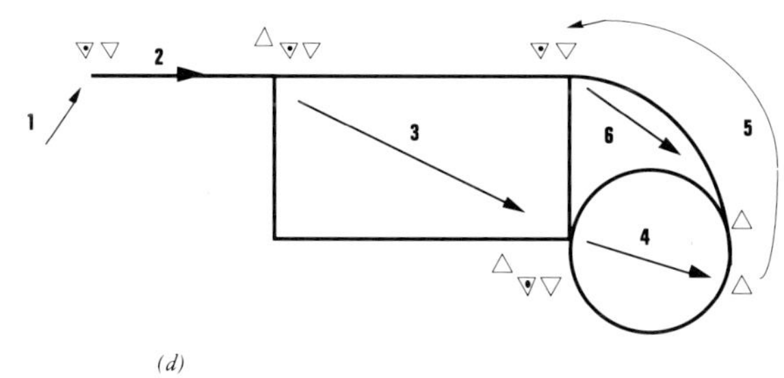

Figure 2.9 (above)
The benchmark comparative tests: (a) drawn freehand; (b) drawn using a drawing board; (c) drawn using a MacDraw II; (d) drawn using the modified configuration which employs both hands (below) key of symbols used

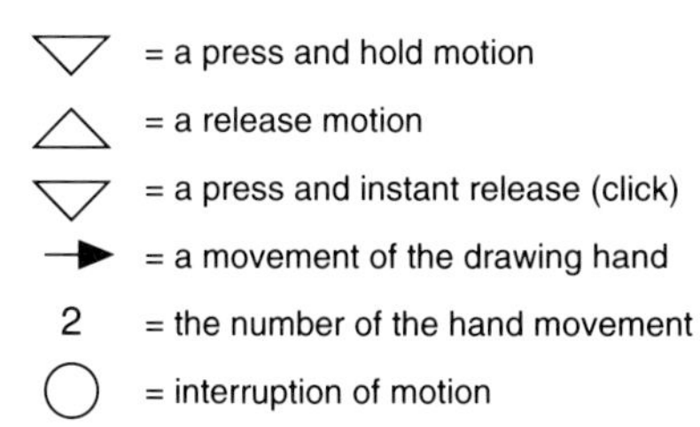

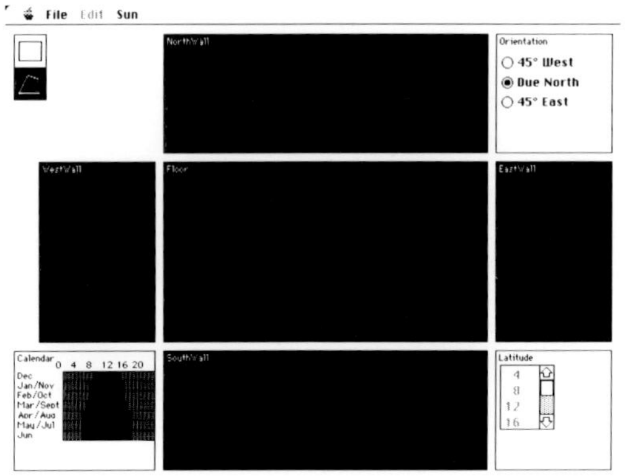

Figure 2.10
The interface for the Sunlight Design Tool

Figure 2.12
Window shape needed to cast the patch of sunlight specified

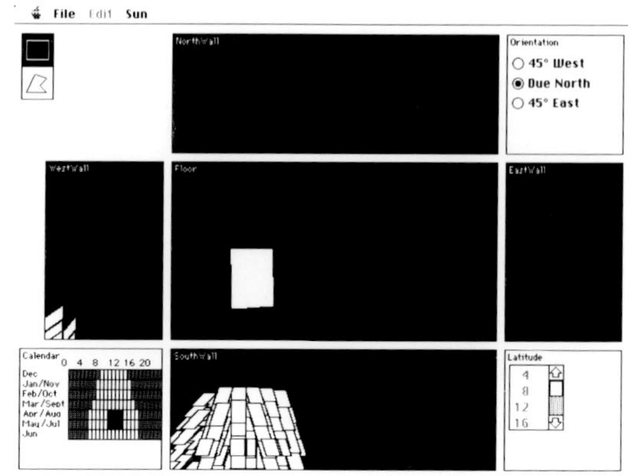

can draw any desired window shape on the walls of the room and the tool immediately shows the areas of sunlight cast for the times, location and orientation specified (Figure 2.11). Alternatively, and more interestingly in the context of the present discussion, the user can sketch a desired patch of sunlight to which the tool responds by showing the shape and location of the window(s) needed to cast a patch of sunlight of this particular shape (Figure 2.12). This clearly gives the architect access to a real design tool; window locations can be chosen to give a desired performance characteristic.

The application is only a prototype and lacks obvious real-world sophistications such as complex room shapes and fine control over orientation. But the principal is established, and that is the important issue. However, we believed that the tool was actually sufficiently well developed to aid students of architecture in their understanding of sunlight penetration into buildings. In order to test this contention we devised an experiment which was described in some detail by Wood *et al.* (1989). Put simply, we took a group of first-year architecture students and tested their ability to predict sunlight behaviour by giving them drawings of rooms and asking them to predict patches of sunlight or window locations. We then let them loose on the Sunlight Tool, allowing them to play with drawing windows and patches of sunlight as they wished. What we did not tell them was that there was a second test of their ability to predict sunlight behaviour, to see whether it had improved as a result of using the tool.

We devised a scoring system to assess the student predictions based on a target centred on the correct answer. What we found is interesting. As a result of using the Sunlight Design Tool for a matter of 15 or 20 minutes the students' performances in predicting sunlight behaviour increased significantly (Figures 2.13 and 2.14).

Figure 2.13
Student scores before using the Tool

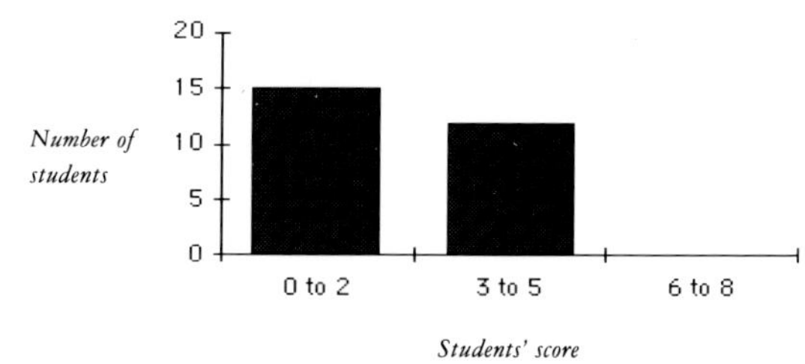

Figure 2.14
Student scores after using the Tool

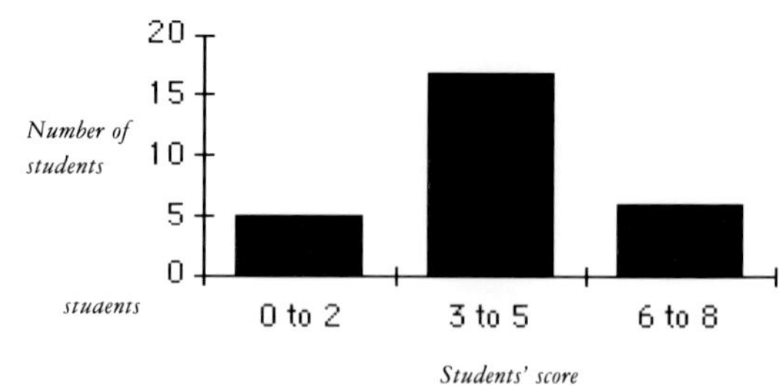

Now, we do not wish to overclaim, but the worth of this kind of application as an aid to design education appears to be significant.

We also asked students to give opinions about various aspects of the exercise just described. One

Figure 2.11
Patches of sunlight cast by windows drawn onto a wall

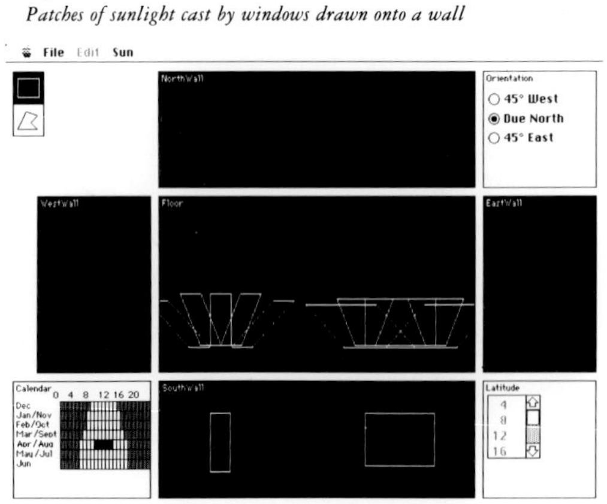

interesting set of answers relates to the students' assessment of the application as a design aid. They tended to rate the Tool highly in this respect and the vast majority could envisage using a more sophisticated version of the tool to augment their design development skills. Their ratings are shown in Figure 2.15. Again, too much should not be read into this result, though it might be worth mentioning that all the test papers and questionnaires were filled in anonymously and the data were analysed by someone who did not know the students concerned.

Figure 2.15
Student ratings of the application as a design aid

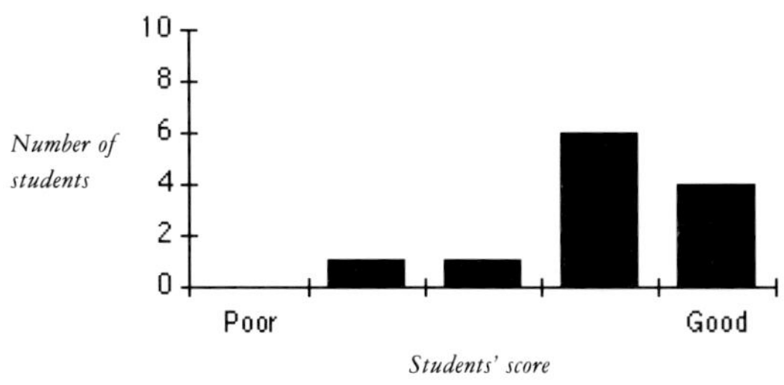

Discussion

The kind of approach to tackling design concerns of a technical kind described above has been identified by some as being a ripe target for expert systems work in the construction industry. An obvious development would be to link the kind of application described here to a drawing–modelling CAD package, the aim being to give the designer interactive feedback about the technical performance of the building as it is being developed in the CAD application. This is the aim of Docherty, who is working with Sockolay to link the Archipak program to AutoCAD.

This is one way of approaching the problem; there are others which are worthy of consideration. But whatever approach is adopted, from both an educational standpoint and from the view of the architect who is concerned with designing buildings (which embodies a complex interaction of problems) it seems clear that there is considerable merit in developing the kind of tool described here.

Concluding remarks

What we have tried to address here is the difficult but interesting problem of using computers in a helpful way during the early stages of the design process. It is well understood that the potential of computers has been realized during the intermediate and later stages of the process: draughting and modelling applications are now quite mature and present the designer with powerful tools once initial design proposals have been established. But, like many others, we are concerned with examining the possibilities offered by computers in helping the designer arrive at these early proposals. Simply tacking a 'sketchy' front end onto an existing draughting–modelling application might be like making silk purses out of sows' ears: potentially interesting as an idea, but maybe not the place to put your money.

We are concerned that what goes on in the early stages of a building design be given thorough and due recognition before we finally establish computer-based tools for aiding the designer in arriving at sketch proposals. We have tried to draw attention to what we believe to be interesting lines of thought and worthwhile areas of discussion of this kind of development.

Acknowledgements

The authors wish to acknowledge the kind support of Apple Computer UK who funded the major part of the investigations into architectural drawing and design described in the first part of this chapter. The full report of this research project is given by Jenkinson (1990).

As noted above, the Sunlight Design Tool mentioned in the second part of this chapter was developed at the University of Oregon under the direction of Professor G.Z. Brown. We also wish to acknowledge the assistance of Professor Brown's colleague at Oregon, Professor B. J. Novitski, who aided the Liverpool University Graduate Student, David Wood, in the development of the Tool.

Finally our thanks go to the students at the Liverpool School of Architecture and Building Engineering who agreed to be guinea pigs in return for a cup of coffee.

References

Brooks, H.A. (ed.) (1985) *Le Corbusier Archive*. Garland, New York.

Brown, G.Z. (1990) Desirable interface characteristics of knowledge-based energy software used by architects. *Proceedings of the ASHRAE Annual Meeting*, St. Louis, MO.

Eastman, C. (1989) Architectural CAD: a ten year assessment of the state of the art *Computer-Aided Design,* Butterworths, London.

Jenkinson, L.A. (1990) *Architectural concept drawing and design*. M.Phil. Thesis, Liverpool University.

Le Corbusier (1957) *The Chapel at Ronchamp* (English transl.). Architectural Press, London.

McKim, R.H. (1972) *Experiences in Visual Thinking*. Brooks Cole, Monterrey, CA.

Negroponte, N. (1970) *The Architecture Machine*. MIT Press, Cambridge, MA.

Negroponte, N. (1975) *The Soft Architecture Machine*. MIT Press, Cambridge, MA.

Pauly, D. (1985) The Chapel at Ronchamp, in *Le Corbusier Archive*. Garland, New York.

RIBA (1965) *Architectural Practice and Management*, RIBA Publication, London.

Sockolay, S. (1990) Archipak version 3.3: an integrated program and database for environmental, climatic and thermal design. University of Queensland, St. Lucia, Queensland, Australia.

Van Sommers, P. (1984) *Drawing and Cognition.* Cambridge University Press, Cambridge.

Witte, O. (1988) Evaluating software for 'the friendly Mac', *Architecture*, October .

Wood, D.J., Brown, A.G.P. and Brown G.Z. (1989) A sunlight design tool. *Proceedings of the ECAADE Conference*, School of Architecture, Aarhus, Denmark.

Learning From Volume Processing: Working For a Three-Dimensional Database

Juan Carlos Sabater and Albert Gassull
Universitat Politécnica de Catalunya, Barcelona

Introduction

We discuss here a selection of the activities taking place at the Vallés School of Architecture, Department of Composition, Politechnical University of Barcelona. Originally our activities with computers (Apple Macintosh) involved undergraduate students, but recently we started working at the Master's degree level.

Our position is now well defined but it has been formulated gradually through the continuous and progressive use of computers in our work. Working with Apple Macintosh computers does not refer to teaching drawing programs (although we believe that the Mac facilitates self-learning and intuitive sense). We try to 'normalize' its use by integrating it in different tasks by suggesting its use in a range of programs and by sometimes letting the visual transcriptions suggest new approaches.

The visual system of values developed by the Modernists (now history) and available through photography, cinema and video is part of our visual language. We must use this to facilitate the understanding of an argument, to discover the inherent values of architectural organization, to hold and manipulate the virtual illusion derived from pencil work and to anticipate the life of a building, to prolong, to dilate or simulate the architectural experience. In fact, the virtual modelling of a building, or a group of buildings that has not been built, increases the relation with historical studies because it divulges more, and in a more precise way. It gains specific weight in the realm of critical and historical analysis.

It is precisely in this area of knowledge that we work at the Vallés school, and, although it seems a play on words, we believe that the program's own 'architecture', especially for three-dimensional drawing, indirectly invites one to think of certain formulations and values of architecture, or at least suggest them. Certainly this is not the place to talk about the capabilities of the Macintosh, but we have to acknowledge that a large part of our work is based around these. The use of certain programs, especially those which process volumes (spaces), takes us back to 1918 tendencies, i.e. to the foundations of modern art. Thus a step forward, paradoxically, relates to the earlier breakthrough in architecture.

This is the place, (we all share the same experience) to remember that analogy, which is the basis of the Apple protocol development, is surely the relation most used by students of architecture. To detect the relations of similarity and to operate through guess work, or by successive transformations is a very familiar experience for architectural students.

We initiated our activities with a MacPlus using programs such as SuperPaint, MacDraw and so on. The very brief period in which we dealt with them was sufficient to determine most of our future decisions.

First, there is some simulation when axonometrical views are drawn with two-dimensional computing tools. Nevertheless, several documents could be obtained from an original document and only one menu order. We saved most of them – it seemed a pity to put them in the 'wastebasket'. We grouped different sets and identified them with different various concepts. Thus a range of documents collected could be used to enhance some of the categories of the architecture of the 1950s, as 'the only practical space', or the resonances of Dutch 'plasticism', or the activities of maintenance and hygiene, and so on. A simultaneous understanding was grasped economically on one screen. We called it the 'new technical reproducibility' (Figure 3.1).

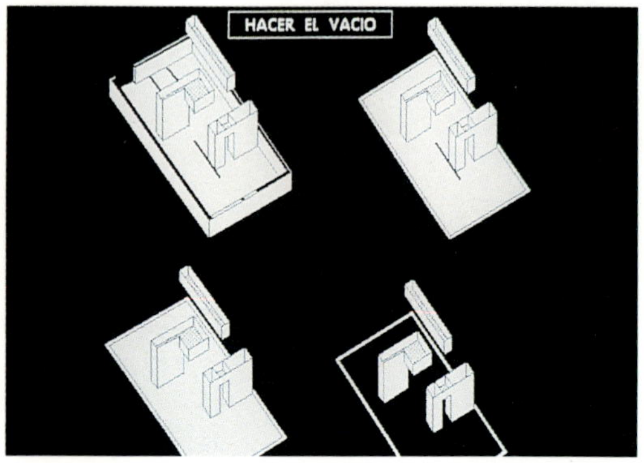

Figure 3.1
Architectural analysis of a 50-foot building

Figure 3.2
View from the 'loo' in the, at that time, unbuilt Vallés School of Architecture

A new school of architecture

Meanwhile our school decided to move into a new building. When the project was ready, we had been entrusted by the staff to draught some perspectives in order to complete the presentation of the model and the whole project for the media. We did more. We also prepared a small HyperCard, and a VideoWorks presentation to show some inner and outer walks, to show daylight details and to explain the way that we understood the school would develop as a structure. We called it 'neither flesh nor skin'.

Journalists could choose given positions in the future school and each had their particular view. The chosen situations varied between the hall, the library and the corridor – one of them asked for the view from the loo (Figure 3.2). We also rendered the drawing with 'Studio 8'. When the journalists left the presentation, they could pick up more than an impression, an imprint, because we plotted the chosen views for them.

We used Architrion for the first time in its 3.5 version. There we got the idea that these kinds of procedures actually anticipate the life of a building.

Multimedia discovering

Dynamic iconography can facilitate the reading of critical and analytical architectural texts. Its systematization in HyperCard could mean a new way of reading. Generally, visual aids are needed when one reads an article – views and plans are required. But often they are not easily available because of their relative place in the book or the main text. Thus we suggested that our students illustrate an article or other similar study by a kind of 'dynamic iconography'.

The starting point is to précis the article. We can then choose from the ideas in it and call upon images, fuse them. By movement and other manipulation, we simultaneously demonstrate the new facilities and the matter referred to.

We believe that this kind of work, which implies a deep understanding by the illustrator, provides a better, faster and simpler exposition for other students. The material can be reinforced and extended by future students. It is particularly appropriate when the arguments give opposing views or a comparative analysis. The new arrangement introduced through the visual documents allows a clearer reading of the text whilst respecting the order of the discourse.

'Lutyens' architecture restudied' is the title of an article published in 1969 by Allan Greenberg. We understood this title as a challenge in the sense that with our computers we can restudy not only Lutyens' architecture but Greenberg's analysis of it. In his essay there are a number of provocative ideas which are difficult to grasp. Dynamic iconography not only makes these ideas accessible but allows one to employ them actively. They can be developed to the extent that even Greenberg's analysis can be criticized.

This work is not concerned with reconstructing or simulating the domestic architecture of Sir Lutyens but with restudying his drawings alongside the arguments of Greenberg's text.

> In Little Thakeham, there is an almost symmetrical disposition of rooms within a square or a symmetrical H plan.

By introducing a mould form, a counter form, we can show the shape.

> The pergola, as a garden element, is also an element of the whole composition.

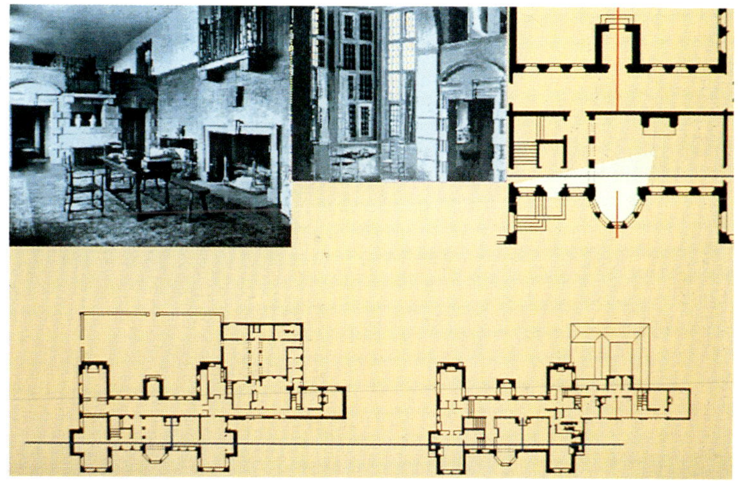

Figure 3.3
Screen with two scans and three plans. Sir E. Lutyens' Little Thakeham

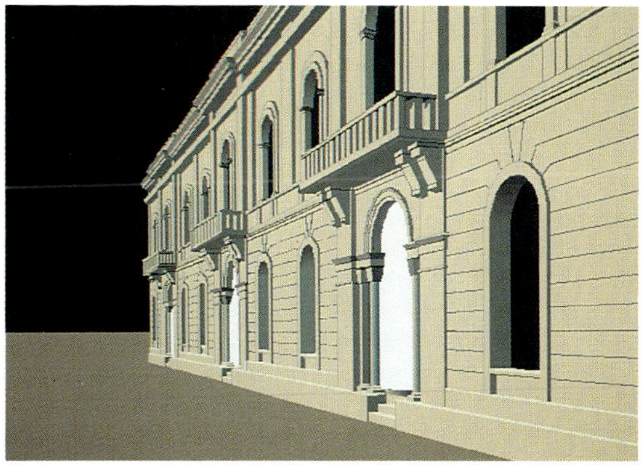

Figure 3.4
Lateral view of third-class model housing of Cerda's first project. 1855

The two main axes can be used to relate the superimposed plans of the ground floor and the first floor.

As Greenberg argues, the crossing of the main axes is occupied by a solid mass.

The axial conflict between the main axes and the inner ones can be seen in the hall, where the inner axis of the piece should be understood only by the position of the fireplace and door to the corridor, which merely trisects the north wall of the hall.

Neither reading dominates, and attention constantly oscillates between the two.

The juxtaposition of axes at different scales can be better understood in an internal view. But if an axis is a unidimensional reference on a plan, in a view it should be seen as a geometrical plane (Figure 3.3). So we have a conflict of the two systems – the main transversal, which also corresponds to the inner system of the piece, and the main vertical – and the inner axis, determined by the balcony and the fireplace.

Whatever view we choose we will find the same conflict between the inner axes of the piece and the main axes of the whole. Each axis is fixed by ensembles of different kinds of elements which, at the same time, define the walls.

The elements also operate ambiguously as a kind of furniture. While the fireplace and balcony above have their double on the west side wall, the bay window and the stairs can be understood either as interior objects or as extensions of the space.

Superimposed on this plan and symmetrical system of axes is an independent and circumambulatory circulation pattern. The solid mass, at the crossing, dislocates movement from the axes and separates guests and servants on either side.

Although the entrance door is on the main axis, movement is deflected off axis. This could be understood as an arbitrary question of style but, if the main transversal axis is lost in the wall of the corridor, the circulation articulates a sequence of spaces, where a variation of the volumetric quantity of space can be simultaneously registered on both plans.

Some of the schemes derived from the principle of compelling movement either on or off an axis–axial complexities – are almost always used to articulate transitional areas and are related to particular circumstances in each plan, or in each transformation in the menu order.

Modelling Cerda's first unknown plan for Barcelona

The beta version (1.0) (or original documents) of Cerda's plan for Barcelona was recently discovered. A student from our School rescued them from the archives. What he found was a kind of balance of the knowledge about the city and the housing in the middle of the last century. These papers, perfectly indexed, (about 500 manuscript folios), illustrate in a very precise way what was for Cerda the ideal city house. The plans of the different models of housing are combined with their disposition over blocks and squares.

Our virtual modelling of these houses was a successful attempt in classical language simulation (Figure 3.4). The courts, and the inner spaces of the working class housing, surprised us with their extreme rationality (Figure 3.5), particularly the communal houses, which look like some of the proposals from the

Figure 3.5
Working class housing model of Cerda's plan. View from the court

Figure 3.6
Central view from a court, 1865

extinct Italian 'tendenza'. The views we simulated also concerned the combinations of models proposed in the main project, forming blocks of detached houses or ranges of terraced houses. Streets were formed by simple repetition of the models. At a certain point in the simulation we were more interested in relating it to the text than in determining exactly the architecture precisely in all its details. We created (generated) views to illustrate the seminal subject of the inner court in the house, for both lighting and the renewal of the 'air mass' (Figure 3.6).

We also created views to show how Cerda could establish the homologous relationship from the secondary rooms to the main one, and to the court and to the unbuilt space between houses.

When we stopped working on the virtual model construction, we arranged a Supercard to test how images could be called upon from the text and vice versa.

There is still a lot to do because the text is a manuscript and must be transcribed with caution, and generating views is a long process which also involves colouring.

The 'house for an artisan' was a project never done by Le Corbusier

The aim of this work was to simulate a set of interior views manipulating the internal geography. The most determining elements of the interior were moved into three different positions. The entrance door, the balcony and the stair, in their respective new positions, configure very different impressions for the viewer depending on the viewpoint.

I will now look at why this way this new project could not be accepted by the author!

How we use Architrion

Architrion as a three-dimensional software package is capable of managing a complete project up to the cost estimate. We do not believe that this should be its function in a school of architecture. Thus we use it to explore the history of architecture. Most of the exercises that we have done have dealt with Modernist 'avantgardes', basically because of their structural affinity with the strategy that this software follows. Since it is a volume (space) processor the user is obliged to deal only with solids, with mass. The void, i.e. the relationship between the boundaries of the mass items, is obtained by default. Whatever solid the user wants to obtain must first be reduced by intellectual abstraction, to prismatic items whose section at first is a parallelogram. It is very easy to infer how architecture underwent its *de-naturalization*.

Not even further than when it held up the principles of the Dutch Elementarism. It did not matter whether they were pillars, columns or beams, because they were solid items.

This may be quite a reductionist view, but we believe that students must profit from it by restudying the principles of the Modern Movement in a different way, more practical and more experimental. It possibly also increases their understanding of Modern Movement concepts dramatically. This process not only tests the software to represent students' projects but represents other architectures to test their knowledge.

On Adolf Loos

As much a determining factor as the cladding in the architectonic experience of Adolf Loos is the height of

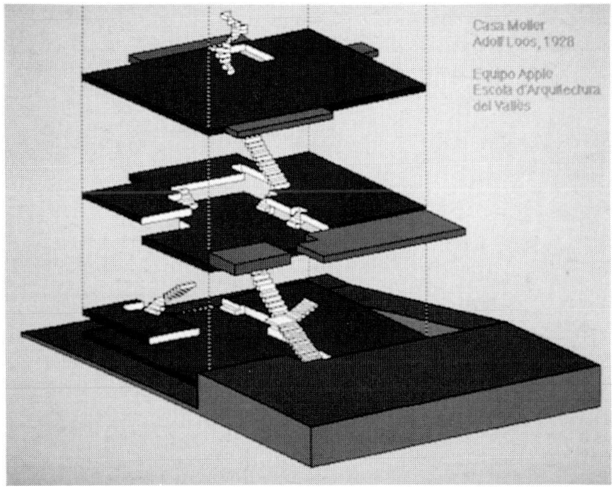

Figure 3.7
The Raumplan, Adolf Loos 1928

the rooms, the furniture (built into recesses in the walls) and the way of entering, with its close attention to privacy.

The height in 'Raumplan' is very precise, to two decimal places, which in computer terms is even more precise. In our opinion, the best way to handle this precision is to maintain the space in such a way that it can be constantly monitored. For the students, to construct the 'Raumplan' houses on the computer involves continuously testing the plan and section, for the gradient of privacy which is established by the 'Raumdurchdringung' or strategy of interpenetrating pieces.

Simulating, by obtaining interior views, the spatial experience of a 'visit', especially when the project has never been built, demands bravery and respect, but without doubt if we initiate such a process we shall eventually have a complete set of plans for the first time. A comparative measurement of the different versions of the plans for each house, which have been published, can lead to new projects, and therefore new simulations.

It is well known that Adolf Loos did not like to draw plans. He did not think the medium was precise enough. Most of his 'Raumplan' houses do not have reliable drawings because he used to modify them during construction. Less well known is his thought that, 'the day when chess will be played in three dimensions will be the moment when the architect will plan directly in space' (Loos, 1929) (Figure 3.7). Tectonics does not play any role in his architecture.

Honesty in construction did not mean anything to him. What really concerned him was the mass, the solid, in static equilibrium or not, all the rest being space. Architrion works this way. We could even say that 'Raumplan' means a kind of 'three-dimensional cartography'.

On Van Doesburg's counter-construction, 1923

We said that there is a structural affinity between the volume processor and the way in which Modernists (avant gardes) expressed themselves, even though, as an abstract idea, Neoplasticism, later Elementarism, only came to be expressed by axonometry. This was considered as a two-dimensional expression, controlled by the principle of permanent opposition. Some of the Neoplastic ideals are still seminal nowadays.

We can re-live in colour (remember that the functionalists did not have this possibility with black and white photography) the experience of the real counterbalanced relationship of lines and planes. We can realize that there are no vertical nor horizontal dominants. Counter-construction from a certain point of view is nothing but an anti-static painting.

Three of these unsettled counter-composition models were in constant movement since they where exhibited for the first time in Paris, in 1923. Nowadays they appear as a phase of work which can be, and must be, explained after the event. No one doubts that it represents a way of thinking. Nevertheless, an explanation, *a posteriori,* can reinforce this vision. Opposed to the classical, it is an 'abstract' notion of composition and plastic expression. It is also in contradiction to the fact that fundamental standard elements of nature and architecture are predominant everywhere. In fact, abstraction is that which takes place within the boundaries of individual thought. Thus, to conceive of three-dimensional space as defined by the faces which involve it, rather than by mass, suggests that it can be viewed in two ways, spatial or plastic. Among others, the 'tools' for the very conspicuous situation are the virtual alignments between voids and solids. All the surfaces are equivalent and their masses lose significance, the only significance being that of the lines. The walls start to

Figure 3.8
Counter-construction, unknown view, 1923

Figure 3.9
Frank Lloyd Wright's Barton house, 1903

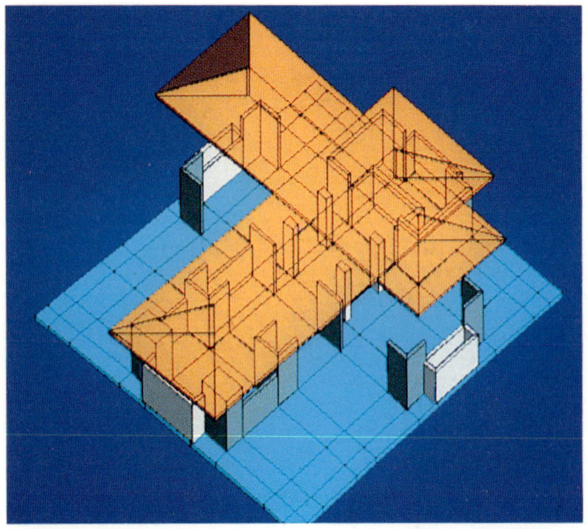

look like cardboard. Their materiality has vanished. Rasmussen offered advice on this matter in 1926, and Bruno Reichlin called it 'de-naturalization'. Otherwise axonometric was instantaneously static, a rigid composition, isolated within the boundaries of the plane. More abstract than painting, the virtual building by a volume processor as a new mental behaviour represents nowadays the same reluctance of the institutional iconographical corpus as Elementarism did in the 1920s. Seventy years later axonometric projection is the easiest way to obtain a utilitarian drawing view. With a discreet quantity of them (about 1000) the counter-construction reaches its birthday in entire freedom (Figure 3.8). Living without the hindrance of gravitation the object becomes the subject through the multiple points of view we choose. Actually it has won its own right to do without gravitation.

A very consistent structural discipline

In Frank Lloyd Wright's work there was a geometric premise rather than personal spatial insight (intuition). Some authors noted in his writings his argument about the plan as a solution and the elevation as an expression. Probably this sentence guided our subconscious for dealing with the next two exercises.

> One of the topics of his architecture is the very characteristic intersection of square and cruciform translated into three dimensions. Another is that the first principle of any growth is that the thing grown be no mere aggregation. Authors such as Manson, McCormac and others have commented that in the Froebel patterns the parts have surrendered their identity to the whole (Manson, 1958; McCormac, 1968).

We can always read the basic form of the plan on a tartan grid. From most Prairie houses it is possible to abstract a perfect tartan. In most houses (Prairie houses especially), the shape of the predominant figure is the form of a cross within a cross. Thus, a typical pattern consists of two interpenetrating cruciforms breaking through a square. The grid underlies the little Barton house of 1903 – the plan is composed of crosses, one within another.

The organization is revealed frontally as a succession of layers standing one behind another (Figure 3.9). This was one of the ways that Wright used to establish an interdependence of interior structure and external shape.

A very consistent structural discipline lies on this grid. The elements, i.e. the typical items in the Prairie houses such as the main piers of the porch and the exterior walls, represent the outer figure. Likewise, the bay window, the flower boxes and the extended verandah representing the inner components, also submit rigidly to the pattern. For Wright this was a basic premise: parts added, porches, verandahs and balconies, should not be sensed as additional but should seem intrinsic, as an extension of the inner structure. The position of end pieces suggests that the main volume of the building stands within the grid rather than around it.

The meaning of his thought concerns the harmonious relationship between plan and elevation, but also reveals how he took into

Figures 3.10 a), b), c): Jean Nouvel Theatre in Tokyo

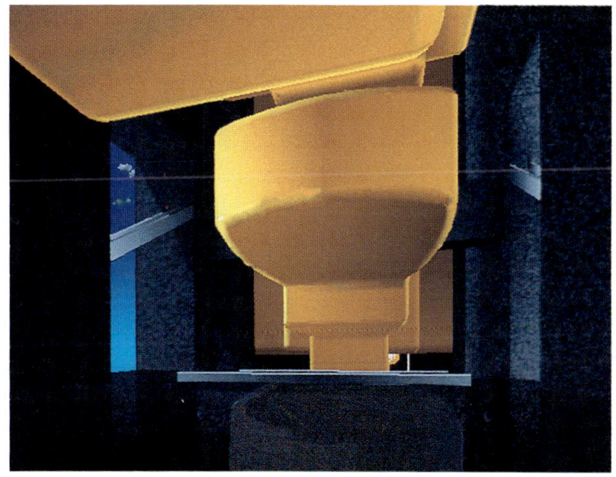

b)

consideration the perceptual difference between seeing the whole pattern from above and grasping the overall form of a building from its perimeter.

Certainly we must not forget that the screen of a computer can always be used as a grid. It can be thought of as the nursery-school aid, the table-top ruled with a grid. The discipline of a grid, combined with modular components, is not only associated with Wright. Durand, at the end of the eighteenth century, provided his pupils at the Ecole Polytechnique with an array of abstract room-shapes, which could be arranged on squared paper to make ideal symmetrical designs.

This is the only discipline which can encompass the complementary practice of removing the servitude and leaving the strength to be transformed into powerful competitiveness. Willpower alone is not enough to plan, to draw or implement detailed three-dimensional programs.

The need for certain analytical practices with regard to the anatomy of Wright's aesthetic could represent to the future user a kind of given discipline, such as the T-square was. This will always remain with us, as a mental capacity, one of the strongest structural disciplines in the history of architecture, and we surely start to associate this strategy with the volume processor. We proposed working with *Architrion* to know the anatomy of Wright's aesthetic better.

Effects in architecture

The virtual modelling of a model is not usual (Figure 3.10). The laws for solid modelling do not correspond with those of the real construction. In a certain way it is an advanced starting point for simulation. Actually the real model was stolen and there was no way to explain the building properly without another model.

Reflections

For Cézanne virtual space was the habitat of his mind. He was gifted in such a way that attentive watch and spatial composition were the same thing. Leonardo da Vinci was only able to see what he transferred to the canvas or drew with the help of a transparent glass. He used to create primary illusion, space appearance. We would like to lead the way between Leonardo and Cézanne.

With a very long step forward in time we can end this chapter with a quotation from Theo Van Doesburg's writing from *Intuition towards Certitude* (Van Doesburg, 1930):

> That which today bestows a cultural value on painting is mathematical order or, rather, arithmetical control. Mathematics has represented not only the basis of all science but also the foundations of art during the great epochs. As soon as the artist uses elementary forms as a means of expression, his work is not merely 'modern', but universal.

References

Greenberg, A. (1969) Lutyens architecture restudied. *Perspecta, 12.*

Loos, A. (1929) Josef Vaillich. *Frankfurter Zeitung,* No. 216, March 21st.

Manson, G.C. (ed.) (1958) *Frank Lloyd Wright to 1910: The First Golden Age,* Van Nostrand Reinhold, Toronto.

McCormac, R. (1968) The anatomy of Wright's aesthetics. *The Architectural Review*, February.

Van Doesburg, T. (1930) *From Intuition towards Certitude*, Paris.

c)

Architecture as Space and Matter: Exercises in Architectural Composition and Interpretation

Antony Radford
The University of Adelaide

Context: theory and practice

The integration of theory and practice in education was expressed by the educationalist Dewey (1936) as 'the question of duly adapting to each other the practical and the utilitarian, the executive and the abstract, the tool and the book, the head and the hand'. The best-known attempt to bridge the theory–practice schism in architectural education has been Itten's proposal for a basic course at the Bauhaus, the celebrated German school of architecture and the arts which lasted just 14 years from 1919 to 1933. The aims of Itten's basic course were as follows:

- to prepare students for further work by relieving them of obstructive attitudes and preconceptions;
- to provide an introduction to, and the necessary theoretical background for, future courses; and
- to provide the means and some ideological background for a broader range of educational experiences than had previously occurred in design education (Cross, 1983).

Itten's preference was to keep the relationship between the theoretical and practical aspects of the course freely interacting. He 'single-mindedly pursued in his own classes the relationship between theory and practice, and attempted to build up a pedagogy of suitable exercises based upon the exploration of this interaction' (Cross, 1983, p.50). A similar purpose lies behind the development of computer-graphics-based pedagogical exercises in architectural composition and interpretation, but unlike many of Itten's Bauhaus exercises these set out to operate directly in the realm of *architectural* design, and deal explicitly, although in an abstract way, with the built environment.

To work well, such integration needs an embracing theoretical framework of the whole, a model of the nature of architecture and architectural knowledge that transcends the boundaries of fields or projects. The model need not necessarily be 'right' in an absolute sense, merely heuristically useful in providing a conceptual framework by which students can understand the whole.

The long-established metaphor of language has been found useful in teaching, expressed in a loose model which separates the idea of a 'syntax' (e.g. elements and composition) of architecture from the 'interpretation' (e.g. environmental, social and economic performance) of architecture, and concerns itself with mapping relationships between the two. Viewing design within this model, architects appear to work with 'languages of architecture' and 'languages of plans and other representations' of architecture. The acquisition of a level of literacy in these languages, and competence in the skills and techniques involved in their application, can be partly taught directly and partly acquired through experience. 'As in learning a language, we do not acquire all the "rules of the game" by having them explained to us as explicit rules of grammar. We learn to speak a language, as language teachers know, by process of total immersion in the given language, at best in the country of origin' (Abel, 1981, p.210).

The aims of a beginners' course on the making and interpretation of form, then, encompass a combination of theory and practice in relation to design and the representation of designs. Through the course, students should achieve the following:

- relate theoretical ideas about the metaphor of design-as-language to the practice of design;
- learn about abstraction and mapping between different representations of designs by using physical models, computer graphics and hand graphics;

- gain experience in manipulating form; and
- gain experience in the design and execution of a presentation of design studies.

The exercises are accompanied by lectures and tutorials describing the metaphor of language and its history, and analysing examples of architecture, landscape architecture and urban design in terms of this metaphor. These sessions are also used to discuss the nature of some of the representations used in architecture (plans, axonometrics, physical models etc.) and the means of their production.

The metaphor of language

The activity of design in architecture involves both the interpretation of a set of needs or desired performances in terms of a design, and the organization, composition, and transformation of combinations of (physical and symbolic) elements of buildings. The metaphor of language has been used more or less literally since the eighteenth century by theorists, such as Durand in France (Durand, 1817–19) and Elmes in England (Elmes, 1823), exploring the nature of graphic and architectural design, and was particularly popular in the early nineteenth century, coloured by the adversarial simplifications of the Battle of the Styles. Design theorists such as March, Stiny and Fleming have explored the metaphor through formal shape grammars and Wojtowicz and Fawcett's *Architecture: Formal Approach* (Wojtowicz and Fawcett, 1986) brings together diverse strands from the syntactic tradition. Mitchell in *The Logic of Architecture* (Mitchell, 1990) presents a clear exposition of design as logical operations within a language and includes a useful bibliography.

The book *The Language of Architectural Plans* (Oxman *et al.*,1987) sets out a series of themes on and exercises in the syntax of architecture, concentrating on the nature and importance of the plan as an abstraction of architectural designs. Students at the Universities of Sydney and Adelaide in Australia, the Technion in Israel, and other institutions have followed versions of and developments from the syntactic studies proposed in that book.

The essential *formal* elements of architecture are space and matter. Both are equally important: the space between walls is to be designed as well as walls, the space between buildings as well as buildings. Ching in the introduction to his book *Architecture: Form, Space and Order,* widely used as a text for beginning architecture students, writes of 'the essential elements of form and space and those elements that control their organisation in our built environment' (Ching, 1979). The edges of elements can be manipulated: hard or permeable boundaries can be given to space, colour and texture given to matter. The operations on these elements are transformations to and additions of space and matter which are subject to ordering systems: axes, grids, proportions, the precedents set by formal prototypes. These elements and operations are the architect's means to compose an infinite variety of forms of buildings and urban spaces. A categorization consists, then, of the following (Radford *et al.*, 1989):

1 Objects
space
matter
are subjected to

2 Operations
- transformations
- additions and subtractions
- grouping

to produce

3 Relationships
- part to part
- part to whole
- whole to whole

under various

4 Ordering systems
- atomistic (additive) systems (such as fixed vocabularies and rules about the assembly of components)
- holistic systems (formal types and precedents and referential systems such as grids and axes)

This categorization is hierarchical both within each category and across categories. Within categories, for example, spaces are made up of component spaces, transformations are made up of simpler transformations, grids are made up of sub grids. More important is the hierarchical structure across categories. Anything can be regarded as an object and the categorization applied to that object. For example, if a grid is regarded as an object, there can be operations on grids within ordering principles for grids. There is no necessary top level or bottom level in the hierarchy.

In designing, architects do not operate solely with this knowledge about syntax and composition. They use abductive knowledge extensively, e.g. that an intention of designing a building which will be appropriate for a cold climate can be mapped onto a building form which is oriented towards the sun, is highly insulated and is not overshadowed. This abductive knowledge defines the characteristics of an *intentional*, i.e. intention-based, design space which is independent of any particular stylistic language of design. Thus the formal parameters above can be met by buildings designed in, for example, modern, post-modern or 'high-tech' styles of architecture. Simon (1975) observed that style is one way of doing things, chosen from a number of alternative ways. Design in a given style can therefore be characterized as being concerned with the production of designs which belong to a space defined by the rules of syntax (a process of syntactic and grammatical generation), but which also belong to a space of designs which accord with some specified set of intentions (a process of abduction, mapping interpretations to forms). Different designers interpret statements about design intentions differently in the design world, and there is no difficulty in accepting multiple interpretations.

The scope of this series of exercises is to explore the formal design world and to map *back*, via annotations to drawings, to *interpretations* of the design worlds. The annotations are important; they emphasize that the formal compositions are to be regarded as abstractions of the built environment and not as mere patterns of abstract form, and they relate strongly to students' observations of corresponding patterns in the 'real' world of buildings, the city and landscape. Moreover, these interpretations can be regarded as potential *intentions* for other designs. In later work the students map *forward* from such statements of intention to an intentional design space.

Computer graphics as a medium for learning about making form

These ideas can be explored using conventional media: pencils, paper, the drawing board. However, a drawing on paper lacks internal structure in the representation of entities; it is an assembly of notations, or marks. There is no built-in way to reorganize these marks or to maintain the coherence of sets of marks as elements; it is the experience of the designer which imposes the structure on marks. In order to teach about design, a better medium is one which can both explicitly represent the operations of design and maintain some internal structure in the representation of entities while undergoing transformation. Computer graphics systems fulfil this need admirably. Further, there is a correspondence between the syntactic operations which computer graphics systems allow on shapes and assemblies of shapes and the syntactic operations which a designer carries out in the development of architectural compositions. Computer graphics can therefore allow a directness and clarity in the execution of the operations of design which cannot be achieved with manual media. This, combined with the ease and speed of its application, allows the concatenation of experience through a rapid completion of a sequence of exercises. The resulting *structure* of the computer graphics representation contains syntactic information which can be interpreted through an active exploration of the structure by taking it apart and examining both the parts and the operations by which the parts are combined.

Images on paper are devalued versions of the computer models from which they are drawn, because in the act of transferring from computer memory, to printer, to paper, the structure and the ability to operate on that structure have been left behind. That is why students should learn with the computer.

Other advantages with computer graphics are the ease of execution of the operations, the sense of security given by the knowledge that any experiments can be carried out on one of multiple copies of the model, and the crisp quality of the resulting prints, all encourage adventurousness and contribute to a willingness to experiment and explore. Importantly, the presented result is developed directly from these experiments, whereas with manual drawing experimental work is usually redrawn for final presentation.

Clearly, if we wish to use the structure and operations of computer graphics in the teaching of such design literacy, the student must first be knowledgeable in computer graphics. Fortunately, literacy in computer graphics at the necessary level is rather easier to achieve than literacy in design. The media used for carrying out the exercises have been two-dimensional drawing programs such as MacDraw and Canvas on Apple Macintosh computers and Autosketch on MSDos (IBM PC and similar) computers. Other programs such as ModelShop, Autocad and Caddsman have also been used by students working directly with three-dimensional models.

Although most of the learning about the making of form does and should take place with the computer, there is also value in mixing hand and computer drawings, and physical and computer models, in a single set of exercises. Computer three-dimensional models have different qualities from and do not replace physical three-dimensional models, and computer graphics two-dimensional abstractions have different qualities from and do not replace hand sketches. If the

Figure 4.1
The operations of design are mapped on to operations of modelling within a computer graphics system. Few graphics systems yet offer the desired degree of directness in these operations, but the derivations and multiple representations are much clearer than with manual techniques

media are mixed, students learn about the contrasting characteristics of the different representations and where and how to exploit these characteristics in their work. If at the same time they seek examples of 'real' built form (directly experienced in the world around them and indirectly seen through photographs) which exemplify aspects of composition and interpretation which arise in their explorations, students learn to relate a variety of abstractions to the built environment.

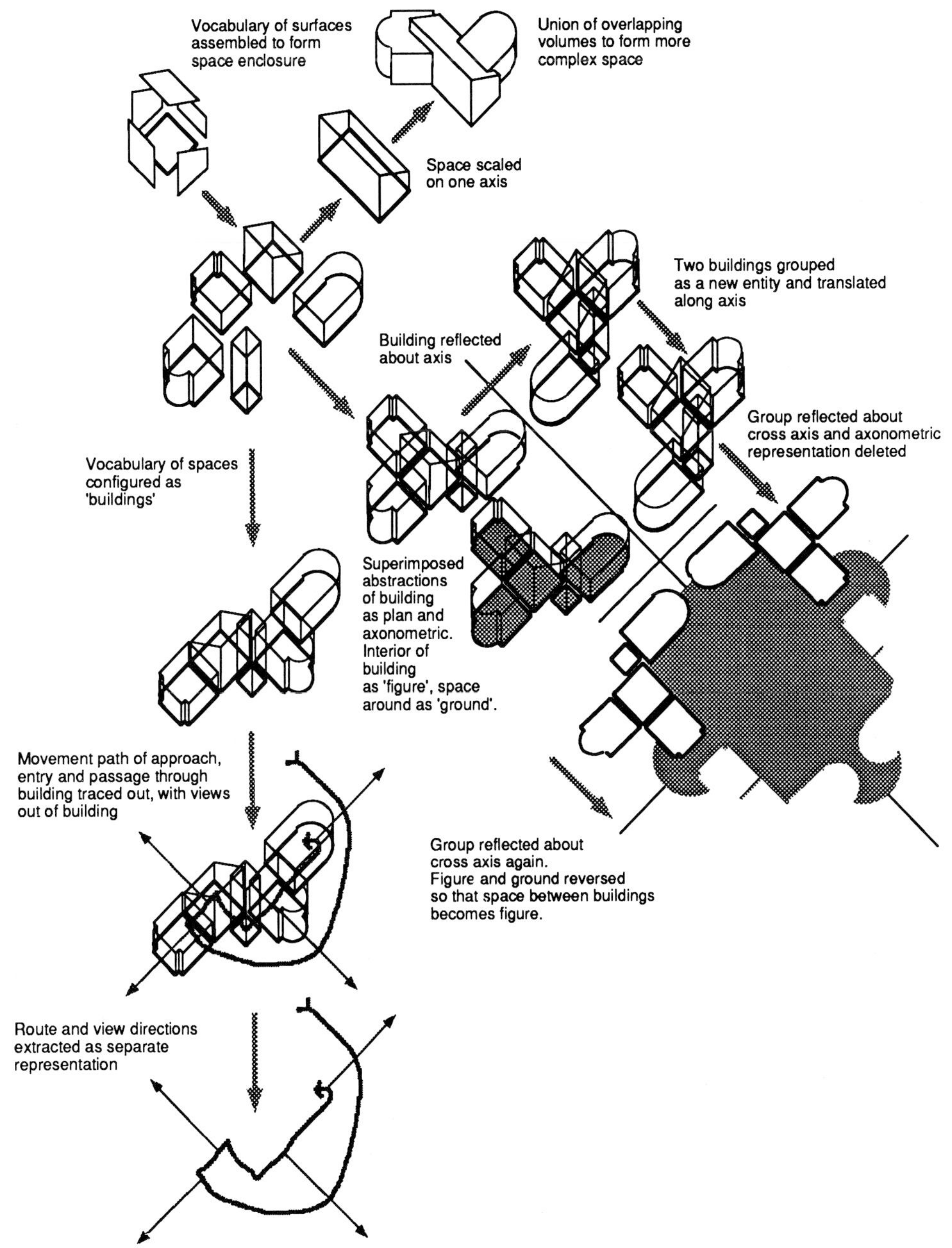

The operations of design are mapped on to operations of modeling within a computer graphics system. Few graphics systems yet offer the desired degree of directness in these operations, but the derivations and multiple representations are much clearer than with manual techniques.

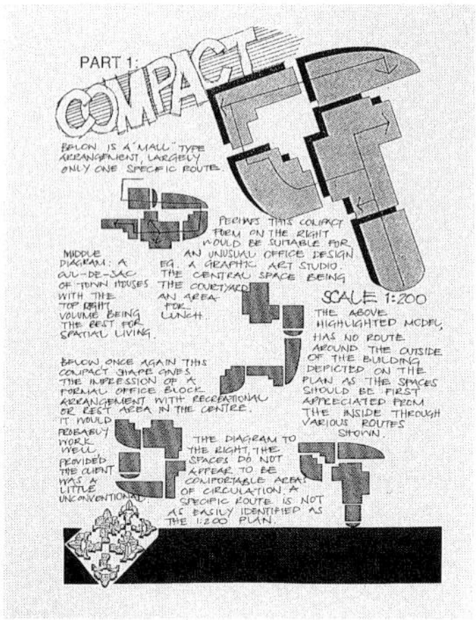

Figure 4.2
Exercise 1, Part 1.
Complete A4 sheet showing some compact arrangements of a vocabulary of five spaces with hand-written annotations relating the designs to building function types. The vocabulary is developed through hand sketches, computer drawings and physical models used in parallel. Students are encouraged to imagine themselves inside and moving through and between the spaces. (Julie Daw, University of Adelaide, 1990)

Figure 4.4
Exercise 1, Part 3.
Extract from a sheet exploring volumes which 'emerge' in the overlapping of the original vocabulary of spaces. The computer graphics image was printed and pasted to a black backing sheet before contrasting hand graphics and annotations were added. In this and other examples the sheets submitted by each student form a set with consistent labels and graphic qualities. The notion of 'emergent' space applies to any spatial pattern which arises out of operations on the original representation and which is not explicitly modelled in the representation. (Jen Smit, University of Adelaide, 1989)

Figure 4.5
Exercise 2, Part 1.
Extracts from two sheets showing two compact (above) and two articulate (below) arrangements of five physical elements. In this exercise the row of post and lintel objects and the group of columns each count as one element. As in Exercise 1, students are encouraged to regard the objects as part of the built environment and to imagine themselves walking through the compositions; the annotation to the lower assembly suggests that it 'can be seen as a greenhouse (pergola, flower beds), courtyard, garden, gym or rooftop recreation area...'. (Rastko Sarac, University of Adelaide, 1990)

Figure 4.3
Exercise 1, Part 2
Translation, rotation and reflection applied to an articulate group of spaces, with inversion of figure and ground in the central image. The importance of designing the layout of the presentation is demonstrated in this example, where the arrangement of the sheet is derived from the operations. The spaces designed by different students suggest very different styles of architecture. (Debra Longin, University of Adelaide, 1990)

Two exercises

Over the years many exercises have been developed and implemented for teaching these ideas in a continuing research and teaching programme. The two described here are the most directly related to the notions of architecture as space and architecture as matter. For other exercises, particularly those concentrating on the plan as an abstraction of architecture, see *The Language of Architectural Plans* (Oxman *et al.*, 1987).

Exercise 1

Part 1

Develop a set of five three-dimensional volumes representing spaces in a building to a scale of about 1:200. Explore arrangements of the spaces in compact and articulate forms. Select and draw a set of some compact and articulate arrangements in plan, or in plan with projected three-dimensional form, also to a scale of about 1:200. Define on at least one plan a route through the spaces, from outside through a single entry to all the spaces. Add notes to the drawings suggesting possible interpretations.
Limit: one A4 model, two A4 drawings.

Part 2

Repeat one 'articulate' and one 'compact' group in arrangements using translation, reflection and rotation, using a smaller scale where necessary to fit. Consider particularly the 'left over' space between the assemblies. Add notes to the drawings suggesting possible interpretations.
Limit: two A4 drawings.

Part 3

Overlap some or all of the spaces to make new spaces which 'emerge' from their combination. You may use any space more than once. Repeat parts 1 and 2. Add notes to the drawings suggesting possible interpretations.
Limit: two A4 drawings.

Exercise 2

Part 1

Make a set of five three-dimensional volumes representing objects (matter) in a building to a scale of about 1:100. They can be a row of columns, a platform, a horizontal plane, a vertical plane with or without regular openings, or discrete cubes or cylinders. Explore arrangements of the objects in compact and articulate forms. Select and draw a set of some compact and articulate arrangements in plan or plan with projected three-dimensional form, also to a scale of about 1:100. Define on at least one plan a route through the objects, from outside through a single entry to a point amongst the objects. Add notes to the drawings suggesting possible interpretations.
Limit: one A4 model, two A4 drawings.

Part 2

Repeat one 'articulate' and one 'compact' group in arrangements using translation, reflection and rotation, using a smaller scale where necessary to fit. Consider particularly the 'left over' space between the assemblies. Add notes to the drawings suggesting possible interpretations.
Limit: two A4 drawings.

Part 3

Overlap some or all of the spaces to make new spaces which 'emerge' from their combination. You may use any space more than once. Repeat parts 1 and 2. Add notes to the drawings suggesting possible interpretations.
Limit: two A4 drawings.

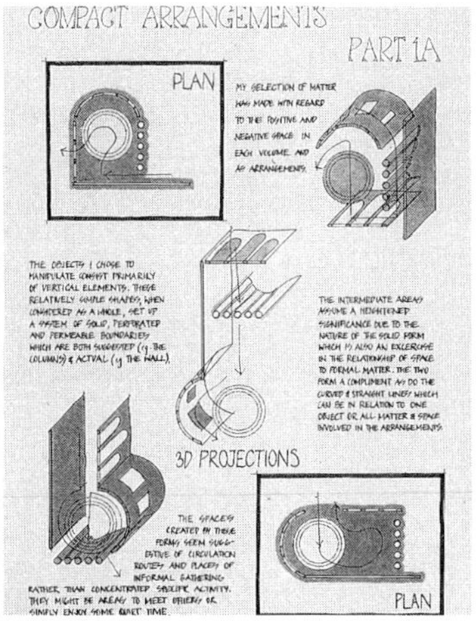

Figure 4.6
Exercise 2, Part 1.
Compact arrangements of matter with hand-drawn projections from computer graphics plans to suggest three-dimensional form. The mixing of and experimentation with techniques is encouraged in the exercises and students are shown examples of earlier work. Colour can be applied by using a pen plotter for the computer graphics drawings or in the added hand work. (Sian Jones, University of Adelaide, 1990)

Figure 4.7
Exercise 2, Part 1.
Physical model of a composition of five elements, in this case projected from an A4 backing board. A computer model does not serve the same purpose as a physical model and the use of both together, with reference between them, is a fundamental part of the exercises. The small size of the models allows them to be raised easily to eye level and also to be pinned vertically alongside the drawing sheets in a display of work. The precision needed for such small models to look satisfactory is also a good learning experience. (Alexander Wilkinson, University of Adelaide, 1990)

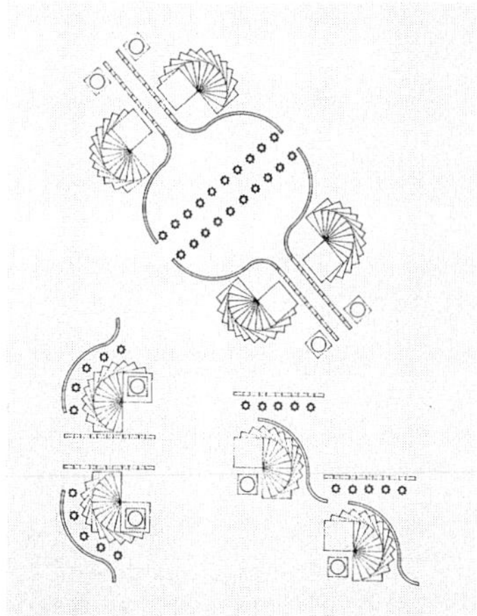

Figure 4.8
Exercise 2, Part 2.
Extract from a sheet showing some different arrangements of the elements shown in the physical model, in each case translated and/or reflected in small groups. (Alexander Wilkinson, University of Adelaide, 1990)

The submission requirements are as follows.

1 There must be a title sheet for the series.
2 The use of computer graphics must be apparent.
3 The use of hand graphics must be apparent.
4 The use of physical models must be apparent.
5 Each part should be presented on one sheet, which means that students have to be selective about what to include.

The assessment criteria are the following:

1 conformity with the submission requirements and required scope of the studies;
2 the content of the submission;
3 the explanation of content through annotations;
4 the organization and graphic design of the submission; and
5 The graphic skill demonstrated in the submission, including model making and computer graphic skills.

Discussion

There is, of course, an intended correspondence between the exercises on 'space' and 'matter' and the fact that both require the preparation of physical models as well as hand and computer graphics. Both two-dimensional and three-dimensional graphics programs have been used; the three-dimensional program is not necessarily better, since it loses the value of working with the plan as abstraction. The quick 'hand' projection of a plan into three-dimensional form is an effective compromise.

Initially, many students tend to produce large-scale images of the kind they see in the traditional studio situation, where work is 'pinned up' on studio display boards. What is required in this program is closer to the scale of book illustrations than that of traditional architectural drawings. The change of scale from the expected format is useful in that it makes explicit a number of aspects of graphic communication which are often left implicit, such as the effects of changing scale, medium and expected reading context on the choice of appropriate format, layout and style. The conjunction of manual and computer graphics techniques being used within the same group of students to carry out the same project proves mutually illuminating. In the process of learning about planning and abstractions, they also learn about graphics: with hand graphics, the subtlety, flexibility and expression of hand work; with computer graphics, the design and development of the image within the vocabulary of a system, and the possibilities and pitfalls of desktop publishing. It is noticeable that the most successful hand-drawn images are those that do not attempt to emulate the precision of computer graphics, while the most successful computer images are those that do not attempt to capture the subtlety and idiosyncrasy of a hand sketch. The concentration of form and content in the small space of the book format, and the possibility of paying undivided attention to the relationships between line quality, style and medium, proves valuable in the exploration of the expressive and communicative potential of simple ink and pencil line work and the comparative effects of adding colour and pattern.

There is now considerable experience of working with these exercises. The supporting activities set up around them, including the accompanying lectures and discussions, the criticism provided during progress of the work, and the opportunities for students to learn from the work of their colleagues during the exercises, are of great importance. The work is reported by students to be highly self-motivating and interesting, and the experience appears to be of value for both very able and less able students.

Figure 4.9
Exercise 2, Parts 1 and 2.
Extracts from three sheets showing an axonometric view of a configuration of five elements and two groupings of the same (above) and different (middle) configurations. The hand-written annotation accompanying the axonometric describes the route: 'The path first passes the block which marks or hides the entrance. It is at the block that the path turns to face the door, thus the approach to the door is always straight on and not oblique. The door marks the entrance, the point of passage from the plain "exterior" to the layered, complex "interior". The colonnade links the door to the platform .... The sail covers the last part of the journey to the platform and intensifies the feeling of arrival. At first the sail is high above the path and the colonnade, as progress is made the sail drops close to the ground, above the platform the sail is at its lowest. The platform is the focus of the journey; it is set apart by the process needed to reach it, by its height above the ground and by the presence of the sail. 'The upper group' reads as some sort of hotel/motel, each part being a room with ablutions located on the platforms and the areas between the door and platform as the main living space....' In the middle group, 'This space acts as a courtyard, node of activity, meeting place. ...The smaller "places" could act as bars/coffee houses or just as smaller more secluded places to be. The sails in these places would reinforce these ideas of "cosy" space. This is a place to meet and be in.' (Peter Schumacher, University of Adelaide, 1990)

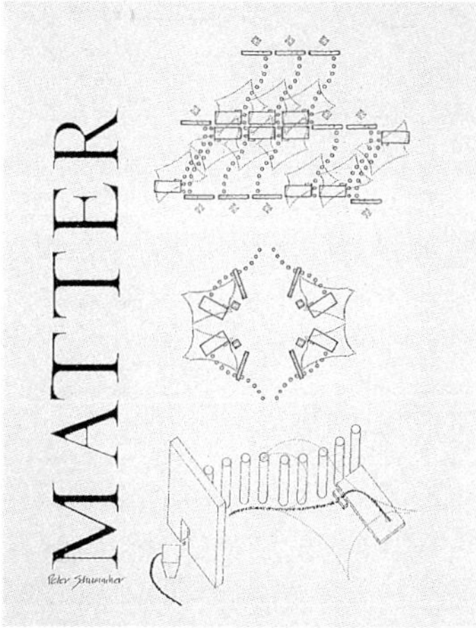

Acknowledgements

I am indebted to Robert Oxman and Rivka Oxman of the Technion, Israel Institute of Technology, for their collaboration in the original research and development of the Language of Architectural Plans teaching program and their critical role in the formulation and implementation of earlier versions of these exercises. I am also grateful to Deborah White, Sam Ridgway and John Gasper at the University of Adelaide for their contribution during the teaching of the program at Adelaide, and to Deborah White and Robert Woodbury for their comments on a draft of this chapter. I also acknowledge, with thanks, the contributions of the students whose work is illustrated here and the many others who have now participated in these studies.

References

Abel, C. (1981) Function of tacit knowledge in learning to design, *Design Studies,* 2 (4), 209–214.

Ching, F.D.K. (1979) *Architecture: Form, Space and Order.* Van Nostrand Reinhold, New York, p.6.

Cross, A. (1983) The educational background to the Bauhaus, *Design Studies,* 4 (1) 4352.

Dewey, J. (1936) The significance of the school in education, in Mayhew, K. C. and Edwards, A.C. (eds), *The Dewey School,* D. Appleton Century, New York, London.

Durand, J.-N.-L. (1817–19). Précis des leçons d'architecture donnés à l'Ecole Royale Polytechnique. Reprinted by Verlag, Nordlingen, 1985.

Elmes, J. (1823) *Lectures on Architecture: comprising the history of the art from earliest times to the present day.* Priestly and Weale, London.

Mitchell, W.J. (1990) *The Logic of Architecture,* MIT Press, Cambridge.

Oxman, R., Radford, A.D. and Oxman, R. (1987) *The Language of Architectural Plans,* Architecture Media Australia, Melbourne (10A Beach Street, Australia 3207). (Republished in Europe as a Report of ECAADE, Education in Computer-Aided Architectural Design in Europe, Eindhoven University of Technology, Eindhoven.)

Radford, A.D, Oxman, R. and Oxman, R. (1989) *Expert Systems and Architectural Formal Knowledge, Proceedings of Expert Systems in Architecture, Building and Construction, University of Sydney Department of Architectural and Design Science.*

Simon, H. (1975) Style in Design, in Eastman, C.M., *Spatial Synthesis in Computer-Aided Building Design,* New York.

Wojtowicz, J. and Fawcett, W. (1986) *Architecture: Formal Approach,* Academy Editions, London.

Computer-Aided Design or Computers and Design

Alan H. Bridges
Department of Architecture and Building Science,
University of Strathclyde

Introduction

The question usually posed in relation to computers and the teaching of architectural design is 'How can we use computers in the design studio?' Such a question presupposes an existing structure for teaching design and that computers can be made to fit into that structure. A more appropriate question might be 'How may we teach design in the computing studio?' The full potential of computing in architectural design will only be realized by the creation of new models of the design process appropriate to the new design medium. These new methodologies need to reflect the nature of the design medium being used rather than simply transferring the techniques of the traditional design media to the computer. An analogy with another art – theatre – illustrates the point. At the beginning of this century drama was transformed by the introduction of the new technology of the cinema. Actors, directors and producers had to find a way of working in the new medium and, initially, simply carried over theatrical conventions into film. This response to technological change is quite usual; only a few years previously the response to the introduction of the still camera was to imitate painting. CAD is at an equivalent stage of development and programs which automate traditional draughting are well established in practice. However, in the way that we now realize that cinema is not merely theatre done with machines, CAD is not just architectural design done with computers. Adaptation requires not only an understanding of the nature of the medium but also a reappraisal of architectural design theory. It is for these reasons that academics concerned with the teaching of CAD have been rereading many of the classic architectural treatises. In this chapter some of the special characteristics of computer-augmented design are discussed and parts of a computer-based course in architectural design theory taught at the Technical University Delft and the University of Strathclyde are described. The course syllabus is outlined in an appendix.

Types of drawings

Traditional drawings on paper are different from computer-based drawings in a number of significant ways. The traditional, pencil-aided design (PAD) drawing is essentially unstructured – each line is drawn independently of every other line. Thus, if the drawing subsequently requires modification, individual lines have to be erased and redrawn. In a CAD drawing the elements of the design are represented by a set of 'graphic primitives' (such as lines, rectangles, polygons, arcs, circles etc.) arranged in a two-dimensional co-ordinate system. It is thus possible globally to change a rectangle of one size for a rectangle of a different size (or for a quite different shape, say a circle), or to make copies of the shape in various ways. The second main difference is the concept of scale. PAD drawings are produced to specific scales, 1:100, 1:50, 1:20 etc., often entailing the redrawing of many elements at a different size with no real difference in their information content. A CAD drawing is stored in the computer at full size and different scale drawings are produced by the computer drawing system which modifies its full-size data appropriately.

These two specific features of CAD enable a drawing to be manipulated in a way that relates uniquely to the medium of computing. As shapes can be made up from graphic primitives we have a choice in the way in which

Figure 5.1
Parties and diagrammatic plan of S. Ivo, Rome (1642)

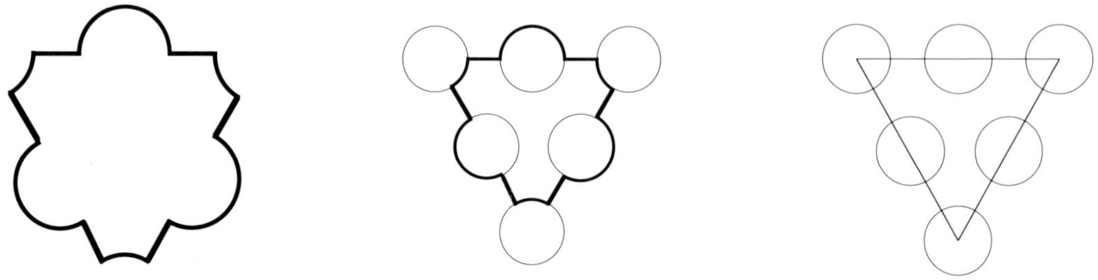

Figure 5.2
Parti for Palladio's villas, together with diagrammatic plans of Villa Thiene at Cicogna and Villa Badoer at Fratta, Polesine

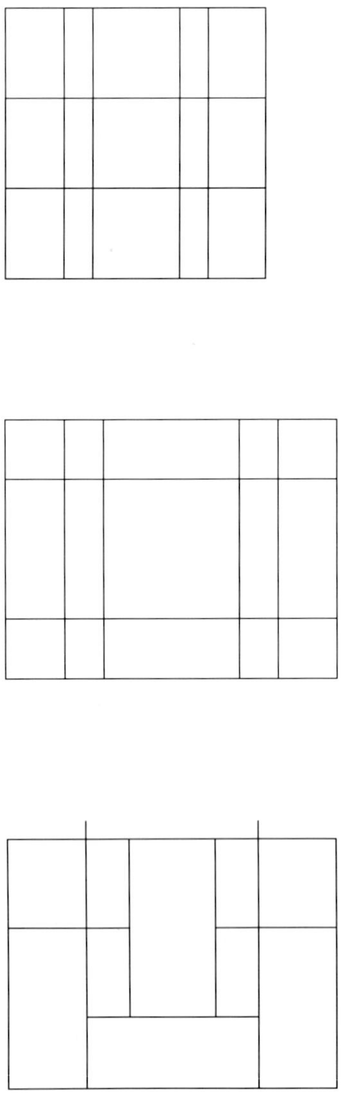

an object is defined. To take a trivial example, a triangle might be seen as a shape consisting of three connected lines or, alternatively, as a three-sided instance of the polygon primitive. Furthermore, the way in which dimensions can be specified enables us to define shapes 'parametrically'. That is, rather than specifying fixed lengths for lines we can define lengths relative to other elements in the drawing. For example, we can embed Palladian theories of proportion into our system by specifying that rectangles should have sides in the proportional ratio 1:2 (or 2:3 or whatever). If we define the unit length as the 'independent variable', after our specifying the length of that side the computer will calculate the value of the 'dependent variable' automatically. One shape definition (rectangle with proportions 1:2) thus leads to the possibility of an infinite number of 'instances' of that shape by the specification of different values for the independent variable. The independent variable(s) define the 'parameters' of the shape and this form of shape modification is known as 'parametric variation'. Mitchell *et al.* (1988) have described the development of a customized CAD system (Topdown) for the exploration of parametric variations. This shell has been used successfully at Delft and Strathclyde but in this chapter we concentrate on experiences of using a much more basic facility – the 'layer' structure provided with most computer drawing systems. This facility is used to set up ordering grids which are then used as formal design generators.

Geometry and grid

Geometry is a fundamental component of design, and computers provide a convenient medium to explore it in two or three dimensions. Whilst geometry in one form or another exists in all buildings, to use it creatively as a formative generator the student must be aware of a number of underlying principles.

The most fundamental application is the use of basic geometrical figures (circle, square, triangle etc. in two dimensions) to determine the built form configuration. Combinations of elements (e.g. a circle and a square) can be used: such figures do not even have to exist physically but may be implied by other figures. Combinations can include different degrees of overlap: one figure may be adjacent to, overlap or be entirely contained within another figure. These geometrical combinations can themselves then be further combined.

Combinations can be made with similar geometries, for example, two circles, three triangles etc. of the same or different sizes. The square is the most commonly used figure, partly because in certain combinations it produces larger versions of itself. The nine-square format assembled from three rows of three squares is one of the classic formative geometries. Palladio's villas are based on a nine-square plan, modified by the insertion of extra divisions to make a non-regular 5 x 3 plan, and Durand shows a 'formule graphique' using 2 x 2, 3 x 3, 4 x 4 and 5 x 5 square generators. Variations can be made on any of these plans by removing certain component parts, modifying the sizes of component parts or substituting other shapes for the squares.

The Palladian villas all derive from a single partie developed from an analysis of the requirements of an Italian villa: loggias and a large hall in the central axis, two or three living rooms or bedrooms of various sizes at the sides and, between them and the hall, space for smaller rooms and staircases. The Villa Thiene at Cicogna, built during the 1550s, shows the pattern

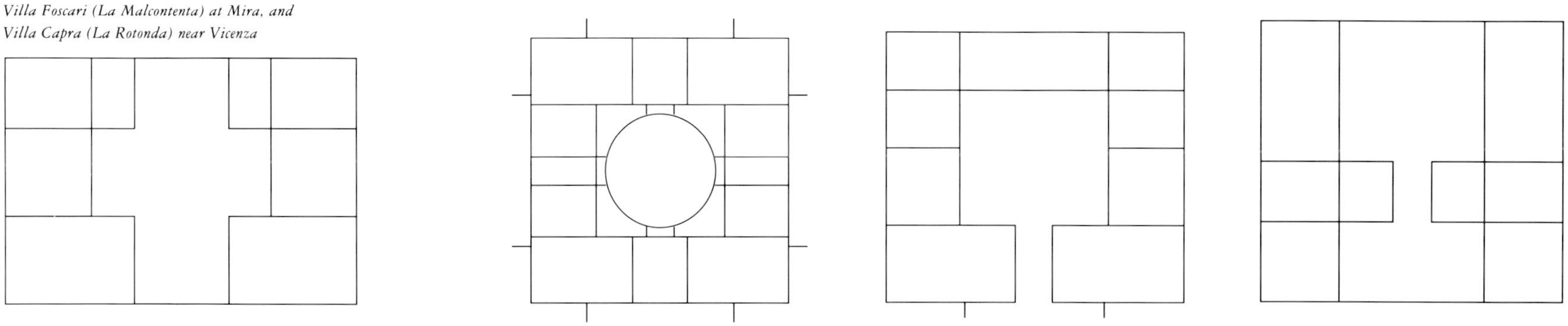

Figure 5.3
Diagrammatic plans of Palladio's villas: Villa Cornaro at Piombino Dese, Villa Eno at Fanzola, Villa Foscari (La Malcontenta) at Mira, and Villa Capra (La Rotonda) near Vicenza

most clearly. The rooms, together with the porticos, are defined by a rectangle divided by two longitudinal and four transverse lines. The Villa Badoer at Fratta, Polesine (*c.* 1566), follows the same pattern, but with one portico now placed outside the cube of the building. The Villa Cornaro at Piombino Dese (1566) is essentially the same scheme inverted with the two small rooms on each side of the hall joined to form larger rooms with their axes at right angles to the hall. The staircases are moved to the wings, leaving an almost square hall of the same width as the porticos. When the staircases are brought inside alongside the small rooms the hall takes on the cruciform shape of the Villa Foscari at Mira (La Malcontenta, 1560). The most regular realization of the geometric pattern is seen in the Villa Capra near Vicenza (La Rotonda, 1570).

Forms can be generated using parts of the basic geometric shape, such as half a circle; or geometries can be obtained by locating elements at the corners of an implied larger geometric shape. Certain combinations or reductions will result in particular proportions and proportion-generating systems can be a subject of study in themselves.

Topological relationships can be found between apparently quite different buildings such as Palladio's Villa Foscari at Malcontenta of *c.* 1550–60 and the Villa Stein de Monzie at Garches by Le Corbusier (1927). Rowe (1976) shows how both are conceived of as single blocks and, allowing for variations in the roof treatment, are of similar volume, each measuring 8 units in length, by 5.5 in breadth, by 5 in height. There is also a comparable bay structure. Each house contains an alternating rhythm of double and single spatial intervals in the form ABABA, with proportions 2:1:2:1:2. Each house, read from front to back, displays a comparable tripartite distribution of lines of support. Both are built following strict laws of proportion. Le Corbusier carefully indicates his relationships by an apparatus of regulating lines and figures and by placing on the drawings of his elevations the ratio of the golden section, A:B = B:(A+B). But, if Le Corbusier's façades are for him the primary demonstrations of the virtues of a mathematical discipline, with Palladio the main demonstration is in the plan. All the interior spaces of Villa Foscari (except for the stairs and the length of the main hall) are integrated according to the proportions 1:2:3:4. Wittkower (1952) also shows how this same proportional integration applies to the portico as well. The layout is basically two suites of three rooms each and two staircases arranged on opposite sides of a main hall. The basic module is a 16 ft square: the larger rooms in each suite are 16 ft x 24 ft (i.e. proportions of 2:3) and the smaller rooms are 16 ft x 12 ft (i.e. 3:4). The height of the rooms is determined (in accordance with the 'first rule' in Palladio's *Primo Libro,* ch. 23) by adding the length and breadth and dividing the total by 2.

Another series of configurations can be developed through the manipulation of geometries by simple translations and rotations. Translations which result in overlaps create a third figure from the combining of the two other figures. The development of apparent complexity through these simple operations is well illustrated in the work of Peter Eisenman.

Grids are developed from the repetition of basic geometries. Multiplication, combination and subdivision of elements all produce relative complexity from simple basic elements. Grids may be irregular, with the spatial divisions differentiated by size, proportion or location. Another aspect of grids is the relationship between the generating series (which may

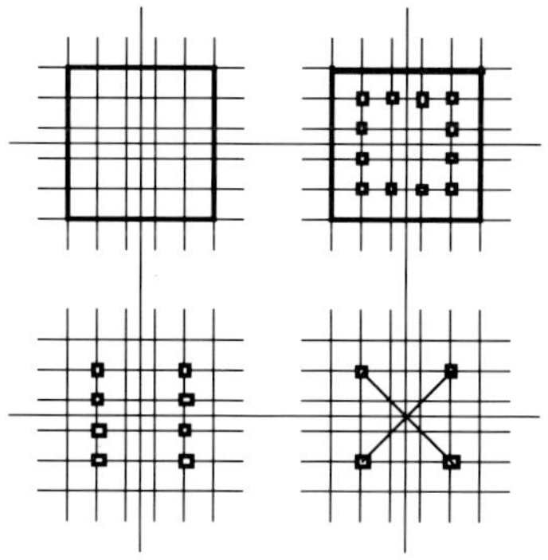

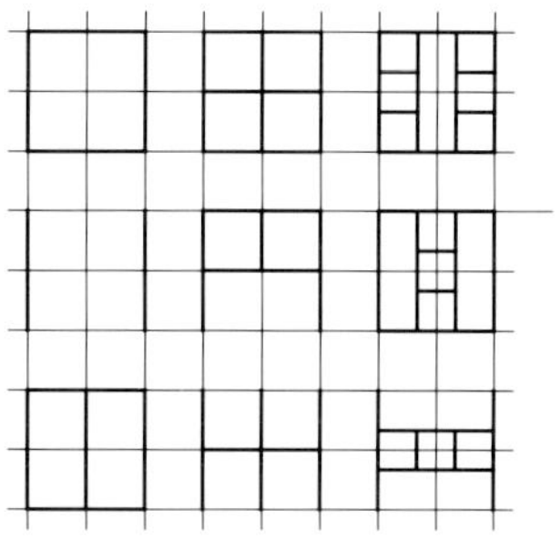

Figure 5.4
Parties from Durand's 'Formule Graphique Applicable aux Edifices Publics Voutés dont les parties sont destinées à des usages différents'

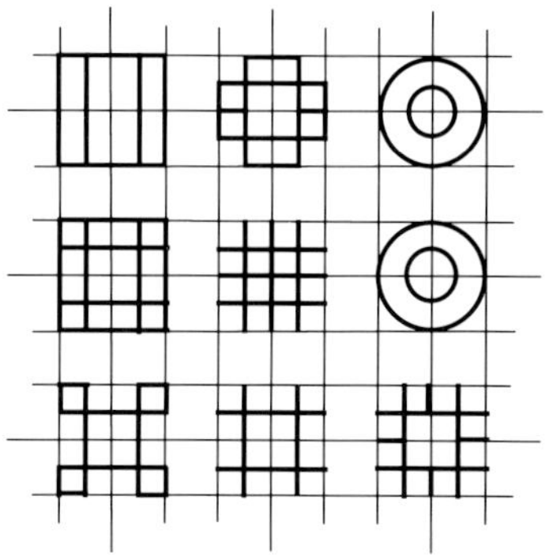

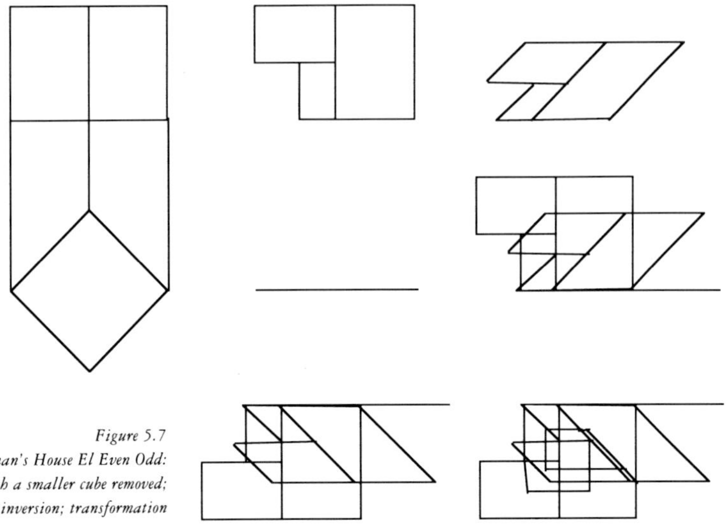

Figure 5.7
Analysis diagrams of Peter Eisenman's House El Even Odd: elevation of a tube; the cube with a smaller cube removed; axonometric; superimposition; inversion; transformation

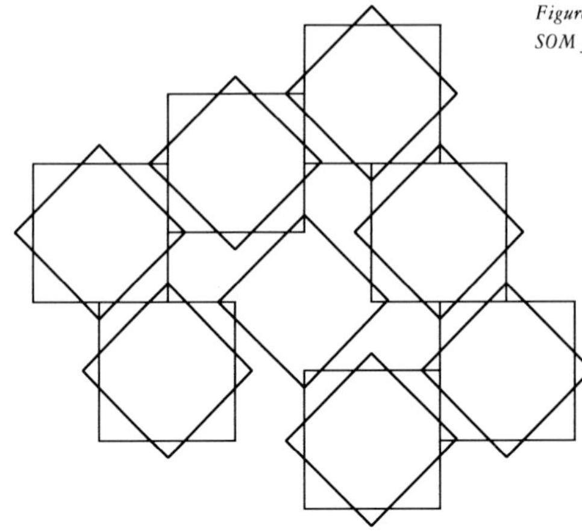

Figure 5.8
SOM field theory grid

Figure 5.5
Diagrammatic plan of Villa Stein de Monzie at Garches

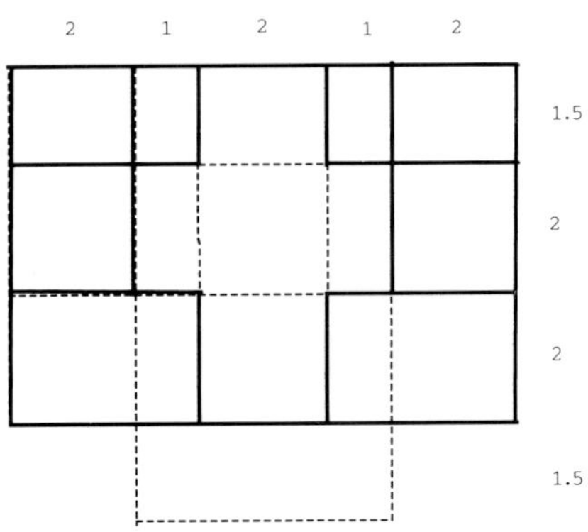

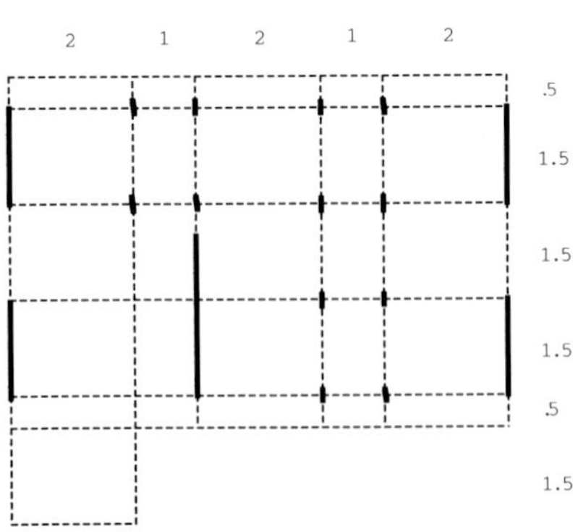

Figure 5.6
Diagrammatic plan of Villa Foscari at Malcontenta

or may not be orthogonal to each other). For example, if the relationship is orthogonal with all intervals in both series equal, a square grid results, whereas two orthogonal series each with more than one equal interval will create a rectangular tartan grid. Like basic geometric figures grids can be combined or manipulated by rotation, translation and overlapping. Figure 5.8 shows SOM's 'field theory grid' used at the Architecture and Arts Building, University of Illinois, Chicago, Circus Campus. In this design the major module was produced by placing an 80 ft square over an 85 ft square at an angle of 45°. Each of these star-shaped modules houses one studio. Grids can be further transformed by disrupting their continuity (maybe to define a major space) or part may be dislocated and rotated. Grids need not even be made up of straight lines.

Precedents from architectural theory

The tripartition seen in Garches and Malcontenta is a classical division of space: it can be seen as marking the difference between the internal and external sections of a work. It divides a building into three parts, two border parts and one enclosed. The 'whole', states Aristotle, is tripartite: it has 'a beginning, a middle and an end'. Tripartition underlies the Vitruvian classification of temples (*De Architectura* Bk 3, ch. 2). The first two types – 'in antis' and 'prostyle' – are similar, both having a front part, usually pilasters or free-standing columns, attached to the main unarticulated volume (the 'cella'). The third form is 'amphiprostyle': this has columns both (amphi) front and back, i.e. a portico at each end. Last is the 'peripteral' temple with columns all round (peri): this plan is divided in three from every view. These three generic styles may be represented by a formula, each letter standing for an architectural part.

Vitruvius defined more kinds of temples by adding parts and/or rows of columns (or deleting them). All can be derived from the same formula of tripartition. What is interesting is not so much Vitruvius's typology of buildings but his system of classification, which contains an implicit method for generating plans. This is more easily seen if we represent these basic types symbolically – ab, aba etc. This may be seen particularly in Cesariano's 1521 edition of *De Architectura* – the first translation of Vitruvius into vernacular Italian. It contained an extensive commentary and many illustrations. The figures relating to the grid and tripartition can be found in the series of illustrations to Vitruvius's Book 3.

The grid is used in a number of ways – generally and specifically – and in regular or irregular units. Referring to the Cesariano plan we see an example of a square grid dividing the plan into seven parts:

A B C D C B A

the middle unit (D) being made up of two identical B units, giving

A B C B B C B A

which is classically tripartite – a beginning part B between A and C, a middle part BB between C and C, and an end part B identical with the initial part. The whole may therefore be condensed as follows:

<u>A B C</u> <u>B B</u> <u>C B A</u>
a b a

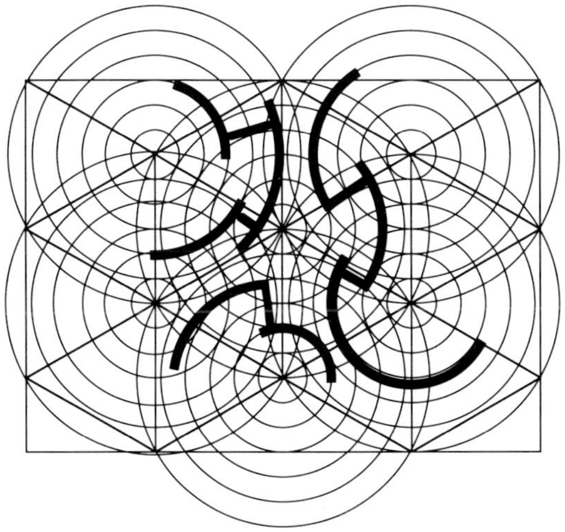

Figure 5.9
After a drawing by Paolo Portoghesi

We can transcribe Cesariano's plan in its entirety with his notation, adding an X where no notation is provided.

ABC D CBA
BHL E LHB
CLK X KLC

DEX F XED

CLK X KLC
BHL E LHB
ABC D CBA

As a next step we can rewrite the plan pattern, simplifying it to demonstrate, as before, its tripartite theme:

a b a
b c b
a b a

Here we find the Aristotelian tripartite schema expressed in the most elementary way. We also find the Vitruvian temple formula. This 'square and cross' pattern is one of the most predominant formal patterns of classical architecture since the Renaissance and is often referred to as the 'mother taxis formula'.

The formula may be expanded by inserting an intermediate part between the end and middle sections. This permits us to demonstrate the workings of the 'production rules' of classical architecture and to relate the formula more easily to specific buildings.

a b c b a
b c d c b
c d f d c
b c d c b
a b c b a

It is possible to apply further productions such as deletion of parts, fusion of parts, addition of parts and substitution of parts (by hierarchically embedding other parts). Further, we can translate the rectangular grid into a polar grid and apply similar productions. Some possible results of these operations are briefly listed.

1 Deletion of parts

c b c b a b c b a a b c b a
c d c b d b b b b b
c d f d c c d f d c c c c f c
c d c b d bbbbb
c b cbabcbaabcba

2 Fusion of parts

a <u>b a</u> a B
|b |c |b into
|a |b |a B C B

a b |a B B
|b c |b into c
|a <u>b a</u> B B

a |b a a C a
b |c b into b b
a b a a b a

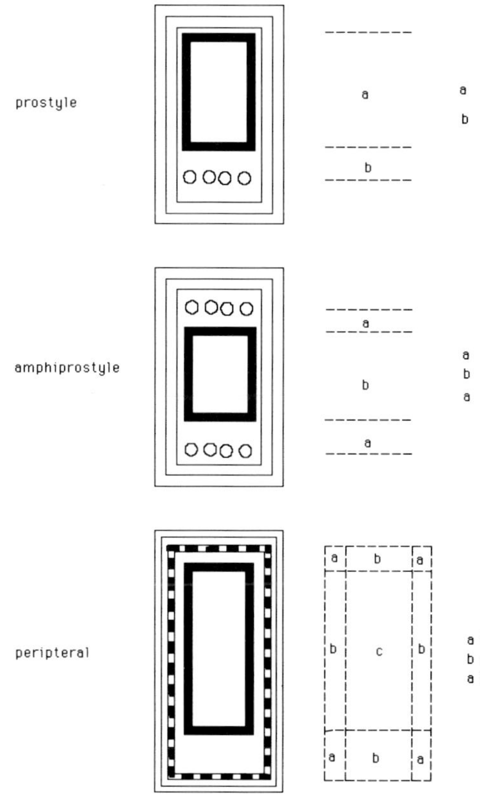

Figure 5.10
Vitruvius' typology of buildings

Figure 5.11
Grid pattern (after Cesariano, 1521)

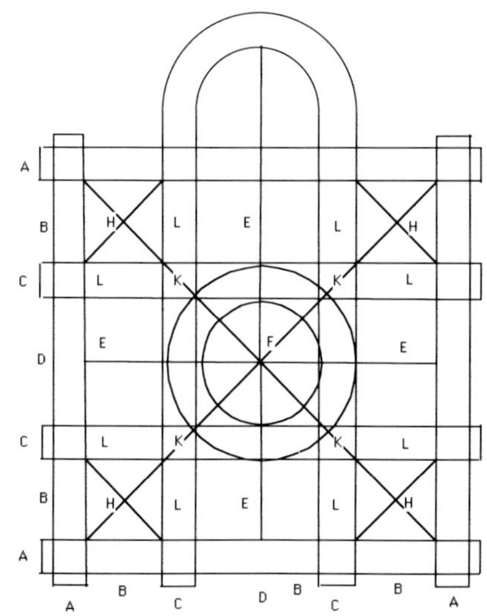

3 Addition or repetition of parts

```
a b c b a
b c d c b
c d f d c
c d f d c
b c d c b
a b c b a
```

4 Embedding of parts

```
                d e d     d e d
                e f e  b   e f e
                d e d      d e d
a b a
b c b   into     b    c    b
a b a

                  a    b    a
```

5 Translation to polar grid

```
                           b c b
                         a     a
a b c b a              b    d    b
b c d c b                   c c
c d f d c     into     c d f    d    c
b c d c b                   c c
a b c b a              b    d    b
                         a     a
                           b c b
```

A number of plans of classical architecture follow these kinds of patterns: for example, Bramante's plans for S. Pietro in Rome and his Tempietto (S. Pietro in Montorio) bring together rectangular and polar formulae to create hybrid formal patterns integrating grids and tripartition schemata. From the Renaissance on, taxis and its normative schemata have controlled an architectural composition by setting up contours, regulatory lines or planes, that plot limits defining the parts within which the architectural elements lie. Towards the end of the eighteenth century another way of specifying the divisions of a work became dominant: specification by an axis rather than by an outline. It is presupposed here that the architectural members of the section indicated by the axis are laid out – balanced – around the axis in bilateral symmetry. A comparison of the Cesariano diagrams (1521) with figures from Durand's *Précis* (1819) is revealing. This shift from contour to axis marks a step towards abstraction and facilitates the application of multiple taxis formulae on the same object, one laid over the other.

Guadet (1894) introduced the notion of axial drawing and proposed a *méthode à suivre* (echoing Durand's *marche à suivre*). The famous Durand plate shows an analysis of a Grand Prix project of Charles Percier annotated by Durand to show a method of design by composing elements on grid sections directed and organized by axes. Elements of 'design by prototype refinement' may also be found in Durand's work. He typically adapted other architects' designs, tailoring traditional arrangements to accord with his own ideals and reducing all compositions to standardized elementary forms, such as circles and squares, made up of a repetitive pattern of basic units. Durand not only 'corrected' originals, but also reduced plans to abstract diagrams and very rarely acknowledged either the original author or the building's original function. The *marche à suivre* illustrates all these aspects. Percier's 'Monument destiné à rassembler les différents académies' of 1786 was one of the most famous academic designs of the late eighteenth century.

Durand published Percier's project in 1805 as a prototype for an Institute, systematizing the proportions of the plan and omitting the platform and obelisks. He extended the steps the full length of the wings and made three smaller entrances in place of one large one. The entrance hall was subdivided to mirror those of the other three wings; the corridors were aligned and the doorways were reduced in size. The elevation was also modified. In 1813, in the revised edition of his lecture course, the *Nouveau Précis*, this simplified project becomes the model for the 'Marche à Suivre dans la Composition d'un Projet Quelconque' where no specific function is designated.

Durand taught his students the *mécanisme de la composition,* which involved the use of a grid to order the fundamental disposition of elements in the plan. Columns were to be placed at intersections, walls on axes, and openings at module centres. Durand showed how to apply this method to all parts of the building and how those parts may be combined in a specific project. Although the solution of the plan was always the primary concern, the application of combinations to façades, general volumetric studies, roofing, and parti generation was also taught. Combinations provided the solution to any architectural problem.

The use of the grid in design was not, of course, Durand's invention. The first signs of this shift may be traced back to Cesariano's 1521 edition of Vitruvius where the famous Vitruvian man is superimposed on a grid!

Conclusion

I do not wish to give the impression that grids dominate architectural design entirely. It is simply that, within the confines of this short chapter, they provide a convenient example. My main objective is to demonstrate that computers provide a convenient medium within which to explore design ideas. Our use of the computer follows the traditional processes of the design studio – learning by doing – but the flexibility of the medium and the possibility of easily manipulating designs (without destroying intermediate solutions) extends the possibilities far beyond those of the traditional studio.

The course is presented as a series of workshops, each beginning with a 45-minute lecture and continuing with a practical session of one and a quarter hours. A wide range of software is used, but the chosen hardware platform is the Apple Macintosh and all the illustrations for this chapter were produced with Graphsoft's MiniCAD.

Appendix – Architectural design and theory syllabus

- The readability of form
    - spatial elements
    - figure/ground relationships
- Energy fields of forms
    - Arnheim/Portaghesi theory
    - modification of forms
- Order in building
    - repetition by addition, division, series
    - proximity of elements
    - common enclosure on ground
    - alignment and series
    - progression
    - hierarchy: centrality, axiality, orientation
- Contrasts
    - positive, negative: solid/void, convex/concave,

- curved/straight
- light, dark: light/shade, absorbent/reflective
- large, small: wide/narrow, high/low
- horizontal, vertical

Complexity
- divergence from norm
- breaking of symmetry
- anomalies in regular patterns
- distortion of familiar patterns

Contradiction
- collision of two or more formal systems
- deliberate breaking of rules

Regularity
- rhythm and repetition
- order and monotony

Relationships between objects
- axial symmetry
- asymmetrical balance

Composition of the object
- articulation
- continuity
- faces and corners

Definition of space
- depths of space
- density of space
- opening of space
- spatial juxtaposition/interpenetration
- geometry

Assembly of forms
- linear organization
- centralized organization
- radial organization
- grid organization
- cluster organization
- plan libre

References

Cesariano, Cesare di Lorenzo (ed.) (1521) *Vitruvius, De Architectura Como.*

Durand, J.N.L. (1819) *Précis des Leçons d'Architecture,* Firmin Didot, 1819, 1817, 1821. Reprinted by Uhl Verlag, Unterschneidheim, 1975.

Guadet, J. (1894) *Elements et Théories de l'Architecture.* Librarie de la Construction Moderne, Paris.

Mitchell, W.J., Liggett, R.S. and Tan, M. (1988) The topdown system and its use in teaching, *Proceedings of the Acadia Conference 1988.*

Palladio, A. (1738) *The Four Books of Architecture* (Ware's edition). Reprinted by Dover, New York, 1965.

Rowe, C. (1976) *The Mathematics of the Ideal Villa and Other Essays.* MIT Press, Boston, MA.

Serlio, S. (1619) *Tutte l'Opera d'Architettura et Prospettiva de Sebastiano Serlio.* Bolognese, Venice.

Vitruvius (1914) *The Ten Books on Architecture,* (trans. M.H. Morgan). Dover, New York.

Wittkower, R. (1952) *Architectural Principles in the Age of Humanism.* Revised edition, Academy Editions, London, 1988.

Teaching Computer-Aided Design at The Open University

Philip Steadman
Centre for Configurational Studies, Faculty of Technology, The Open University, Milton Keynes

Introduction

In 1987 the Open University launched a new undergraduate course on CAD. The course is offered by the Design Discipline of the Faculty of Technology. It is thus not a course offered to architecture students – we do not teach architecture at the Open University – but is part of a range of general engineering courses. It does however include a large element of architectural CAD, and for that reason will I hope be of some interest to architectural educators.

It is perhaps necessary to explain a little about the way the Open University works, since we are so different from conventional institutions of higher education. We teach mature students, most of whom are in employment, and study part-time in their own homes. The main medium of teaching is via correspondence texts – books and booklets. We also use television and radio broadcasts, audio and video tapes, experimental apparatus sent to students through the post and, increasingly in the last few years, microcomputers which students use at home. All these media are supported by a network of part-time tutors all over the country who mark students' written work and give face-to-face tutorials.

The University works on a credit system. Students may choose from any of a wide range of courses to make up their own 'degree profiles'. The normal pattern is for students to take one credit a year. Six credits are needed for an ordinary bachelor's degree and eight credits for honours. Our CAD course is a half-credit course, i.e. it constitutes one sixteenth part of an honours degree. It is a 'third-level' course, roughly equivalent to third year undergraduate level in conventional universities. It represents in total some 200 hours of study time, spread over nine months.

Our students come to the CAD course with a great variety of backgrounds and interests: some are designers or draughtsmen, some work in engineering and manufacturing occupations, some are studying electronics and computing courses, some are teachers of craft, design and technology. We have therefore designed the course to be very wide-ranging in the areas of application covered: graphics, architecture, mechanical engineering, electronics. We have also tried to make it a course which is accessible to complete beginners: it assumes no prior experience of either computing or design. However, this has not prevented us taking many of the topics to some depth, as I shall demonstrate.

The course has three main components (see Appendix). The first is a textbook, *Principles of Computer-Aided Design* (Rooney and Steadman, 1987). As the title indicates, this provides much of the theoretical and mathematical background to the subject. The book is supported by 'study guides' – booklets which offer supplementary teaching with 'self-assessment questions' and pencil-and-paper exercises. The second component is a series of five one-hour videotapes. The third component is a large suite of software called CADPAC – most of it specially developed, but including one commercial package – together with very full supporting documentation and exercises. There are three other short booklets. At the very beginning of the course comes a basic introduction to computers and to design. At the end of the course there is a discussion of the implications of CAD for designers' work practices, and of the economic and social benefits and costs of the technology. Students are also provided with an edited collection of papers on expert systems and artificial intelligence in design, which can be updated as this research area develops.

Those of us responsible for the course felt that we only wanted to teach the subject if we could include a large element of practical hands-on computing experience. In the

Open University this meant in effect providing a machine for each student at home. (We try to keep the costs to students very low, and could not expect them all to buy computers for themselves.) Cost constraints were obviously critical, although at the time we were planning the course in 1985–6 the prospect of one machine per student was just about becoming an economic proposition.

The kinds of option open in the price range were the BBC Micro or the Sinclair QL. A more suitable and powerful alternative then became available: the research machine NIMBUS PC1, with colour monitor and mouse. The PC1 has a single disc drive and 576 K of memory. The University bought 200 NIMBUS machines which are loaned out and returned each year. This places a limit on the number of students admitted annually. Nearly 1000 students have gone through the course in four years, the extra 200 being students with independent access to other NIMBUS machines.

We were ahead of much of the rest of the University in home computing, but more recently the University has formed a policy and adopted a general MS DOS IBM-PC compatible standard for student microcomputers. We are converting the CAD course to meet this specification for 1991, of which more later.

The CADPAC software was developed for the most part in-house by my colleague Jeff Johnson and a team from our Academic Computing Service. It is of two main kinds. Some programs emulate the operation of real CAD systems but in simplified form. For example, in the electronics part of the course the student designs the logic and creates the physical layout for a printed-circuit board (PCB). In the mechanical engineering exercises the student uses finite-element methods to study the conduction of heat through a flat plate of complex shape, or designs a four-bar linkage to act as a door hinge and tests its motion dynamically. The student does not use a full computer-aided electronic design system, or a full finite-element package, but instead goes through a form of tutorial in each case. The basic logic and concepts are clarified and the key points of the respective design processes are explained, but inessential details are omitted.

The second type of software uses computer-aided learning techniques to convey some of the requisite geometry and algebra. For example, one series of exercises concerns the two-dimensional spatial transformations – translation, rotation, reflection, scaling – and their matrix representation. The student is able to manipulate a shape within a co-ordinate system interactively. Meanwhile the matrix form of the corresponding transformation is displayed at the bottom of the screen, and the matrix elements change value as the shape is moved. Another example of this approach is in the teaching of the geometry of curves. Again, the student can manipulate curves interactively and see the relation to the corresponding polynomial functions. This linking of algebra to geometry has proved to be a powerful teaching device, especially for those design-oriented students who find it easier to approach mathematics in a visual graphical way.

The total study time occupied by the software is a nominal 70 hours, and so it is only possible to give the briefest kaleidoscopic overview here. The course starts gently with paint systems and graphic design. This is followed by a section concerning the layout of equipment in kitchens, which is similar to the commercial packages used by kitchen design studios and manufacturers of kitchen units. The student can design a layout and have the program evaluate it according to ergonomic and other functional criteria. New plan outlines can be created, and the library of fittings and furniture can be edited.

The third part of the CADPAC software is entitled

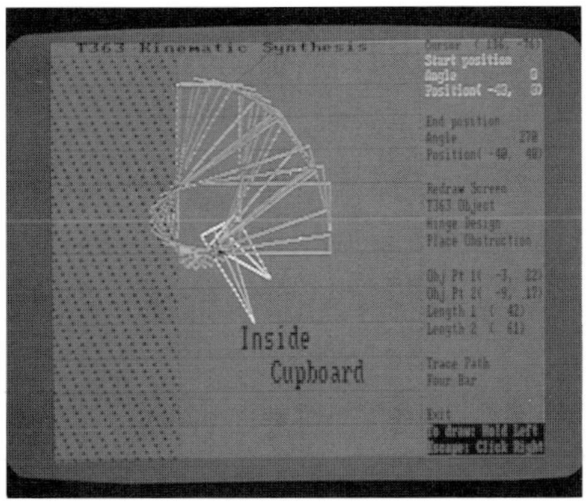

Figure 6.1
Experimenting with rotation and transformation

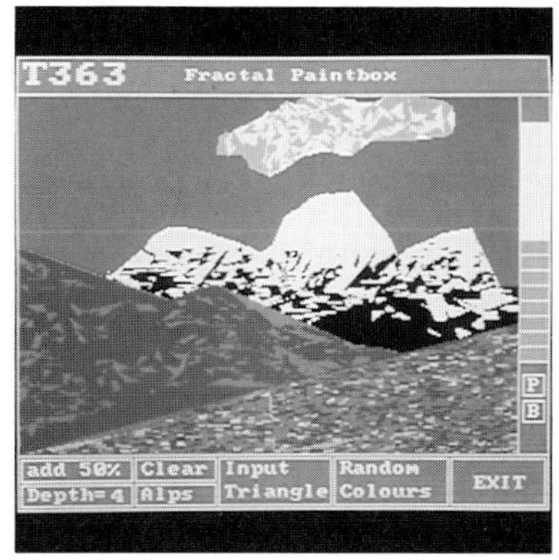

Figure 6.2
Paint exercise

'Computer Graphics and Design', and goes behind the scenes to consider some of the underlying theory and mathematics. I have already mentioned two-dimensional transformations and their matrix representation. Other sections deal with co-ordinate systems, graphical data structures including linked lists and the geometry of perspective.

Part four makes use of a commercial two-dimensional draughting and three-dimensional modelling package, SCRIBE MODELLER from Ecotech Design of Sheffield, developed by Cedric Green. The student makes a simple engineering drawing of part of a gearbox, and builds several solid models including a model of a Greek temple. One of the assignments which the student completes and sends to the tutor is a model built using SCRIBE. This assignment is submitted on disc. (Cost constraints prevent us from equipping students with printers or plotters.) The topic varies from year to year, but typically students are asked to design and model something like a set of chess pieces, or a box of children's toy building bricks.

I have referred already to the contents of the fifth and sixth parts of CADPAC, which are devoted to mechanical engineering and electronics respectively. I shall not dwell on the details, since the focus here is primarily on architecture, but pass on to the seventh and final part, called 'Advanced Concepts'. This is intended to make students think about the future of CAD. Some sections deal with rule-based pattern generation, cellular automata and fractals. Other sections are concerned with automated design synthesis, drawing examples from spatial layout in architecture and in electronics. They introduce ideas about solution spaces, search trees, heuristics and optimality. A final section introduces expert systems and their application to design problems. The student is able to enter rules and facts to an expert system shell. The principles are illustrated with implementations of P. H. Winston's forward-chaining BAGGER system for packing groceries in supermarkets and I now turn briefly to the use of video in the course. The capacities of the NIMBUS, for all its virtues, are obviously limited, and so we use video to give students a kind of surrogate experience of large commercial CAD systems in practical use in industry.

We have filmed some relatively extended sequences showing designers at work at the machine; interviews with architects, engineers and electronics designers who use CAD; and sequences exploring the special manufacturing and design issues arising in different industries, to show how these affect the application of computers. Another use of video is in a series of studio-based demonstrations using physical models of some geometrical aspects of computer graphics and solid modelling. These include the principles of algorithms for hidden-surface removal, ray-tracing and Boolean operations on shape primitives. The last tape of the five is devoted to advanced computer graphics and 'the search for realism', and contains interviews conducted in some of the leading American and Japanese graphics research laboratories.

I described how the University had decided on a new policy for home computing, and that the CADPAC software is being rewritten this year (1990) to run on IBM PC and compatible machines. New features are being introduced at the same time. (The opportunity is also being taken to update some of the text and video, especially those parts relating to advanced graphics and artificial intelligence). One consequence of the software conversion is that the quota of student numbers, imposed by the University's stock of NIMBUS machines, is now lifted, since many Open University students have acquired their own Amstrads or other PC compatibles. The number of students provisionally registered for the course in 1991 is

Figure 6.3
Kitchen design

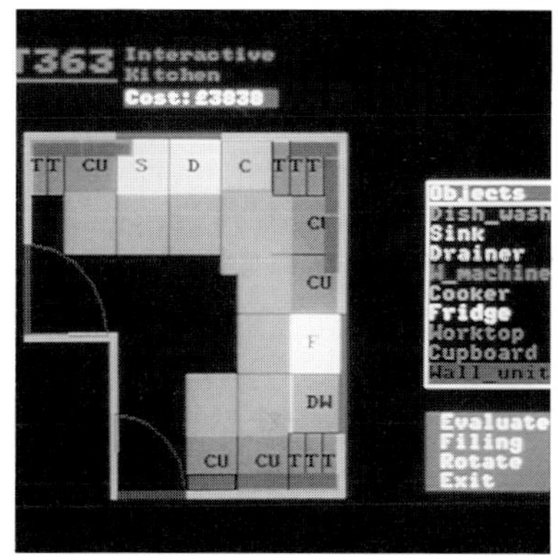

Figure 6.4
Greek temple using a saibe

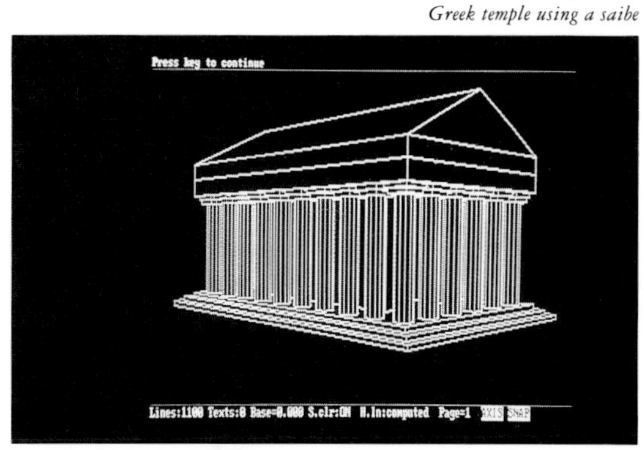

650. We hope that the new software will also be of wider interest and commercial potential outside the University.

What have we, the team responsible for the course, learned from the experience? We have learned many things, but I shall pick just one point. Our greatest challenge was to try to teach both computing and design to students, many of them complete beginners, working alone at home with very little tutorial supervision. Such success as we have achieved in this is due to the very great care, attention and effort that has gone into designing, documenting and testing all components of the course, but especially the software. The documentation is very full. At many points it takes students through actual sequences of mouse operations or key-presses, showing by diagrams what should be expected on screen at each stage; at other points it stands back to explain principles and teach more general issues. Both software and documentation have been extensively tested, first by fellow academics and then by paid teams of student testers. As a result, it *has* been possible to get students learning both the theory and the practice of CAD for themselves, by themselves.

The academic team responsible for the Open University CAD course included Alun Armstrong, Nigel Cross, Mike Dooner, Chris Earl, Jeff Johnson, Ray Matela, Joe Rooney and Philip Steadman. Enquiries about the course and the CADPAC software should be addressed to the T363 Course Manager, Christopher Pym, Design Discipline, Faculty of Technology, Open University, Milton Keynes MK7 6AA.

Reference

Rooney, J. and Steadman, P. (eds) (1987) *Principles of Computer-Aided Design.* Pitman, London.

APPENDIX
Contents of the course

Text

Introduction to CAD
Textbook: *Principles of Computer Aided Design*
Ch 1 'Representing objects' element methods)
Ch 2 'Representing relations'
Ch 3 'Graphical techniques'
Ch 4 'Draughting systems'
Ch 5 'Wire-frame modelling'
Ch 6 'Surface modelling'
Ch 9 'Solid modelling'
Ch 11 'Kinematic analysis'
Ch 12 'Electronics—logic and layout'
Ch 13 'Architecture—spatial layout'
Ch 14 'Realism in graphics' Artificial intelligence
Ch 15 'Geometry in motion'
Expert systems and CAD
Implications of CAD

Exercises

1 Graphic design (painting systems)
2 Architectural design (furniture layout in kitchens)
3 Representations and transformations (data structures; 2D transformations and matrices, perspective)
4 Draughting and modelling (exercises with Scribe Modeller)
5 Engineering design (kinematic synthesis; curve design; finite-element methods)
6 Electronics design (logic; testing; PCB layout)
7 Advanced concepts (automated layout; rule-based synthesis; expert systems)

Video

1 Computers in design/using the Nimbus
2 Graphics and draughting (in architecture and mechanical engineering
3 Modelling (solid modelling; surface modelling; finite element methods)
4 Analysis (energy in building; simulation of circuits; geo-metrical analysis in process plant design)
5 Advanced graphics (ray- tracing, 'the search for realism')

Computer-Aided Design Media: A Comparative Analysis

William J. Mitchell
Harvard University Graduate School of Design

Methods of geometrical description

Underlying any design medium is some method of geometrical description – some strategy for using geometrical entities to describe three-dimensional physical artefacts (Mitchell, 1990). In traditional media these geometrical entities are represented by physical tokens such as graphite marks on paper, cardboard cut-outs or machined blocks of wood. In a CAD system they are represented symbolically within the framework of a Cartesian co-ordinate system, and display hardware is used to translate them into visual equivalents.

Symbolic descriptions may be based upon two-dimensional or three-dimensional Cartesian co-ordinate systems, and may take points, lines, surfaces or solids as their primitives. (See Mortenson (1985, 1989) and Hoffmann (1990) for details.) This yields seven basic possibilities (all of which are well known), as shown below.

TABLE 7.1

	Two-space	Three-space
Points	Pixel images	Voxel models
Lines	Line drawings	Wire frames
Surfaces	Polygon plans	Surface models
Solids		Solid assemblies

Point (spatial enumeration) representations

The idea of a pixel image representation follows directly from that of a two-dimensional, finite, integer Cartesian co-ordinate system. A value specifying some spatial quality is simply associated with each addressable point in the plane. For display, these values are interpreted as pixel intensities or colours (Figure 7.1). Thus, for example, a floor plan can be represented by serial numbering the constituent rooms, associating a serial number with each point to specify the room within which that point is located and employing a colour-coding scheme for display of the plan as a mosaic of coloured room shapes. Similarly, the site for a building can be represented by numerically describing elevation, soil conditions, hydrological conditions, vegetation and so on at each point. The generalization to voxel models of three-dimensional spatial configurations (similar to the voxel models used in medical imaging) is obvious. Quadtree and octree techniques can be employed to reduce the very large storage demands that these types of representations tend to make (Samet, 1989a, b).

Pixel and voxel representations are collections of samples. At some chosen density they describe a region of space comprehensively. The denser the sampling lattice and the more information allocated to the description of each sample, the more accurate the description will be. Sampling theory (Shannon's theorem in particular) provides the basis for determining the sampling lattice density needed for adequate representation of details of some specified size.

Boundary representations

Other than some specialized applications in site analysis and interior space planning, however, such exhaustive point-by-point descriptions of spatial configurations are rarely necessary or appropriate in practice. Since buildings normally consist of areas and volumes that are (for practical purposes) homogeneous between well-defined boundaries, it is usually far more effective to describe them in terms of the properties and relationships of spatial boundaries. These boundaries

Figure 7.1
An image consisting of discrete pixels

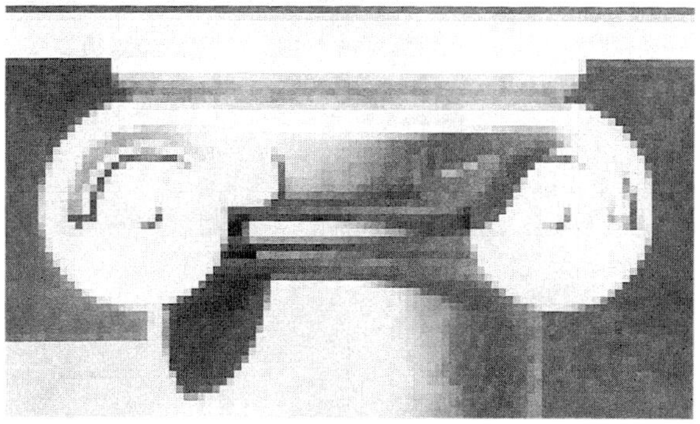

form a hierarchy: zero-dimensional points bound one-dimensional lines, these lines bound two-dimensional surfaces and these surfaces bound three-dimensional volumes. A cube, for example, is a solid bounded by six square faces. Each of these faces is bounded by four straight edges, and each of these faces is bounded by two vertices. The complete boundary structure consists of eight vertices, twelve edges and six faces, such that three edges are incident on each vertex and each edge divides two faces.

A representation of this type has two parts (although in practice they may not be clearly distinguished): there is a *topological* description of the connectivity (and perhaps orientation) of vertices, edges and faces, and there is a *geometrical* description – a specification of how these elements are embedded in space. For example, a simple structure of straight lines in space might be represented as a relation of connection on a set of points stored as a matrix or as a list of point pairs (the topological part), together with a set of co-ordinate triples specifying locations of those points in space. Editing operations on that representation might change the topology by adding or deleting connections, or the embedding by changing co-ordinate values.

The simplest type of building description based upon this abstraction strategy is a two-dimensional plan, section or elevation consisting of straight lines, arcs and other curves arranged on a planar surface. Each straight line is represented by its end-point co-ordinates, and instances of other types of curves are specified by means of additional parameters that describe shape between the end-points. The associated repertoire of editing operators provides (at least) for inserting, deleting, extending and trimming lines of various types, forming line relationships such as parallels, perpendiculars and tangents, grouping lines into selectable subshapes, and copying and transforming these subshapes. CAD systems based on this type of data structure, and oriented towards input, editing, storage and hard-copy production of precisely constructed line drawings are conceptually and functionally related to traditional manual draughting practice. The topological part of the descriptions that they maintain is minimal – usually consisting merely of associations between vertices to specify lines – and most of the stored information consists of co-ordinate values and coefficients specifying how vertices and lines are embedded in two-dimensional space.

A wire-frame model consists of lines embedded in three-dimensional space. (The idea had its origins in Italian Renaissance perspective construction, and some Renaissance perspective drawings look uncannily like output from a wire-frame modeller.) The data structure and editing operators of a wire-frame modelling system are closely analogous to those of a two-dimensional draughting system, but the viewing system must additionally provide for projection of lines onto a two-dimensional display surface, and the interface must incorporate some technique for specifying locations in the three-dimensional co-ordinate system. Procedures for producing the parallel and perspective projections normally used by architects simply apply appropriate rules for converting three-dimensional end-point co-ordinates of lines in the model into two-dimensional end-point co-ordinates of lines in the projected drawing. (The crucial point here is that, under parallel and perspective projections, straight lines always map into straight lines.) Conversely, the interface applies rules for converting two-dimensional co-ordinates specified in some construction plane into the three-dimensional co-ordinates of the model.

Figure 7.2
A Lambert-shaded image produced from a plane-surface model

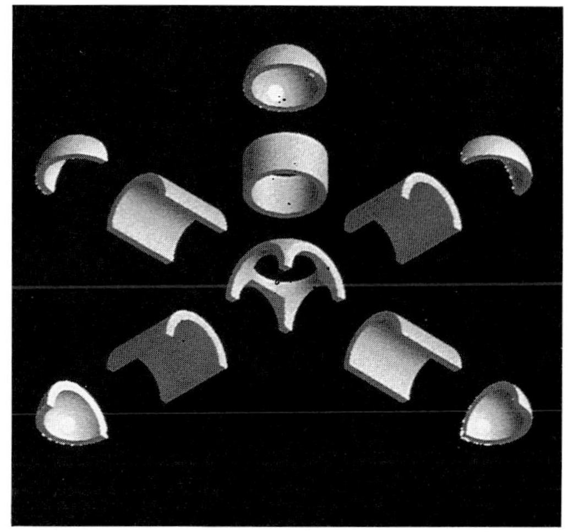

Figure 7.3
A smooth-shaded image produced from a curved-surface model

Wire-frame models can represent the essentials of a building's geometry in elegantly sparse and economical fashion, but they are too radically abstracted to serve as the basis for generation of sophisticated displays and analyses. In particular, they contain insufficient geometrical information to allow automatic removal of hidden lines in projected views or the production of shaded renderings. This can be remedied by extending the topological part of the data structure to record not only associations of points to specify lines, but also associations of lines to form circuits that bound closed surfaces. Thus a building is represented as a collection of surfaces (rather than a collection of lines), much as in a cardboard or chipboard physical model. In the simplest case the surfaces are all planar, and any curved surfaces are approximated by small planar facets. More sophisticated systems also provide parametrically described cylindrical surfaces, spherical surfaces, spline surfaces and so on.

Three-dimensional surface models provide the basis for realistic simulation and detailed exploration of a proposed building's visual qualities (Foley *et al.,* 1990). By means of appropriate surface-sorting techniques they can be used to produce perspective views in which hidden surfaces are removed. If a direction of incident light is specified, then it is straightforward to produce simple shaded views by calculating surface normals and shading surfaces in accordance with Lambert's cosine law (Figure 7.2). This technique can be extended to provide smooth-shaded images of curved-surface objects (Figure 7.3). (The basic idea is to interpolate intensities or surface normals between points on a curved surface.) Photorealistic renderings of both exteriors and interiors can be produced by introducing additional surface and lighting parameters and calculating surface intensities by means of ray-tracing or radiosity procedures that take account not only of light directly incident on surfaces, but also of light inter-reflection between surfaces in a scene, so reproducing extremely subtle effects (Figure 7.4). These renderings can be matted into scanned or video-captured images of sites, so that the building is convincingly shown in context (Figure 7.5). Animated sequences can be produced by rendering successive frames corresponding to the positions of a camera moving through the building.

The two-dimensional equivalent of such three-dimensional surface models is a map or plan represented as either a loosely packed collection or tightly packed mosaic of closed polygons. The geometrical part of the two-dimensional polygon model is basically the same as that of a corresponding draughting system model, but the topological part records considerably more information – associations of edges into polygon boundaries, adjacencies of polygons and so on. Graph theory – particularly that part dealing with planar graphs, their embeddings in the plane and their duals – provides a theoretical basis for many of the associated operations and algorithms (Baglivo and Graver, 1983). This richer and more specialized representation supports area, density and cost calculations, filled-polygon graphics and other functions that are useful in space planning, facilities management and geographical information systems.

In three dimensions, the idea of boundary representation can be extended another step by recording (in the topology part of the data structure) not only the associations of vertices which bound edges and the association of edges which bound surface facets, but also the association of surface facets which enclose solids. Thus a building is represented as a collection of

Figure 7.4
A ray-traced image of an architectural interior

Figures 7.5a) and b)
A computer-generated image in context. On the left is a scanned photograph of Palladio's Villa Rotonda, showing the dome as actually constructed. A synthesized image of the different dome that Palladio originally designed has been substituted in the image on the right

solid 'building blocks', much as in a wooden or polystyrene physical model. Typically, a solid modelling system provides a vocabulary of parametric solid primitives (box, cylinder, prism, solid of revolution, etc.), operators for inserting and deleting solids, geometrical transformation operators for assembling them in space and spatial set operators (union, intersection, subtraction) for building complex solid shapes from simple ones (Figure 7.6). (The spatial set operators suggest an alternative way of organizing the data structure – as a constructive solid geometry (CSG) tree in which shapes are described as Boolean combinations of simpler shapes.) In architectural applications of solid modelling techniques, solids can be used to represent both physical elements such as columns and slabs and enclosed voids such as rooms. An architect can employ the available operators to shape and assemble construction elements and spaces in a very direct sculptural way.

Since an assembly of solids is a geometrically complete description (in the sense that it is always possible to determine whether an arbitrarily specified point is within an arbitrarily selected solid), volumes, centroids and surface areas can be calculated, arbitrary sections can be cut and inadvertent spatial clashes between elements can be detected. Furthermore, material properties can be associated with solids so that their structural and thermal properties can be analyzed, typically by means of finite-element methods. Finally, the properties of joints and connections between solids can be described so that structural, kinematic and other analyses of assemblies of solids can be performed.

In order to simplify implementation problems and reduce computational demands it has been usual to assume various topological and geometrical restrictions in the implementation of solid modelling software. Some practical solid modellers only deal with prisms, and others only with plane-faced polyhedra containing no holes. More general systems allow curved faces and holes, but frequently exclude such complexities as intersecting holes. But the range of solid shape types that might be of interest to designers is extraordinarily extensive (Koenderink, 1990), and so there has been a strong tendency to generalize solid modelling software as increasing theoretical understanding of the solid modelling problem and the growing availability of computation power and better implementation tools have progressively opened up the possibility of doing so.

It has also been usual to assume that all bounding surfaces of solids will be closed oriented manifolds embedded in three-dimensional space. In other words (roughly speaking) the bounding surfaces are always deformable into planes without tearing. This excludes self-intersecting surfaces, coincident edges, hollow shells, dangling edges and the like (Figure 7.7). But there is increasing interest in non-manifold modellers that handle three-dimensional objects of the type shown in Figure 7.7 and provide a designer with the flexibility to build solids incrementally from points, lines and surfaces (Wesley, 1980; Weiler, 1986; Hoffmann *et al.*, 1987; Gursoz and Prinz, 1988; Hoffmann, 1990).

Yet another extension of the boundary representation idea (one that is of growing interest as the computation power at our disposal increases) is to add a fourth dimension – time dimension. In other words, points are specified by co-ordinates x,y,z,t to embed them in four-dimensional space–time. Vertices specified in this way sweep out lines in four-dimensional hyperspace as t is incremented, lines bounded by these vertices sweep out surfaces, surfaces

Figure 7.6
Spatial composition using union and intersection operators

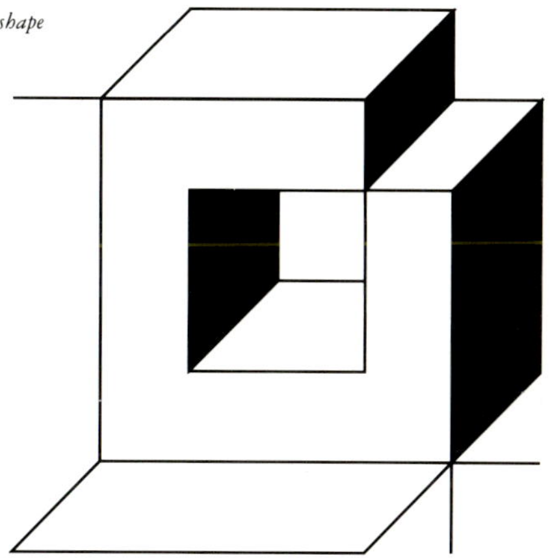

Figure 7.7
A non-manifold three-dimensional shape

bounded by these lines sweep out solids and solids bounded by these surfaces sweep out hypersolids. Pairs of wire-frame, surface or solid models at times *t*1 and *t*2 can serve as keyframes that bound animation sequences – just as points bound lines, lines bound surfaces and surfaces bound solids.

Shape instantiation and selection

A structure of physical tokens becomes a medium when tools are provided for manipulating those tokens. Taking graphite lines on paper as the tokens, together with pencil and eraser as tools, yields a medium for hand sketching, for example. If we control the pencil by a parallel bar, adjustable triangle, scale rule, protractor, dividers and compasses we obtain a draughting medium. Cardboard polygons which can be cut out with a matte knife, translated and rotated in space, and glued together, provide a simple three-dimensional modelling medium.

In a CAD system, the corresponding step is to provide operators for manipulating the data structure. At the very least, a designer needs operators for instantiating, selecting and deleting geometrical entities. Thus draughting and wire-frame modelling systems provide for constructing representations by instantiating straight lines, arcs, splines and so on, surface modelling systems provide for instantiating various different types of surfaces and solid modelling systems provide for instantiating solids from some vocabulary.

Most CAD systems provide for selection of geometrical primitives, and sets of primitives, by pointing at them with a cursor or enclosing them with a selection rectangle. Selected sets of primitives can then become operands perhaps of a deletion, duplication, translation or rotation operation. This is usually thought to be sufficient for a designer's purposes, but it is not. A designer needs to be able to operate not only on shapes that were explicitly instantiated (and are thus recorded directly in the data structure) but also on emergent instances.

Consider, for example, the shape shown in Figure 7.8. We might see it as a square and two right triangles, and so we might construct it by instantiating a square and two right triangles. More laboriously, we might construct it out of eight straight lines of equal length plus two diagonals. But we can also read this shape as a whirling configuration of four overlapping polygons shaped as shown in Figure 7.9. We might want to select one of these polygons in order to operate on it in some way, but a traditional CAD system does not allow us to do this. (Such a system may provide divide operations and other operations for restructuring representations, but this does not help fundamentally, since dividing lines into smaller parts will destroy the capacity to select the original figures.)

It is feasible, however, to implement systems that allow direct selection of emergent shapes (see for example Nagakura,1990; Stiny, 1990; Tan, 1990). The basic idea is to treat selection as a recognition problem, i.e. as the converse of instantiation. We want to be able both to instantiate and to recognize shapes in a chosen vocabulary. If only squares and triangles are in a designer's shape vocabulary, then the shape shown in Figure 7.8 will be constructed and manipulated accordingly. If only knife-blade quadrilateral forms like that shown in Figure 7.9 are in the vocabulary, then the shape shown in Figure 7.8 will be constructed and manipulated differently. If squares, triangles and knife-

Figure 7.8
A line figure constructed by instantiating a square and two right triangles

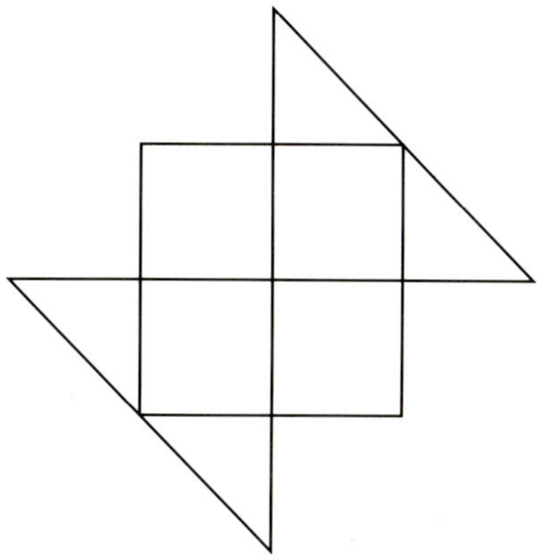

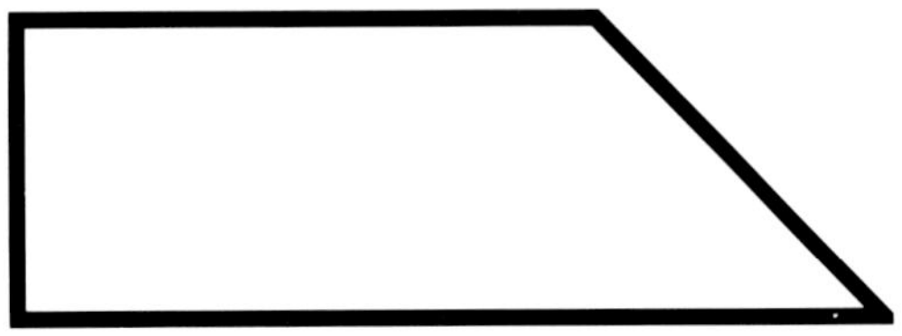

Figure 7.9
An emergent subshape

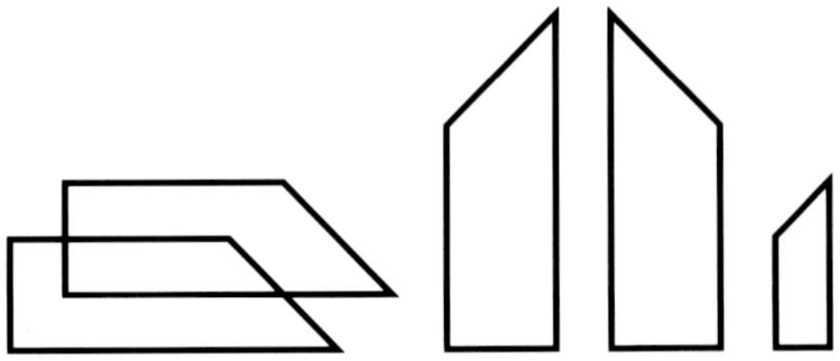

Figure 7.10
Translating, rotating, reflecting and scaling a selected shape

blade quadrilaterals are in the vocabulary, then there is a choice of ways to put the shape together and a choice of ways to take it apart.

There is a close analogy here with physical three-dimensional models, e.g. those made with Tinkertoy, Meccano or Lego components. The ways that we can take them apart are determined by the ways that we can put them together using available types of elements. But a pencil drawing has no such fixed atomic structure, and can be taken apart in ways that do not depend on how it was constructed. This is the principal source of the pencil drawing's extraordinary flexibility and versatility as a medium for design exploration, and probably the main reason why it has not been supplanted in this role by CAD systems. But the introduction of emergent shape recognition capabilities into CAD systems should go a long way towards making the 'D' stand for 'design' rather than just 'draughting'.

Transforming and combining shapes

In general, a designer needs tools for transforming and combining selected shapes (i.e. for performing unary and binary operations on them). Physical design media usually provide very limited repertoires of such tools, but CAD systems can provide much wider repertoires, including both tools that have direct physical counterparts and others that do not.

Most fundamentally, the rigid components of a physical model can be translated and rotated to desired locations and orientations in space. Two-dimensional drawn shapes can also be reflected and scaled. Correspondingly, most CAD systems provide for copying, translating, rotating, reflecting and scaling selected shapes, as shown in Figure 7.10. The primitive-instancing approach to geometrical modelling depends on providing a sufficiently large vocabulary of shape types together with the capacity to perform these basic unary operations.

A more elegant way of providing the representational flexibility that results from a large vocabulary is to provide a much smaller vocabulary of basic shapes together with binary operations for combining simple shapes to make more complex ones. For example, the union, intersection and subtraction operations can be defined on closed polygons and closed solids, as shown in Figure 7.11. Since the shapes that result from these operations may themselves become operands, enormous ranges of possibilities can be generated within this sort of system.

An initial vocabulary of shapes, together with a repertoire of shape operators, establishes a shape algebra for a designer to explore. Application of union, intersection and subtraction (relative complement) to a vocabulary of solids yields a Boolean algebra, for example. The set of shapes that can be constructed by application of the operators to the vocabulary is the carrier set of the algebra (i.e. the universe of available shape possibilities), and the operators provide a transportation system for moving around in the carrier set by instantiating, deleting, transforming and combining shapes.

A medium has the right basic structure for a particular design purpose if its underlying algebra has appropriate shapes in its carrier set, and if the algebra's formal properties facilitate exploration of that set. Consider, for example, the difference between the types of design explorations that you can carry out with cardboard models manipulated with a knife, straight-

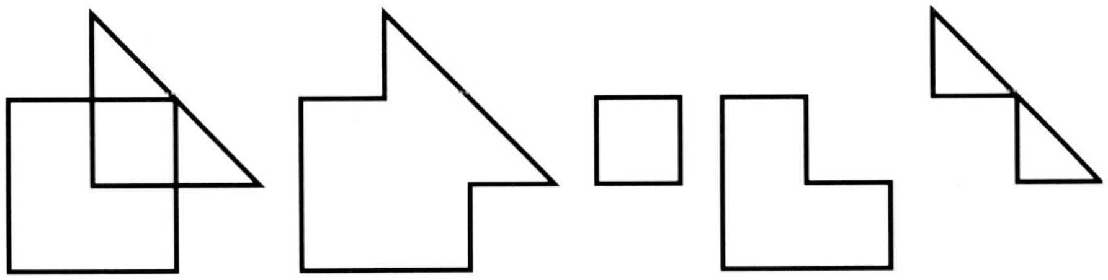

Figure 7.11
Union, intersect and subtract operations on a square and a right triangle

edge and glue-gun and those that you can carry out by shaping wet clay on a potter's wheel, or the difference between what you can do with a NURBS surface modeller that provides for tweaking of surface control points and a solid modeller organized around the operations of constructing profiles and then performing translational and rotational sweeps.

Real-time feedback

Abstractly specified shape algebras can be implemented by combining actual tools and materials into systems that behave as required – just as an algebra of numbers can be implemented as an abacus or as a four-function electronic calculator. A given shape algebra may have many different implementations using different technologies. These differences are important, since they establish the speed and efficiency with which explorations can be carried out and the character of the feedback loop between the designer's sensors (which yield knowledge of the current state of the design) and effectors (which control the design tools), and hence the effectiveness with which a design process can be directed.

In manual sketching, for example, you see the line emerging from beneath the point of the pencil, and your hand controls the pencil's location, angle and pressure to obtain the line that you want. In laying on a watercolour wash you see a growing pigmented area of variable density, and you adjust the speed and spacing of brushstrokes accordingly. In a typical current CAD system you see a rubber-band line on the display screen and your hand controls the position of the mouse in order to locate the line as required.

What actually happens in a CAD system is that user actions (such as mouse movements) are interpreted as operations on the data structure, and then the data structure is reinterpreted as a new display. When this happens fast enough the effect of real-time feedback is produced. Thus, by using different types of user actions to control operations, and by interpreting the data structure in different ways, the implementer of a CAD system can present the same shape algebra in many different ways.

For example, different input hardware and display combinations can be employed to sense different types of actions and provide different types of feedback. The ubiquitous mouse can be replaced by a pressure-sensitive and angle-sensitive cordless stylus, used in conjunction with a display software that varies displayed line qualities in response to variations in stylus pressure and angle. (The system might then behave much like a pencil, but it does not have to: pressure might control line hue, angle might control saturation and speed of movement might control brightness.) Voice commands may be used in place of hand gestures to control operations. (If you think that architecture is frozen music, you might want to sing a design.) Audio and tactile feedback can be added to visual feedback, or might even replace it. (Imagine a system for a blind sculptor.) Recently there has been intense interest in so-called 'virtual reality' systems which combine head-mounted stereo displays with datagloves, datasuits and similar devices for interpreting bodily movements: these allow you to 'pick up' full-scale three-dimensional geometrical entities and 'carry' them to where you want to locate them in space (Benedikt, 1990).

As workstation speed increases, systems with richer real-time feedback become feasible, and these begin to structure design processes that are not just faster than but qualitatively different from those that we have known until now. It is becoming standard, for example, for draughting systems to feed back relational information as rubber-band line and similar operations are performed: the designer is instantly notified when a selected line approaches tangential relationships with existing arcs, parallel and perpendicular relationships with existing straight lines and so on. (The Ashlar Vellum draughting system pioneered this idea, and it has already been widely imitated.) Surface modellers are increasingly providing real-time adjustment of lighting and viewing parameters, particularly through use of specialized shading, ray-tracing and radiosity chips. Some solid modellers running on powerful workstations provide real-time Boolean operations: you can push two solids together and see the resulting union, intersection or difference taking shape.

Serial computing devices are inherently limited in their capacity to provide real-time feedback, but parallel computation can provide a way of overcoming this limitation. Consider, for example, the task of updating multiple views of an object when some change is made to its geometry. With a serial machine, the views must be updated in sequence, and the more of them there are the longer this will take. But, with a parallel machine, a separate processor can be allocated to maintaining each view. Future CAD systems are likely to provide multiple viewing and analysis 'agents' that simultaneously monitor the evolving design and provide as many parallel streams of feedback as the designer wants.

Virtuosity

Virtuosity in a medium depends firstly on the capacity to form a structural conception of the object that is to be represented and to map this onto the token structures and construction operations provided by the medium, and secondly on sufficient sensor–effector co-ordination skills to allow facile generation of the required token structures. Thus a traditional life class develops virtuosity by teaching students to analyse the structural complexities of the human body, to map the conceptions that emerge from this onto structures of linear contours that can be produced with a pencil and to produce these contours with swift and confident hand gestures controlled by an attentive eye. A draughting class teaches students to analyse the way that a building is put together, to map their conceptions onto sequences of construction operations executable with draughting instruments, and (the trivial part in this case) to handle the instruments. We recall tales of the Zen watercolour master who motionlessly studies a complex scene for many hours, and then suddenly renders its essence with a single swift perfectly executed stroke.

In CAD, skills in formation of structural conceptions of objects and in mapping these conceptions onto the constructs of a given system are equally important. Effective use of a draughting system to construct a plan or elevation, for example, often depends on recognition of repeating parts and the structure of the repetition, followed by shrewd use of copy-and-transform operations. Effective use of a surface modeller may depend on the ability to see a building as a collection of translationally and rotationally swept profiles. And effective use of a solid modeller may depend on the capacity to see complex shapes as unions, intersections or differences of simpler ones. Such skills can be developed (as in a life class) through practice in construction of representations of conceptually demanding objects, such as major works of architecture.

Early CAD systems provided such primitive interfaces (e.g. keyboard commands and storage tube display) that they virtually eliminated the need for hand–eye skills. But as systems provide increasingly broadband interfaces, and are able to interpret increasingly complex gestures and to provide much richer forms of feedback, the need for hand–eye skills returns. In future, skilled users of CAD systems may be much like musicians playing demanding instruments – able to execute complex gesture patterns, attuned to all the nuances of the feedback that flows from them, and ready to make subtle adjustments in response.

Conclusion: uses for a thousand million instructions per second (MIPS)

I have suggested that any CAD system which we employ as a design medium can usefully be characterized in multilevel fashion. First, we can consider the capacity of the underlying data structure to represent topological properties of designs and their embeddings in two-dimensional or three-dimensional space. Next, we can take note of the shape vocabulary that is supported, and the tools that are available for instantiating and selecting shapes in the vocabulary. At a still higher level we can consider the formal properties of the shape algebra that is defined by the shape vocabulary together with the available operators for transforming and combining selected shapes. Finally, we can consider the way that the interface presents the underlying formal structure by providing real-time feedback in response to commands and gestures. A designer must first understand the system at a basic structural level, and second be able to co-ordinate hand and eye in the ways that the interface demands.

Learning to use a CAD system to represent designs is not, then, so very different from learning to draw or model in traditional ways. But the shape algebras implemented in CAD systems need not correspond to those underlying traditional media, and the forms of feedback that these systems provide need not do so either. As commonly available workstations become commonly more available, and as our grasp of the theoretical principles of CAD expands, developers of CAD systems will increasingly emancipate themselves from metaphors of earlier representational technologies — just as the developers of the Sony Walkman far transcended the metaphor of the player piano. The thousand-MIPS workstations that we are promised will open up domains and styles of design exploration which have little connection with those associated with traditional media. The challenge to designers will be to grasp the relationships between architectural intentions and the new means at their disposal.

References

Baglivo, J.A. and Graver, J.E. (1983) *Incidence and Symmetry in Design and Architecture.* Cambridge University Press, Cambridge.

Benedikt, M. (ed.) (1990) *Collected Abstracts from the First Conference on Cyberspace.* School of Architecture, University of Texas, Austin, TX.

Foley, J.D., van Dam, A., Feiner, S.K. and Hughes, J. *Computer Graphics: Principles and Practice* (2nd ed), Addison-Wesley, Reading, MA.

Gursoz, E.L. and Prinz, F.B. (1988) corner-based representation of non-manifold surface boundaries in geometrical modelling. *Proceedings of the RPI–IFIP–NSF Workshop on Geometrical Modelling.* Rensselaerville, NY.

Hoffmann, C.M. (1990) *Geometrical and Solid Modelling: An Introduction,* Morgan Kaufmann, San Mateo, CA.

Hoffmann, C.M., Hopcroft, J. and Karasick, M. (1987) Robust set operations on polyhedral solids. Technical Report 723, Computer Science, Purdue University.

Koenderink, J.J. (1990) *Solid Shape.* MIT Press, Cambridge MA.

Mitchell, W.J. (1990) *The Logic of Architecture.* MIT Press, Cambridge MA.

Mortenson, M.E. (1985) *Geometrical Modelling.* Wiley, New York.

Mortenson, M.E. (1989) *Computer Graphics: An Introduction to the Mathematics and Geometry.* Industrial Press New York.

Nagakura, T. (1990) shape recognition and transformation – A script-based approach, in M. McCullough, W.J. Mitchell and P. Purcell (eds), *The Electronic Design Studio.* MIT Press, Cambridge, MA.

Samet, H.J. (1989a) *Design and Analysis of Spatial Data Structures: Quadtrees, Octrees, and Other Hierarchical Methods.* Addison-Wesley, Reading MA.

Samet, H.J. (1989b) *Applications of Spatial Data Structures: Computer Graphics, Image Processing, and GIS.* Addison-Wesley, Reading, MA.

Stiny, G. (1990) What designers do that computers should, In M. McCullough, W.J. Mitchell, and P. Purcell (eds), *The Electronic Design Studio.* MIT Press, Cambridge MA.

Tan, M. (1990) Saying What it is by what it is like. In M. McCullough, W. J. Mitchell and P. Purcell (eds), *The Electronic Design Studio.* MIT Press, Cambridge MA.

Weiler, K.J. (1986) *Topological Structures for Geometrical Modelling.* Ph.D. Thesis, Rensselaer Polytechnic Institute.

Wesley, M.A. (1980) Construction and use of geometrical modelling systems. In J. Enarnacao (ed.), *Computer-Aided Design: Modelling, Systems Engineering, CAD Systems.* Springer-Verlag, Berlin.

SECTION 2: COMPUTERS IN PRACTICE

INTRODUCTION

PAUL RICHENS

The chapters in this part reflect the real-life experiences of five architectural practices of varied size and structure. The smallest of them (Leslie Fox Albin) has become the pre-eminent champion of the Macintosh way of running a small design business. At the opposite end of the scale, YRM and Arup Associates are substantial multidisciplinary practices deeply committed to the use of 'big' systems, from Intergraph and McDonnell Douglas respectively. In between we have Michael Hopkins and Partners, and Nicholas Grimshaw and Partners, distinguished medium-sized architectural firms that treat their Macintoshes 'as part of the furniture'.

One thing that links the five offices is the exceptionally high 'penetration' of CAD. Everyone is encouraged to use the computer, and nearly everyone does so. The provision of workstations is high – around two to every three architects, sometimes even more. Their experiences do lead to some areas of agreement between the authors. There is a general satisfaction with the accuracy and quality of computer draughting, and its ability to liberate the architect from the tyranny of the tee-square (for example by facilitating the design of buildings on long-radius curved grids). There is agreement that co-ordinating the work of several people is a problem, and solving it can justify the use of a more difficult-to-use system such as Microstation. Practically every output technology *except* pen plotting gets a mention.

But the real fascination of this part is in the *differences* of opinion and practice, and the bald contradictions that emerge. Robert Aish complains that CAD 'has made the ultimate pragmatic response which is to do nothing and accept the existing architectural drawing convention as the communication medium'. Mark Leslie tells us how he communicates with his clients using slides, HyperCard stacks, Director animations and video-on-a-shoestring – practically anything you can imagine except conventional architectural drawings. David Harriss and John Pringle find their Macintoshes better for drafting than for sketching and design. Mark Leslie shows how (with sufficient virtuosity) the opposite can be true.

Mark criticizes some of the older CAD systems for being 'originally devised to help engineers in the aircraft and motor industries'. Robert Aish describes how YRM (in the role of consulting engineers) used just such a system to solve a geometrical problem that the architects could not pin down. The fascination of this story is that the architect is Grimshaw's, where we are told by David Harriss that CAD stands for Computer-aided-draughting rather than Computer-aided-design.

Attitudes to staff training differ considerably. John Hare pushes the people at Arups through seven and a half days of formal training on GDS, and admits to the need for specialists for the more difficult three-dimensional work. The smaller practices minimize formal training and do not want to see the emergence of an 'elite'. Yet it seems probable that what you get out of CAD is somehow related to what you put in – not necessarily formal training or expensive equipment, but enthusiasm, invention, high expectations and (as at Leslie Fox Albin) a positive mania for exploration and improvisation.

What do Architects Expect From Computer-Aided Design?

John Hare
Arup Associates, London

Introduction

The title of this chapter was deliberately chosen to evoke two distinct viewpoints on the topic of computers in architecture, one referring to experiences in working practices today, and the second looking somewhat further into the future. I shall attempt to define the position that my own practice, Arup Associates, has reached after five years of intensive use of CAD, and thereby to state what I believe are reasonable expectations using today's technology and levels of knowledge within the profession. Then, by considering the list of shortcomings that we would like to overcome, I shall go on to define our plans for the coming years and begin to address the question of what we expect from CAD in the near future.

Popular misconceptions

As an architect working in the field of CAD, I find myself confronting a popular myth of just how far our subject has progressed to date. People outside the fields of computing and architecture have been led to a very high expectation of the role of CAD, presumably by extrapolation from the seductive computer-generated imagery used in television graphics. I find myself struggling to decide how to respond to questions such as – It must be so useful that the computer knows what the building will look like? or How does the computer know how strong to make the building? Even very worldly professionals have often been lulled into suspended belief, particularly when confronted by a well-rehearsed and carefully crafted CAD demonstration.

Everyday realities

The achievements of modern CAD systems are considerably more prosaic than either the popular myth or the slick demonstration imply. I do not regard them as in any way trivial, however. We are in the midst of major change in our profession. Many practices have already made strides in familiarizing themselves with the available technology and have begun to automate or at least assist some of the time-consuming tasks that they are expected to accomplish on the way to realizing a building project. The next five years will see the continual evolution of this process as we adjust the ways we work to realize the full potential of the systems we use. Within five years, I expect to see a second round of advances, as the systems themselves improve to take advantage not only of the ever greater capabilities of hardware and the significant strides in software design but equally importantly the greater knowledge of the professional user.

What do we expect of CAD today?

My description of our own experience to date will be taken under the following headings:

- how CAD is implemented in Arup Associates;
- what it achieves today;
- the benefits of CAD;
- what can we expect in the future.

Implementing CAD

Three factors are paramount in the successful implementation of CAD: making workstations easily available, ensuring that they are used by working designers, and recognizing that both these factors will require a continuous level of highly skilled support.

Figure 8.1
Planetarium study, Saudi Arabia
(GDS image manipulated on Macintosh)

Available workstations

Arup Associates began the introduction of CAD in January 1985 with the purchase of a six-workstation GDS system. This was located in a working design group which at that time had about 20 potential users: architects, structural engineers and building service engineers. During the following four years, the system was expanded group by group until it reached its present size of 35 workstations driven by a Prime 6550 mini computer, serving between 90 and 100 designers.

Throughout the process we have tried to meet two goals; firstly that a GDS workstation should be available whenever a designer wishes to use CAD; secondly that each should pay its way by recovering charges against live projects. The target: Each workstation should be in productive use for five hours each working day. Dividing the number of working hours into the annual cost of the system we arrive at an hourly recovery rate, which is applied to the number of hours logged by each project.

Professional users

During the introduction of CAD, Arup was anxious to continue to allow all designers to produce their own drawings, without expecting them to work through CAD technicians. This has given rise to a policy of 100% training in the use of GDS, in the form of a five-day external course supplemented by two and a half days of in-house training. Initially this occurred group by group as workstations were introduced; now it is timetabled to suit the arrival of each member of staff, who generally receives CAD training during his or her second week in the office.

By combining general training with an adequate provision of hardware, each designer is free to choose when to use CAD and when to use manual techniques. The take-up rate is surprisingly high. Of the 90–100 architects and engineers in the office at any one time, more that 70% are competent users of CAD. Of the remainder, the majority do not need to produce drawings in their work. Less than 5% could use CAD but actively choose not to.

Finding metaphors

It is not reasonable to expect all users to master all aspects of a powerful multi-user system such as GDS. To supplement the generalized training a degree of customization is also necessary to handle the most complex tasks in a simple and straightforward manner. These extend from the design of the project database to facilities to combine complex fragments of data at plot time. Over the past five years, we have developed a range of utilities, programs and adjustments to the standard interface to ease the transition to CAD and to extend the capabilities of even the frequent user. Currently, we are bringing these together as a single Arup Associates system, which provides a front-end to GDS and maintains a parallel drawing management database running under the Oracle relational database management system.

What the system produces

Drawings

The most obvious output of the system is paper drawings. Currently we use CAD to produce over 90% of our issued drawings. The non-CAD element consists mainly of certain types of presentation drawings at the beginning of a project and sketches to accompany instructions at the end. Drawings range from small-

Figures 8.2a) and b)
Detailed design studies for an office building in Newcastle

scale location and site drawings through co-ordinated sets of plans and sections to large-scale assemblies and details. Given that the choice of what to draw using CAD is made by each designer, it is interesting to note just how far the range extends. While in a project sense there can be no doubt that highly referenced general arrangement plans are the most cost-effective use of computers, to an individual user any drawing that will require adjustment during its life will show benefit from the transfer to CAD.

Reports

The second output is the non-graphical report. This originates either from non-graphical attributes attached to entities on drawings or from the linked relational database. Currently the main focus for these links lies in drawing management, allowing us to record accurately the location, status and issue history of all drawings held on a project.

Visualization

The third output is of course design and presentation images produced from three-dimensional models. Unlike normal drawings, these are only rarely produced by working designers, being more often the work of members of our computer support unit. They vary from large and intricate models of projects in their surroundings to quicker studies of parts of projects used to help resolve design issues.

Output is achieved via a number of techniques, originally slides and screen dumps to thermal plotters, but increasingly now via transfer of raster data to Macintosh systems for image enhancement, photo montage and painting prior to output using the full range of Macintosh peripherals, either in-house or bureau based.

The benefits of CAD

In its most limited application of two-dimensional draughting, CAD produces obvious benefits to drawing production, in a way that is analogous to the effects of word-processing on document production. These include the ability to adjust layout and appearance freely and to copy and modify previous work. Just as with word-processing, equal dangers also arise from these facilities – the temptation to focus on inappropriate levels of detail or the facility to replicate monotonously rather than redefine.

I should like to point to three less obvious areas, each of which offers enormous advantages to the quality of our work, but require us to adjust our way of working in order to realize the full benefit.

Accuracy

The ability to work accurately from the scale of the whole to that of the part releases us from a process of supplementing graphical representation by mathematical checks. Complex geometrical relationships can be resolved by graphical means rather than by recourse to trigonometry. Dimensions can be checked visually by relationship to other elements of known size without concern about accumulated errors. Parts can be removed, developed in detail and then returned with confidence of their fit. The result of this process is that far more complex forms can be processed with confidence throughout the design development stage, and that architects can be freed to draw what they have designed and not to design what they can draw.

Co-ordination

For Arup Associates, perhaps the greatest benefits of

Figure 8.3
Paternoster master plan context model.
(GDS image manipulated on Macintosh)

Figures 8.4 a) and b)
Details from Paternoster master plan model

CAD arise from its abilities to display the work of several designers simultaneously. Since all related data are held in exact register and to a common scale, each user is free to use any combination of data regardless of the forms of output required by his or her colleagues. More importantly, reference data are always accessible in their most up-to-date form, highlighting conflicts and speeding the process of co-ordination.

Since all drawings can be seen by all other users, used as backgrounds or incorporated into final plots, each additional drawing produced using CAD gives benefits not only to its author but to the entire team, leading as it does to a highly co-ordinated project database. Fully exploiting the value of this database is perhaps the most difficult challenge in the change to the use of computers, requiring as it does an adjustment towards a very collaborative way of working and the mastery of the intrinsically complex operations to be found in multi-user computing environments. We still feel that there is much more to develop.

Graphic quality

The final benefit to which to attention should be drawn is that of graphical quality. Computers represent a new medium, or perhaps we should say several new media. Initially, of course, users are most concerned to reproduce the drawings which existed prior to their introduction. GDS in particular has enormous facilities to replicate the highest standards of draughtsmanship with sophisticated input techniques and excellent control over the appearance of line-styles and text.

However, the most interesting results begin to occur when the style of drawing adjusts to the new strengths of computer media. An example in two-dimensional draughting would be the use of raster fill patterns, which introduce great possibilities for improvements in the legibility of drawings and which tend to preserve relative graphic weights when reproduced at multiple scales. Equally thought provoking is the appearance of two-dimensional graphics on a high-resolution colour monitor, both as a working tool and as a presentation device. As we move into the areas of raster printing and image enhancement, we encounter not only the need to learn skills from other disciplines but also entirely new techniques for which no manual equivalent exists.

What do we expect of CAD in the future?

What is asked for

Given its manifest benefits, I have never encountered much resistance to the take-up of CAD in Arup Associates. The problem now is much more one of trying to find ways of meeting the aspirations of users who, having already derived benefit from certain aspects of the change to computers, are keen to see both the systems they use and their own knowledge develop at a steady pace. Having analysed a number of the requests raised from the users of CAD, I would categorize them into the following main groups:

- understanding better how the systems really work;
- knowing how to find available data;
- having simple access to three-dimensional modelling;
- linking geometrical models to analytical systems;
- achieving higher quality final output;
- having straightforward access to related applications, e.g. word-processing and spreadsheets.

Similar lists can be developed to represent the requirements of the users of our other main systems – cost modelling, engineering analysis and office automation. While these contain certain improvements specific to individual applications, they predominantly share the same concerns. It is my belief that all of these will best be met by moving away from our current methods, based around largely proprietary systems, towards a more generalized computing environment which allows access to each of the functions we now carry out. The characteristics of this future way of working will be as follows:

- consistent interface concepts;
- improved customization environments;
- multi-user graphical and relational databases;
- powerful multi-tasking platforms;
- effective networking.

Actions in the meantime

During the past few months, we have been attempting to define a future policy for our practice which allows these objectives to be met. In so doing, I have become convinced that we are currently in a transition phase, which may last for four or five years, during which time we can only approach our ideal. At the end of this period we can expect to have achieved a far more integrated use of computers. It will almost certainly be based around the powerful personal workstation which is used in a far more relaxed way as a standard piece of office equipment. The signs are very good that the hardware to provide the required performance at an acceptable cost will certainly be available.

During the transition phase, our principal task must be to continue to evolve our current use of computers, and particularly the confidence and expectations of our professional users, while maintaining the productive value of the systems in which we have already invested.

The Introduction of a Computer-Aided Design System in a Medium-Size Practice

David Harriss
Nicholas Grimshaw & Partners, London

Introduction

Nicholas Grimshaw & Partners is a medium-size architectural practice based in London. It was established in 1980 and the current staffing level is 63 employees of whom 47 are architects. We started to look seriously at the possibility of introducing a CAD system into the office in 1987 when we were approximately half our present size.

Although CAD systems were available for architects prior to 1987 we had always considered them to be inappropriate to a practice of our size as they were based on the use of mainframe and mini computers, which were expensive, and the available software was not user friendly. During 1986–7 we also noticed, that there was an increase in the number of potential clients who were keen to know what in-house CAD systems we were using or, alternatively, what plans we had for purchasing a system. The demand for looking at the available CAD systems therefore arose not only from our interest in its ability to improve the efficiency of the office and provide us with another presentation medium, but also from potential clients who believed it would be to our mutual advantage to use CAD on their projects.

The brief

I believe that it is essential that the implementation of a new technology into the workplace is undertaken by a senior member of the organization who is also enthusiastic about making such a change. Many failures in the implementation of computers can be attributed to either ordering an inappropriate system or failing to motivate the staff to operate the new technology correctly. The method of implementation of a new system should never be underestimated.

We spent many hours discussing what our brief for a CAD system should be and the key concepts which came out of these discussions were as follows:

- it should be user friendly and available to all architects;
- it should not require a specialist computer department to run it;
- it should be used on all projects and not just selected ones;
- the system must be capable of growth and change;
- it must be able to produce both general arrangement drawings and production information;
- special consideration should be given to the choice of input and output devices;
- the proposed CAD system must be affordable.

The research

Armed with this checklist I talked initially to other architects who had a CAD system rather than the suppliers, who would probably not give an unbiased view of their products. Approaching other architects was not easy, however, as most of them wished to maintain a level of secrecy about their CAD system.

It was during these discussions with other architects that I was introduced to the Apple Macintosh II machine. Until then I had always considered that personal computers were just 'toys' when it came to CAD as they had insufficient computing power to handle the large data files that CAD generates. However, the Mac II introduced the concept of 'open architecture' in its design, and dealers were encouraged to remove the lid and, to some extent, customize the machine for its particular application.

The 'desktop' or user interface of the Apple computer is also very 'user friendly' and so I was keen to put together a CAD system using the Apple Mac II computer as the basis of each workstation. This decision was to some extent 'putting the cart before the horse' as, according to the textbooks, it is usual to decide on the software first and then find the appropriate hardware to run it on.

The software decision was much more difficult as most packages which were marketed specifically for architects seemed to be based upon the assumption that all buildings are of brick and tile construction! My conclusion was that a general purpose overlay draughting system would be more appropriate.

Turning to the question of input and output devices, I soon came to the conclusion that high-resolution colour monitors would be required to display the information in a way that is easy to see and an electrostatic plotter should be used to produce the drawings. Both these items of hardware are expensive but they offer substantial operating advantages over cheaper monochrome screens and pen plotters.

The system

After about 18 months of research we selected an Apple dealer who was prepared to offer us a 'turnkey' deal by supplying us with all the hardware and software. This has been invaluable in sorting out problems when we were often not sure whether a fault was due to the hardware or the software.

Our standard CAD workstation specification consists of an Apple Mac II (now superseded by a Mac II CX) which is customized with a 100 Mb SCSI internal hard disc and an 8 Mb random access memory (RAM). Each computer is, of course, also connected to a standard keyboard and mouse. The data are displayed on a 19 inch high-resolution colour monitor fixed to a tilt–swivel mechanism. The drawings are plotted on 200 dpi electrostatic plotters, although we also have an A4 laser printer and a dot matrix printer. One advantage of the electrostatic plotter and laser printer is that they are both quiet to operate whereas the dot matrix printer is located in a cupboard as it is very noisy. All the CAD workstations and output devices are connected together on a network in order that they can communicate with each other. The initial software which we used for learning the CAD system was MacDraw but we have since introduced PowerDraw and MiniCad+ as the major CAD packages which are used in the office.

Installation and growth

We initially ordered three CAD workstations, together with a 24 inch electrostatic plotter (i.e. A1 width) and dot matrix printer in July 1988. At that time we employed 25 architects, giving a ratio of approximately

Figure 9.1 Growth of the CAD system

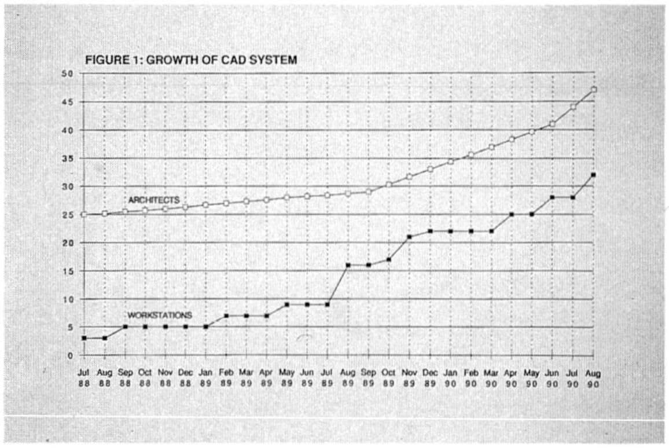

Figure 9.2
Overall view of the Waterloo Terminal (Courtesy of YRM)

Figure 9.3
Inside perspective of the Waterloo Terminal (Courtesy of YRM)

one workstation to eight architects. By the end of 1988 we had ordered a further two CAD workstations, bringing the total up to five. During 1989 there was a rapid growth in the number of CAD workstations within the office and the total increased to 22 workstations bringing the ratio down to approximately two workstations for every three architects (Figure 9.1). Interestingly the ratio of workstations has remained fairly constant throughout 1990 but, owing to the increase in staff, we currently have 32 CAD workstations and an additional 36 inch electrostatic plotter (i.e. A0 width).

Our range of software applications has also increased. The two dimensional CAD packages of MiniCad+ and PowerDraw are still the major users of the system but they have now been joined by Microstation Mac, which is the Macintosh version of the Intergraph CAD software. This has been very useful on our Waterloo International Terminal project as the engineers have developed the structural system on their in-house Intergraph system which they have then supplied to us on disc for direct input into the Microstation Mac workstation. Although this software is much more difficult to learn it is more powerful and has the advantage of being able to measure true distances in three-dimensional space which the simpler two-dimensional CAD packages cannot offer.

The most useful three-dimensional CAD package which we now use is ModelShop, which can produce three-dimensional images extremely rapidly. This package took so long to be released that it appeared that every architect's office in London with Macintosh equipment had a beta version for evaluation!

Other areas of computing, ranging from word-processing (MacWrite II) to project planning (MacProject) and spreadsheet programs (Microsoft Excel), have also 'invaded' the CAD workstations. In addition, we now use the Apple Macintosh computers for electronic publishing in order to produce reports and brochures using Aldus Pagemaker software. To satisfy these non-CAD functions we have ordered two additional machines to act as word-processing workstations, thereby releasing the more expensive CAD workstations to perform their primary function. All our specification information will be produced on the Apple Macintosh machines in future.

We have also purchased an Apple Macintosh II CX machine with a 173 Mb internal hard disc and 8 Mb RAM to act as a file server for the drawings on the Waterloo International Terminal project. This was found necessary in order to establish an audit trail for the large number of drawings on the project and it has also simplified the back-up procedure. The file server enables all the drawings on the project to be found easily and eliminates the need for each architect to keep a copy of every drawing generated on his or her workstation, which would eventually lead to chaos.

The Apple Macintosh machines have not invaded all the computerized functions in the office however. Our accounts department has recently installed a computerized financial package which does not interface with the Macintosh and the secretaries' word-processors are Olivetti equipment which we had already purchased before considering the choice of CAD system.

The network, which was initially installed to connect the CAD equipment, was a simple 'backbone' where all the equipment is connected to a common spine. The advantage of this approach is that it is the simplest (and cheapest) form of network, but there would come a time when the traffic will cause problems

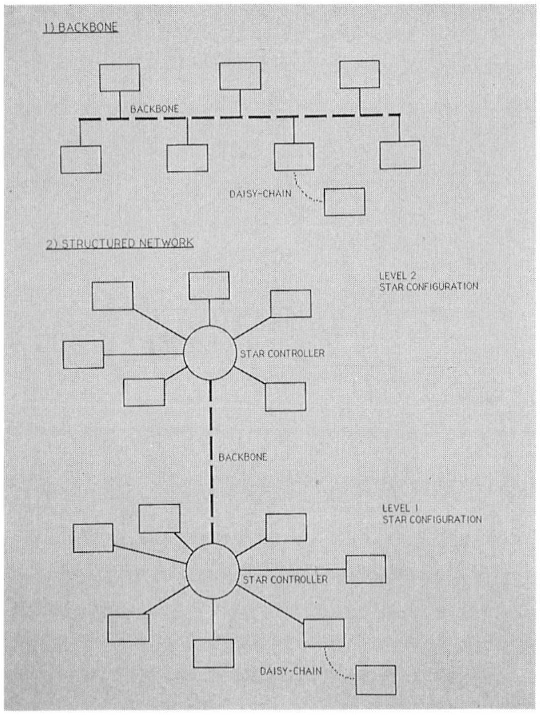

Figure 9.4
Network

as it all has to share a common communication cable.

In January 1990 we moved to new offices located on four floors. This gave us the opportunity to re-evaluate the kind of network we should install. The configuration we adopted is called a 'structured network' with each outlet wired into a star configuration on each floor (Figure 9.4). At the centre of each star is a 'star controller' and these, in turn, are connected to each other by a vertical backbone cable. This network configuration will allow considerably more traffic than the simple backbone. We initially specified 80 outlets to allow for future flexibility yet we currently have a small number of workstations 'daisy chained' together as there is not a convenient outlet to serve them. It is interesting to note that our network contains some 5 kilometres of wire and its installation cost was approximately the same as that of the new telephone system.

Management and control

We have set up a maintenance agreement with our dealer and the electrostatic plotter manufacturers in order to minimize the downtime caused by equipment failures. The equipment is, of course, sold with an initial 12 month warranty period. We also employ our dealer to offer tuition within the office to new members of staff who are not familiar with the Apple Macintosh or the particular CAD software that we use. Most members of staff, however, have not needed any formal tuition.

All software which is not supplied in sealed envelopes from the software house is initially processed through 'virus protection' software. The major culprits appear to be games programs which can do a great deal of damage if they are not initially screened. We have suffered from only one virus to date and that was in the system software which formatted the internal hard discs. This meant that on a specific date none of our computers would work. In fairness to the software suppliers a 'fix' was sent to us by courier from the United States the next day.

Cleaning the workstations (e.g. monitors and keyboards) is the responsibility of the users. We attempted to use a specialist external cleaning company and it was a disaster!

All site survey information is now specified to be provided to us in DXF format which we input, via a translation program, directly into the Macintosh machines. We have also supplied CAD drawings to other consultants on floppy discs in DXF format which appears to be the industry standard for digitized information. It must be remembered, however, that the transfer of data may contain errors and a system of verification and authentication must be introduced to prevent any disputes. (A very useful document on the problems of data exchange has been produced by NEDO (1990).)

As we use the same software on a number of workstations we have obtained site licences which allow us to copy it for our own use at a reduced rate. Unfortunately, PowerDraw does not offer a site licence agreement as each copy is 'dongle' protected. The Copyright Act amendment of 1 August 1989 makes copying software an offence which is punishable by a maximum of ten years in jail. The software houses estimate that only 20% of their software in use is sold legitimately, and to police this unauthorized copying an organization known as FAST (Federation Against Software Theft) has been set up to track down offenders.

Our CAD system does not have any security access

system (e.g. passwords). We believe that security is best served by preventing unauthorized entry into our premises and escorting visitors around rather than using passwords which can often very easily be broken.

Each architect is responsible for regularly backing up his or her CAD data onto 44 Mb cartridges which are kept in fireproof cabinets. We also intend to introduce a system to store all drawings on microfilm so that, if the magnetic data become corrupted, the drawings can be retrieved in another form. Archive CAD data is kept off site.

Another aspect of the CAD system which is currently under investigation is the actual design of the and the appropriate furniture that we should use. Issues such as lighting, cable management and ergonomics should not be underestimated as they will undoubtedly lead to high rates of absenteeism due to fatigue, back pain and repetitive strain disorders if the workstation is incorrectly designed or incorrectly used. I understand that large organizations take these problems very seriously.

The future

The current weak link of our CAD system is undoubtedly the plotting procedure.

Currently, plotting times are extended as the available range of software to run the electrostatic plotters (known as plotter drivers) will only simulate the vector commands of pen plotters. There are tricks to speed up plotting time like removing areas of fill and not using opaque masking, but the solution seems to be for the software houses to produce better plotter drivers.

Our other plotting problem is that we are unable to queue drawings onto a machine which could act as a plotter server. With large drawing issues, this sometimes involves people working all night just to load the next drawing into the plotter. System 7.0 will introduce virtual memory where the computer will be able to use its spare capacity on the internal hard disc as RAM. This will extend the power of the Macintosh by a factor of up to 4.

Conclusions

In conclusion I believe that we have selected the appropriate CAD system for our practice which allows us to undertake much larger and more complex projects using smaller highly motivated teams of architects with powerful tools to assist them. Does CAD stand for computer-aided design or Computer-aided draughting? I believe that in our case it is the latter. We have not thrown away our sketch pads and we still make sketch models. However, once the initial concept (or range of options) is established, the computer enables us to test and change it during the development of the design.

Reference

NEDO (National Economic Development Office) (1990) *Information Transfer in Building and Liability Issues Arising under English Law.* NEDO, London.

Computers and Computer-Aided Design at Michael Hopkins & Partners

John Pringle
Michael Hopkins & Partners, London

Introduction

The process of realizing a building frequently seems to be a lengthy conspiracy to compromise or dilute the original concept – often starting with the client and including engineers, the builder and his sub-contractors, the local authority, the limitations of current building technology and so on. We find that the reality of the average architect's day is that he or she has to 'entrepreneur' the building into a built reality as much as 'design' it.

It is also a process which still involves the production of numerous pieces of paper. The prospect of a bricklayer consulting a computer screen as he builds up a wall is a long way off, and for the foreseeable future we shall still issue drawings and write letters to the contractor, the local authority and the majority of consultants on a job. So how have computers helped us in the task of producing all this paper, remembering that our business is about building buildings and not about computers?

Like most people, at the outset we had quite ambitious ideas about what computers could do for us: they seemed to offer the prospect of a fully integrated drawing, quantity surveying and administration tool. They were also fascinating as we found them watching the screens of our engineers' mainframe computers. The delay when you could feel the system's brain churning through a lengthy operation, or building a rendered hidden-line perspective (usually of a membrane structure), was thrilling. You could see that it was working on its own accord which gave that reassuring feeling that everything was under control. It also produced a visual image that we had never seen before, together with the important part: all the engineer's calculations of a complexity never contemplated previously. With this sort of computing power the prospect of a fully integrated building model, complete with bills of quantities and contract documentation, seemed quite within one's grasp.

A lot of the magic seems to have gone out of it now. Nowadays we just take it all for granted and the wait for the computer to build a perspective seems just an irritating waste of time. We also now know that there are still many things the machine will not do for us, and we complain that it is too slow at doing the mind-numbing tasks it should be good at. In the end it is still up to us to get on with the architecture and work out how to do the drawings – usually in a hurry and preferably without the technology getting in the way.

We have ended up with nothing like the all-embracing nerve centre we might have dreamed of. In reality computers are just another tool, probably a bit more useful than a parallel motion, at the disposal of architects who still design in the way that architects have always designed. We use them casually like a useful piece of furniture or drawing equipment – neither used to their full potential, nor used for all our activities, but nevertheless fully used. So much so that if you were to look through the contents of any hard disc in our office, you would find the typical contents of a filing cabinet or plan chest which needs a good clear-out – a motley selection of the usual letters and drawings, year-out students' projects, perspectives of someone's entry for an architectural competition, computer games and rogue pieces of software that someone has brought in from somewhere.

Computers have only been of interest to us if they can produce something at least as good as, if not better than, we did before. For a long time it seemed to us that for all their sophistication they could only produce a result, with dot matrix printers, that looked little better than a supermarket till receipt, and all the labour that went into hand-crafted drawings still seemed worthwhile because of the superior end-product. However, they gradually infiltrated their way into the office and became recognized as a useful tool at our disposal. As far as CAD was concerned, it was not a case of our office deciding to invest in a CAD system – it was more a case of CAD reversing itself into the office through our existing computer network.

Computers verses bureaucracy

We started with a few 512 K Macintoshes and a laser printer in January 1985. One of the reasons for buying them was that the laser printer gave us something that we could not achieve before: typesetting quality for all our reports and (via Transtext and a photocopier) drawings – as with all architects, presentation quality is very important. However, our main motive in buying computers was initially to streamline our administrative systems.

As always we learn something from each new client and the way that they do their business. We first encountered the Macintosh through one such client, Schlumberger, in Cambridge. Despite having a powerful DECS mainframe system, we noticed that most of the scientists seemed to use their own Macintoshes and thought, or rather typed, directly into them for most of their routine work, because the machine was easy to use. Whilst the people in our office are nothing like as highly qualified as the Schlumberger scientists, we felt that they could just about cope with this additional skill! We also noticed, whilst working for the *Financial Times* and the *Daily Telegraph*, that journalists typed their stories directly into the computer and we felt that, if they could do it, so could we.

Analysis of how architects actually spend their time in the process of running a building contract has produced the sobering statistic that only about 30% is spent on the prime activity of drawing. A further 30% is spent on administration and the rest of their time seemed to be unaccounted for! We recognize that bureaucracy is a tiresome but necessary tool in the construction process and vital to the successful construction of a building. If we lose control over the bureaucracy, then we lose our ability to control the finished product. It seemed to us that we could streamline our administrative system if architects typed everything that they needed to write directly into the computer, without the laborious process of writing it out longhand and sending the typed draft back two or three times before it was correct.

As an experiment with one of our teams, we moved our copy typists onto more interesting jobs and made it impossible for architects to issue a drawing issue sheet or architect's instruction without using a standard form on the machine. We discovered that when composing letters and reports most people did not think much faster than they can type with two fingers (with very little practice), and the advantage of being able to edit their own work is a real benefit; architect's letters or specifications are usually laboured over at length.

Architects could now deal with their correspondence when they wanted, often early in the morning or in the evening, instead of when the secretaries were there. Many liked the smarter lettering which they could produce on the laser printer and conventional pen stencils disappeared overnight. Other people in the

Figure 10.1
A view into the office

office saw that the computer simplified these chores and offered a real advantage which did not exist before and the demand for machines spread through the whole office – about half our current stock of machines are small-screen Macintoshes which are mainly used for administration tasks.

We now also have two portable computers which, although rather large, are useful for meetings and administrative tasks on site, thus extending the principle of cutting the bureaucratic process to a minimum. At consultants' meetings some architects use the last minutes as an agenda, and type in the new minutes while the meeting is in progress and tidy them up afterwards. There seems little point in spending as long writing the minutes back at the office as the meeting took in the first place and minutes can be issued much more quickly. Spreadsheets of schedules are often updated on site very quickly and easily. They are also used by people who wish to continue working at home (without constant interruptions from the telephone and other people in the office), if they want to, making the working day much more flexible.

Computer availability

We have encouraged architects to use computers as much as possible and to make them easy to use, with stand-alone machines dispersed throughout the office. This inevitably leads to a great deal of redundancy in the system and we now have something like 2000 Mb of total disc memory.

One of our main aims was to avoid a computer élite in the office. We did not want a corps of computer technicians working day and night shifts, like a team of engineers nursing the optimum performance out of a massive power plant. We do not have any computer 'experts', but prefer to rely on our dealer for anything that cannot be handled in house. We try to ensure that there is at least one person in every team who knows the basic facts about maintaining the system. Our teams vary in size between six and 15 persons and they tend to operate as fairly autonomous units with their own particular variations on running the computer system.

For us, the computer should be much more like a piece of office furniture or something from the stationery cupboard, and treated with as much familiarity. Our small Macintoshes really represent additional A4 pads of paper, pencils, calculators and filing cabinets; our large Macintoshes are additional drawing boards with parallel motions and a storage system. There is not more than a metre between your seat and the nearest computer.

It is important to us that people should perceive that there is always a computer available whenever they want it and within reach of their workspace and telephone. If it is at all inconvenient to use then it will not be used. As a result, we now have a network of 33 computers for about 60 staff, a ratio of one computer to two persons (it used to be much better when it was nearer 1:1.5). They are rarely used to their optimum performance, neither in terms of the number of hours they are in operation during the day nor in terms of the potential of the software, but this is a necessary redundancy.

All the computers and two laser printers are linked on a 'phone net' network, divided into two zones by a bridge. We use a TOPS network server which gives people the facility to access files on another disc, further reducing the competition to gain access to a particular terminal. At times the traffic on the network becomes a little busy and this is something we shall have to upgrade in the near future. But again, the simplicity and ease of use of the present network ensures that it is widely used, despite its shortcomings.

We have also found that a decentralized system of networked stand-alone machines has proved very reliable and relatively immune from a crash somewhere else on the network. We have not thrown any computers away yet – equipment that is five years old is still used effectively, but its tasks are more limited than those of newer machines with more memory. Backward compatibility of new software has been much better than expected. One of the gratifying aspects is that architects in the office generally perceive that the new technology seems to work and there is not the suspicion found in many firms that it is expected to be more trouble than it is worth.

Software

The emphasis on software is that it should be easy to use, and we will usually forgo some of the more sophisticated features of one package if another will perform 90% of the everyday tasks more simply. Often the more sophisticated packages are more difficult to use; that sophistication may only be fully exploited rarely, perhaps at the expense of more widespread use, if it were not so complicated to use.

It is important that the software allows people to operate in much the same way as they did before. Thus the first drawing programs we used tended to work in an overlay draughting manner, 'tracing' over base plans to create new drawings. It was important that it did not involve a complete change in the way that architects go about setting up a drawing.

We found that most of our architects naturally taught themselves how to use a wide variety of other software, especially spreadsheets, simple drawing software and project planning programs. This happened quite easily without training once the basic operation of the computer had been mastered. This has now spread further to desktop publishing and databases.

Some people show more aptitude than others and usually pick up their expertise by having to accomplish a specific task rather than learning to use a program formally. Almost no formal training has taken place for the vast majority of our software and there is always someone nearby to ask if you run into problems. However, we have had to organize more in-house training for some of our more complicated CAD software so that everyone is aware of the tools that are at their disposal, which may not be immediately apparent, rather than working inefficiently because they did not know that a facility existed. It has also been necessary in order to ensure that the network is properly used as part of the CAD system.

The implementation of CAD

CAD came along very much as an afterthought once our network of primarily administration-based machines had been running for about three years. People had already experimented first with MacPaint and then with MacDraft, MacDraw and Schema software (later ModelShop), and had produced incidental graphics for diagrams in reports. Students from the Architectural Association and other schools, who had done their diploma projects on Schema, began to appear, and their example encouraged other architects to experiment with graphics programs.

The small screens and lack of plotter, however, were an obstacle to working effectively on graphics programs and only limited software was available until about 18 months ago. We constantly find that the output devices tend to limit the potential of the system, but nevertheless they are an essential component as they are the only means of passing information to the outside world. We still have to produce good quality hard copy drawings for the client or the contractor. We find communicating with the plotters is archaic, fax modems are unreliable and the big-screen monitors seem like technological dinosaurs compared with the ultra-compact processors which actually do all the work.

However, the advent of the more powerful Mac II and Mac II CX with large screens enabled us to consider running CAD software which was just becoming available at the time, some of which had originally been developed for minicomputers. We were quite fortunate that we could now launch into CAD using computers which, if all else failed, could still continue to be used for the same administrative tasks as the small computers, and at the same time offered the potential for running some very powerful CAD programs, which only a year earlier required an investment of many hundred thousand pounds.

The main task to overcome in embarking on CAD was finding the right hardware to plot the drawings. A pen plotter did not seem to be the right technology when we were already used to laser printers for written work; the prospect of sticking together sheets of A4 paper from the dot matrix printer would certainly deter all but the most dedicated computer fanatics. We therefore chose the 400 dpi electrostatic plotter; in fact we bought two, which are hooked onto the network. This machine is very quiet (important in our open-plan office) and achieves very fine resolution, and would enable us to continue to print our drawings with the fonts and fill patterns that we were now used to.

CAD software

In terms of software, we started off using MiniCad+, a powerful overlay draughting package: everyone found it very easy to use. It was a simple step from the conventional architect's skills in tracing and preparing drawings, rather than constructing a computer model. In many ways it was a good introduction to CAD for architects used to drawing conventionally, and who were already familiar with the Macintosh.

However, we quickly discovered the limitations of an essentially single-user package. This was the tendency for very large files to be built up of multiple layers which could only be manipulated by one person at a time, with the unfortunate effect of forcing us to 'funnel' a large number of tasks through a single architect. The overall building could not be easily subdivided into minitasks which the whole team could do at the same time (i.e. splitting the building into structure, cores, stairs, façade etc.) without losing some of the benefits of integrating all the elements into a single model which CAD should provide.

This was the very situation we wanted to avoid as it was creating a small number of skilled computer operators with the rest of the team rarely participating in the use of the computer. For the sort of jobs we have in the office and our method of splitting the job into design packages based around trade packages, it was essential that all the different architects could work on the same plan at the same time, if we were to have the benefit of co-ordination which the computer should offer.

Figure 10.2a) and b)
Examples of views created in ModelShop

We have therefore recently started using Intergraph Microstation which structures the drawing process very differently. The building can be split up into smaller subtasks which can be combined together to form a single model by means of a 'reference file' system. This offers the advantage of co-ordinating everything whilst at the same time distributing the workload into a number of packages spread around the entire team. Several computers can therefore work on the same building simultaneously by means of links over the network and all the architects can obtain the benefit of the CAD system. It seems to work quite well, although the complexity of the reference file structure is more difficult to learn and the program is not quite as intuitive as some of the other software we are used to.

Some of this is inevitable once you attempt to integrate several persons' work into a single system, and we foresee that it will become increasingly difficult for many people to understand how to use the more sophisticated network facilities as they become available in the near future. We may have to spend more time explaining how to use the computer as part of a network and some of the instant intuitive use which we have had so far may disappear.

We have found that importing and exporting information between our office and other consultants, surveyors etc. by means of DXF files has worked reasonably well – most of the information seems to get across and the translation between Macintosh and IBM formats seems to be fairly painless. However, direct data transfer to engineers and others who use CAD systems is still very underexploited.

Although Microstation has a three-dimensional facility, we have only used it for two-dimensional work up until now. Almost all our three-dimensional work has been done on ModelShop, which has been relatively quickly mastered by a small number of people in the office. It is a useful tool for visualizing views, especially within buildings, but it is by no means a replacement for models and hand-drawn perspectives. We often use it for setting up hand drawings.

Multi-application documents

One of the greatest benefits of the single hardware and operating system which we have adopted has been the ability to cut and paste between applications. Perhaps the best example of this was a report which we prepared for the House of Commons on the New Parliamentary Building project.

The text was prepared in MacWrite II; original full-size plans and sections were prepared in MiniCad+ (in fact much more suitable than Microstation for coloured architectural drawings in this context) and reduced down to report format; diagrams and block perspectives were drawn in ModelShop, extruded from plans imported from MiniCad+; photographs were scanned using our scanner; images were coloured up using PixelPaint; and the entire contents from the production line were assembled in PageMaker and edited together on the screen, entirely dispensing with the traditional paste-up process. It was all done in colour and printed on a colour laser printer, and was subsequently photocopied in colour. It was satisfying that the same A0 size drawings which formed part of the preliminary design could be imported directly into the report without redrawing.

The ability to carry out a number of subtasks in different applications and then combine them together in another application was all accomplished with little

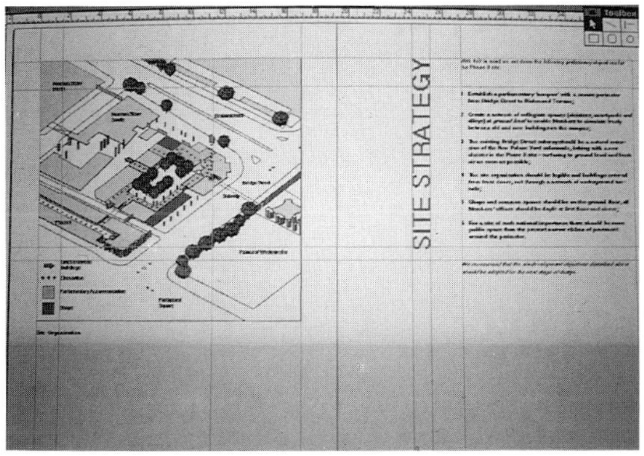

Figure 10.3
The mixing of text and images

difficulty, and we discovered the advantage of having a single system which deals with text, numbers, CAD and graphics.

CAD and architecture

We are concerned about the influence of computer draughting on the architecture produced. Since drawings are built up through a process of overlaying layers, one sees a sort of 'overlay architecture', consisting of two-dimensional layers one in front of another, emerging in the work of some practices. When looking at the flatness of a computer drawing, we see that the temptation is to create subtlety by adding another layer rather than by enriching the layer that is already there.

Whilst computer perspectives are attractive in an abstract way, they tend to be somewhat dull, rather like over-perfect air-brush drawings, and are sometimes not atmospheric enough to be of real use. Somehow they level all projects to the same repetitive standard of quite acceptable but ultimately tedious competence. Trivial ideas can often look just as interesting as the secretly beautifully crafted masterpiece. Students' diploma projects which may in reality be improbable buildings can often look more spectacular than a masterpiece of modern architecture on a computer screen.

Exotic rendered images do not tell you whether a masonry wall is holding the building up or is just a cosmetic veneer on something else: they will not help you tell the client that they are different and why it is important. We often find that only the tactile quality of a model will tell you this. However, computer perspectives have proved very useful as diagrams or snapshots of interior views of the building for reports, but are often not as useful as might be expected in communicating what we think our building is going to look like.

The advent of computers has almost forced our practice into more manual techniques during the development stage of the project, as the elevations often look relatively featureless, and we now make more models than we ever did before and do more specialized hand drawings in the early stages. Perhaps this will diminish as people become more accomplished in drawing with the computer – we already see that different people's 'styles' in computer drawing can be recognized as they become more expert in the basic techniques. At present, the CAD system really comes into its own when the project settles down into the detailed design and production phase and the main parameters are fixed.

We do not use the computer much for 'sketching', but it is useful in the early stages for investigating building grids to use as a base for developing sketch designs. Many of our recent buildings have had curved grids which used to be very difficult to draw manually on a large scale, since this would require a beam compass several metres long. The computer has made it much simpler to develop quite complicated geometries accurately.

One unexpected problem of CAD has been the proliferation of paper. There is still a need to see the result of what one has done on a piece of paper. People seem to sit like zombies mesmerized for hours on end in front of the computer screen, manipulating imaginary grids and co-ordinating commands, but does the end-product still make sense by the standards we are used to? We still need an old-fashioned print-out to check whether it will communicate information to the person who uses it when all the reference files are linked, layers switched on and off and the title block added. As a result we end up with scores of negatives of the same drawing, all slightly different: which one is right? By comparison, the reassuring dog-eared, scratched-out and patched-up one-and-only hand-drawn negative was very straightforward.

In the same vein, whereas the computer offers endless possibilities for examining multiple options or different views of the same thing, it can also generate endless useless work, investigating alternatives which would never be investigated if they were to be carried out manually because it would be too tedious to do so. One sometimes wonders whether any real purpose is served by the computer doing this: were we not better off deciding for ourselves by instinct beforehand? The risk is that computer techniques could create as much irrelevant work as the drudgery they remove. The result is that greater rigour and discipline than ever before is required to use the additional facilities on offer.

Our vision of the computerized architect's office is of the computers replacing many of the tasks of the drawing board and note pad: carrying out more and more of the tasks we always do anyway, adding some we never did before and perhaps accomplishing them slightly more quickly.

Computer-Aided Design in Practice: A Closer Analogue to Reality

Mark Leslie
Leslie Fox Albin, London

Introduction

Most architectural practices invest in CAD systems in the hope that automating the draughting of presentation and working drawings will buy them more time to design by traditional methods. Increasingly they are finding that the nature of on-screen object graphics, even in two dimensions, can greatly improve conceptual thinking by providing a much closer and more dynamic match with reality than mapping a building with lines on paper. As ever faster, easier to use modelling and animation software evolves largely from the world of computer games, architects are finally getting affordable three dimensional concept design software to replace the coloured pencils.

Fundamental issues, such as the play of colour and light over solids and voids, can be juggled and adjusted with unprecedented ease. Both the basic design and sophisticated presentation images and drawings can be derived from a single modelling exercise. As the screen becomes the medium of choice, it creates a fourth dimension of motion and change through time, impossible to simulate with lines on paper. Animated cutaway views and interactive multimedia software has created an entirely new way of conveying design ideas. CAD is now moving beyond the mere automation of routine chores. It is opening up new areas of activity and communication techniques impossible without the technology.

Architects as a CAD-resistant profession

Architects are required by trade to be an unlikely combination of businessman, entrepreneur, politician, project manager and technician. Nonetheless they tend to think of themselves primarily as artists. The very idea of computerized design seems threatening to their central creative role in the design of buildings.

Architects have been resistant to CAD with good reason. Building design is only a very small niche in a much larger industrial CAD/CAM market. The blanket description CAD masks the fact that many products are quite unsuited for building design. Such distinctions seem lost on many sales persons however.

The problems of CAD

The reason why so many CAD systems seem to architects like solutions to other people's problems is that they are. They have often been cut down from systems originally devised to help engineers in the aircraft and motor car industries. These people can justify spending millions of man-hours simulating the geometric, thermodynamic and aerodynamic properties of each machine-tooled component. Once the prototype has been perfected there will be a production run of thousands. For the architect, nearly every building is a one-off. The components are mass produced and already exist in the builder's yard. The geometric and aerodynamic qualities of the brick are well known in advance. Accuracy of up to eight places beyond the decimal point of a millimetre is wasted on a building site.

A further problem for architects is that many of the CAD systems specifically devised for them have been geared around big computers on the assumption that architects tackle conceptual design, design presentation and production information as a single simultaneous exercise and require a single computer program to do the same. These usually store every possible piece of information in a single file. This requires prodigious amounts of processing power for even a simple building.

Figure 11.1
Offices in Mountpleasant.
A ModelShop sketch design. Fundamental issues, such as the play of colour and light over solids and voids, can be juggled with unprecedented facility

Large computer systems tend to suffer from the space shuttle syndrome. They take so long to develop that they are often obsolete before they are working properly. The full potential benefits of their depth and sophistication is seldom achieved as architects seldom have the time to receive the necessary training.

The advantage of personal computers

The fast moving world of microcomputers, by contrast, can rapidly and cheaply incorporate the latest concepts in hardware and software design. Enormous sales ensure that there is economy of scale. Software is of necessity less rambling and more tightly programmed. As a result it is invariably more learnable. The reality of architecture in practice is that more than 60% of even the lead designer's time is spent in meetings and administrative chores. The personal business computer is a broad tool that pre-empts the user from needing one system for CAD, another for the accounts and yet a third just to type a letter.

The particular advantage of the Macintosh

Using traditional tools and methods the complex process of building design is generally broken down into three distinct tasks: conceptual design; design presentation; and construction information. That is, having an idea, selling an idea, and implementing it. Architects prefer to leave themselves room to manoeuvre by not being too definitive with their ideas at the beginning. By slowly building up design information from sketch doodles to sketch plans, through models and general arrangement plans to detailed schedules and specifications, there is a better chance that the right decisions are taken at the appropriate time. Integrated stand-alone CAD systems that store all the required information in a single file sometimes require the architect to commit himself to decisions that he is not yet ready to take. Typically a system might require the designer to specify all components in a library before a single line can be drawn.

The standardized software interface and easy PICT file exchange lets the Macintosh user build up a web of relatively cheap and simple software tools. The myriad tasks of marketing, feasibility analysis, desktop publishing, conceptual design, presentation, production information, project management and office management can mingle inextricably as programs become modules in one giant suite. The whole is greater than the sum of the parts.

Breaking problems down into separate tasks to be tackled by separate tools is less demanding on both the hardware and the operators. It lets designers mirror traditional methods with an interactive matrix of simple software tools each clearly focused at a single task or design phase.

Macintosh – the centre ground

Currently two waves of design software are in collision on the Macintosh. One consists of programs cut down from mainframes and mini-based CAD systems. The other has evolved upwards with the microcomputer. This includes both the home-grown Macintosh software and many exciting products from small innovative companies seeking to escape the limitations of 'games' machines such as the Atari, Amiga and Archimedes. In time they will all fuse into a single stream. Ideally this should combine the auto-co-ordination and depth of mainframe CAD with the breadth, fluidity and ease of use that is the legacy of MacPaint and MacDraw and the Macintosh interface.

Leslie Fox Albin – experience in practice

Beginning with low expectations

Having been involved in the 1970s and early 1980s with the design of 'intelligent building' for multinational corporations, where the mainframe that ran the air-conditioning knew if someone even sneaked out to have a smoke in the loo, I was strongly averse to the idea of letting 'HAL' loose in the design office. The discovery of microcomputing followed from a visit in 1985 to an early desktop publishing (DTP) bureau to get the new partnership letterheads and forms printed. Architectural draughting has much more in common with graphic design than with engineering design. In the first few years the principal advantage of the Mac was that there were no cumbersome engineering CAD/CAM packages to distract architects from the intoxicating simplicity of cheap Mac graphics and DTP programs.

By reviewing the way in which my own small practice has handled some of its key projects over the past five years it is easy to discern with hindsight the milestones that mark our change of attitude from regarding CAD as simply a draughting aid, through discovering its power for presentation and marketing, to using it as the primary initial design tool. Starting with the final stage of working drawings, the computerization of Leslie Fox Albin (LFA) worked its way backwards through the three stages of design. Ink, set-square and drawing boards were dispensed with as early as 1985; pencil and doodle pad are only slowly fading away in 1990. Hopefully LFA's most basic aids to design thinking, such as the back of a cigarette packet, a hot bath, a cool drink, a deck chair at the bottom of the garden and so on, will remain for the foreseeable future.

The central role of human creativity

Although computers are excellent for developing, presenting and implementing a design idea, they cannot actually have the idea. Indeed, very few human designers actually have original ideas. It is fair to say that by cramming both their conscious, and subconscious minds with myriads of seen and admired options and images, their job is to act as a filter to match appropriate pre-digested solutions to the problem at hand. Often the best schemes and ideas float unexpectedly from hidden recesses of the mind rather than by being arrived at through any rational process of deduction. This is often after a good night's sleep or whatever.

Some researchers continue to pursue notions of true 'computer design' with software for automatically deriving and analysing 'best' spatial arrangements. These expert systems merely reflect priorities and presumptions of their authors. The reason that so many hitherto reluctant architects are starting to warm to CAD is the realization that, far from replacing human talent and experience, or the lack of it, computers merely amplify it. Now that-user friendly systems are rendering the white-coated priesthood of CAD technicians obsolete, the creative individual can return to centre stage.

Dynamic design sketching in two dimensions

St Lukes Hospice, Plymouth

In the autumn of 1985, LFA were asked to design the new St Lukes on a magnificent sloping site overlooking Plymouth harbour. This was possibly the first architectural project in England where all the drawings were handled on the Mac. Using a system that cost less

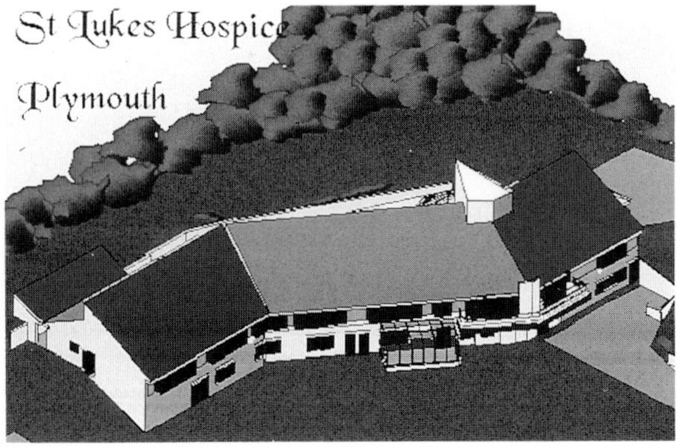

Figure 11.2
St Luke's Hospice Plymouth
Possible the first UK healthcare building to be designed entirely on a Macintosh in 1985, it was awarded the MicroCAD Achievement Award for Architecture in 1987. The original Schema sketch design model was later colour painted in Studio 8

than £3000 LFA used the project to re-define the term 'desktop CAD'.

LFA had just rented their first Macintosh 512, with MacWrite and MacPaint, as an office labelling machine to replace Letraset. The thinking was that title blocks and specification text could be generated and altered more rapidly than by hand stencilling. Labels could be pasted onto pen and ink drawings. The arrival of MacDraw and MacProject led us to suspect that combined with MacPaint and MacWrite these four simple programs constituted an integrated CAD system of unheralded ease of use. If the Macintosh could cope with St Lukes then it should prove even more suitable on our larger but simpler industrial projects.

Conceptual design in two dimensions

LFA had won the commission to design St Lukes in competition with a number of other practices on the basis of an interview and traditional concept doodles. Quick pencil sketches continued to inform the design throughout 1985, as there was no three-dimensional CAD software available as yet. LFA was firmly of the opinion that the true role of CAD was to speed up the production of plans and buy more time for 'design' with coloured pencils.

Although LFA began with no visualization software, object graphics provided a two-dimensional analogue of three-dimensional reality. They are more useful for conceptual planning than pen and ink line drawings. The functional requirements of healthcare meant that St Lukes was designed from the inside out. Bedroom and bathroom plans were evolved in detail before repeated units were assembled into an overall plan. The ability to group a bed, a chair, a medicine trolley and a bath and pull them about on the conceptual diagrams demonstrated the usefulness of CAD for basic space planning. Manipulating objects, rather than lines, is like moving cardboard cutouts on graph paper. The graph paper has magnetic snap points, and the cardboard is rubber. It can be squeezed and stretched.

A striking example of the usefulness of object graphics arose over the issue of manoeuvring beds out of the wards to the treatment bathrooms. LFA had tried to minimize the precious square footage taken up with circulation. When the staff queried the widths of the corridors, it was possible to push a bed object grouped with two nurse objects around the plan, on screen, and thus discover and eliminate potential bottlenecks.

Escaping the bounds of line drawing

Most draughtsmen are conditioned to accept the bizarre conventions of Euclidean geometry. Their universe consists of lines of no thickness that intersect at points of no area. They are more concerned with the infinitely thin boundary between an object and the rest of the universe than with the object itself. Sometimes they struggle to get the best out of CAD. They often produce drawings that are laboriously assembled from lines, as if they were still using a pen. Many programs pander to this conservatism by providing more line editing tools than shape tools. Several drawing stages can be skipped if drawings are assembled from pre-filled and hatched shapes. By building up plans from assemblies of symbols that directly relate to structural components (such as blocks, slabs, panels, windows and doorways) clear design thinking is improved. The creation and alteration of plans is speeded up. Typically, the wall elevation might be constructed by creating building blocks at their actual dimensions, say 175 x 375mm, and duplicating with the grid snap set at the nominal dimensions of 200 x 400mm. The coursing of the joints between the blocks will be perfectly set out automatically. Constructing the drawing is much the same as building an actual wall.

The problems arose with the project from its extended time-scale. Hospices are funded mainly by public subscription. The budget targets change constantly in line with the success of the fund-raising efforts. The brief itself therefore matured over a long period as the staff of the existing hospice found time to evolve their ideas. As the list of required rooms grew longer, the plan changed from 5000 to 12 000 square feet. Six different schemes were drawn up before the hospice committee felt able to go out to tender.

It proved a fortunate choice of project for a CAD test. Instantaneous deletion and alteration is one of the principal benefits of CAD. The ready re-sizing of objects makes ease of alteration one of the particular benefits of MacDraw-type graphics. The sound of razor blades scraping on vellum soon became a distant memory. The danger is that once clients find out how easy it is to make changes, they come to expect it on a continuous basis. The benefit for the conceptual designer is that designs usually tighten and improve through the discipline of continuous redrawing. Previously, however, time and tedium seldom permitted the number of iterations required for a plan to mature fully. Fear of the effort of commitment to ink need no longer hold back the designer.

Experimenting with three-dimensional presentation

In mid-1986, LFA obtained an early version of Schema 3D, a design sketching tool developed for students at Harvard University (since developed commercially by Paracomp into ModelShop). The complete contract package had already gone for a negotiated tender. When the Contractor's minimum figure came back over budget, urgent action was required. Altering the MacDraft plans was straightforward. There was no time for the long series of pencil doodles that had informed the evolution of the original design. The reduced scheme looked reasonably acceptable in two dimensions. Would it work out in three-dimensional reality?

Schema 3D

Schema's 'painter's algorithm' is optimized for speed rather than accuracy. Clearly, a tool which renders in seconds with the odd line misplaced is of far more use for design sketching than one which takes hours with none. Blocks could be duplicated, flipped, tweaked and dragged to rapidly assemble a crude but effective massing model rapidly. Setting up a perspective was as easy as dragging a line from the desired centre of view to the desired standpoint. The hidden-line removal was calculated in less than a minute. LFA used simple outline views as starting points to be worked up into detailed sketches by hand. The proposed new massing appeared unsatisfactory when viewed from ground level in three dimensions. Further changes in the MacDraft general arrangement plans led to a more balanced scheme that could be checked out in Schema.

Using Mac tools in parallel

The two separate CAD tools of MacDraft and Schema were being used in tandem much as an architect might use traditional media of the drawing board and a balsa wood model. This two-program approach was quick and simple, and worked. LFA used the Clipboard to make the next logical step. Soon views of St Lukes were being rendered up in both MacDraft and SuperPaint. Textured

Figure 11.3
Becton Dickinson Labware Building Plymouth. LFA's draughting team of four people and four Mac SEs managed to get this 200,000 sq ft pharmaceutical manufacturing plant on site within eight weeks of briefing the project

Figure 11.4
Becton Dickinson Labware Building The main office block entrance. An image of the Schema site model

bushes, trees and skies could be sprayed on at will. The combination of a $20 modelling package, a £90 paint program with a £500 matrix printer was producing images comparable with those from CAD systems costing tens of thousands of pounds at that time.

Presentation in three dimensions

The Becton Dickinson Labware building

Having used two-dimensional object graphics for both simple concept plan sketching and detailed drafting LFA was determined to move on and capitalize on the possibilities of three-dimensional software, and moving images, to present design ideas and win major projects, whilst retaining the advantages of maintaining a small close-knit design.

The opportunity came in 1987 when the Becton Dickinson healthcare company decided on a limited design competition for their 180 000 square foot Labware manufacturing plant. A major US design build organization was one contender. A large firm that had designed many buildings for the company in England and abroad was another. The problem for LFA was to convince Becton Dickinson that the smallest, and newest, of the competing organizations would in fact be the fastest and most efficient. A two-week deadline was given to produce a coherent plan and a perspective view.

Most briefs and sites suggest several promising design strategies. The time it takes to draw up even a simple scheme by hand usually forces architects to put all their eggs in one basket and present only one. Becton Dickinson specified in their brief that the Labware building should match their adjacent Vacutainer building in every detail. This was flattering to the partners of LFA who had played key roles in designing the original building whilst working for another practice. But it was limiting to their creativity seven years later on. How to reconcile the strictures of the brief with LFA's own ideas? The solution was to use the file duplicating possibilities of CAD to produce two different schemes for a lot less than double the work. This would both demonstrate LFA's productive capacity and show that two identical brown boxes 800 feet long on the same site could make for monotony.

Figure 11.5
Becton Dickinson Labware Building The main stairwell. An image from the MacArchitrion walk through

Presenting with HyperCard

In 1987 Apple began bundling HyperCard free with the Mac. This 'information environment constructor kit' added database search functions and background programming to the abilities of earlier Mac presentation software such as Slide Show Magician. 'HyperTalk,' the built-in programming language, had the unusual merit of being a subset of plain English. LFA could now invent invisible screen buttons by writing HyperTalk 'scripts' such as 'dissolve slowly into Managing Directors Office'.

The Labware commission was secured following a boardroom presentation in which HyperCard's flick-card abilities were used to show two Schema site layout models and two MacArchitrion building models of two radically different schemes: the curved flat roofed scheme requested in the client brief, and a contrasting pitched roof scheme favoured by LFA. On-screen bulldozers cleared the site amidst clouds of dust, steel sprang out of the ground, cladding panels flew together and so forth. The client was sold LFA's preferred option by a more dynamic impression of the architectural concepts than would ever be possible from mere drawings.

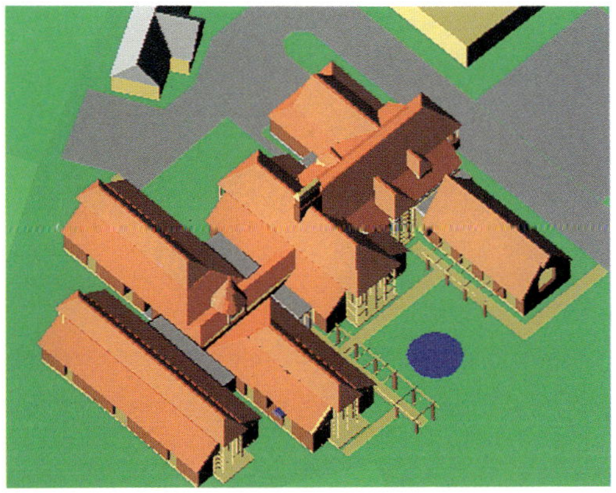

Figure 11.6, 7 & 8
The Maidstone Hospice Kent
A single day's CAD modelling produced a file from which any number of colour shaded perspectives could be rendered for transfer to video

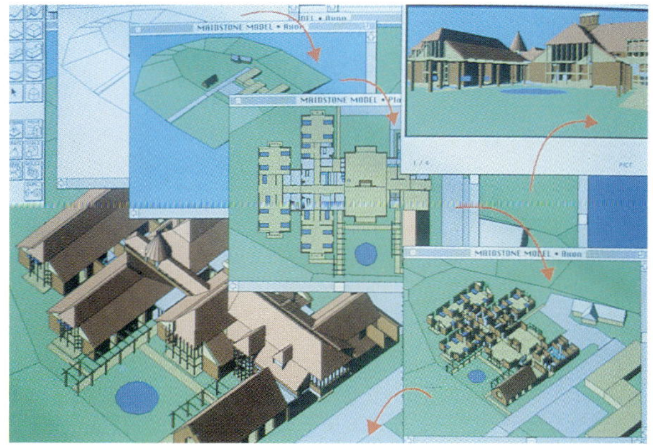

Interactive walk-through

Although the client totally redefined the brief and doubled the size of the building, LFA's draughting team of four people and four Mac SEs managed to get the project on site on 4 January 1988, a mere eight weeks after appointment. Later, time was spent in creating a very detailed MacArchitrion CAD model of the administrative office area. Over a hundred perspective views were pre-processed, saved into HyperCard and buttoned into logical looped sequences. Clicking on the left or right side of the screen might turn one in that direction. Clicking in the centre might move one forward. Clicking on a door, skylight or window, might jump one through it. Floppy discs sent to the United States let us talk the client through the building by phone from the UK. The man-week involved in creating this presentation was equivalent to the time spent setting up a single architectural perspective by hand.

Introducing time, the fourth dimension

A serious drawback of HyperCard was that to optimize its speed as an administrative 'filofax' it was strictly black and white. Luckily it can be buttoned to control other programs when required. LFA coloured up a number of the key views with a colour paint program, Studio 8. This has its own slide show utility, as well as the ability to cycle colours through time. It was easy to create the appearance of night gradually falling over the building and lights coming on, as well as the reflections of passing clouds in the exterior mirror glass. The microcomputer screen introduces the passage of time and the effects of moving light and shadow.

Concept design in three dimensions

The Maidstone Hospice

In early 1989 six practices were invited to produce proposals for the new Maidstone Hospice. They were all given the brief on a Thursday morning with instructions to attend an interview the following Monday. The difficulty for most architects is not design but presentation. Ideas that can be evolved in a matter of hours can take weeks to draw up in presentable form. With only a weekend available, it was safe for LFA to presume that our competitors might only present a few doodle sketches. We were determined to show that the Mac's abilities as both a high speed three-dimensional sketching tool and a multimedia presentation tool would give us the edge in every aspect of the conceptual design presentation and implementation of the project. We resolved to present a videotape 'fly-through'. For the first time the design process would commence entirely on screen. There was simply no time for coloured pencils.

On-screen sketch design

Once the site and existing buildings had been delineated, ModelShop was used to shuffle correctly sized colour-coded floor slabs into an acceptable layout in plan view. In essence this was no different to manipulating the two-dimensional objects when planning St Lukes except that the rectangles were now blocks. Standardized walls, furniture and fittings were duplicated. Modelling the roofs was an exercise in 'origami' using the fold and tweak commands. A single day of CAD modelling produced a file from which any number of colour-shaded perspectives could be rendered.

Figure 11.9
Shannon Aerspace Facility, Ireland. ModelShop permits a virtual world up to 32 kilometres square to be created. The entire Shannon estuary was modelled to set the building in context

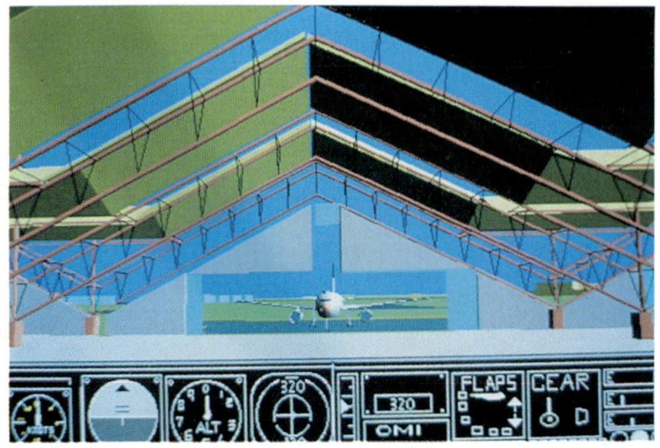

Figure 11.10
Shannon Aerspace Facility, Ireland. An example of an on screen analog design

Figure 11.11
Shannon Aerspace Facility, Ireland. An example of an on screen analog design

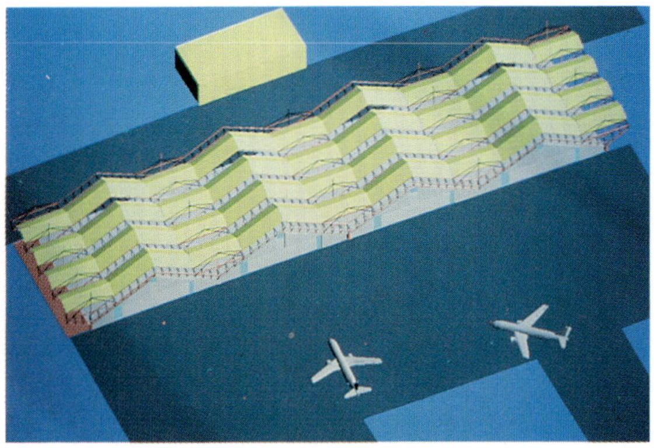

Figure 11.12
Shannon Aerspace Facility, Ireland. An example of an on screen analog design

Getting the images off the screen

One can readily post paper to a client. Posting floppy discs requires compatible machinery at the other end. Videos are now ubiquitous. One of the supposed benefits of multimedia is the linking of CAD to video. Conventional wisdom requires an £8000 slide maker to generate 35 mm transparencies from computer images. Not possessing one of these excellent devices, LFA's only recourse was to a bureau. To our amazement we discovered that the technology required more time to 'Image' the views than we had taken in designing and building the three-dimensional model and saving 70 or so perspectives as two-dimensional 'paint' files. Thus this route was eliminated. A peep under the lid confirmed that a built-in camera and LCD screen lay at the core of the Slide Maker box. LFA raced back to dust off our own slide-making machine, a 35 mm reflex camera on a tripod. Once the slides were back from the 'One Hour' photo shop it was time to start videoing.

Imparting motion with a camcorder

Computer animations are supposed to be either set up on screen using specialist animation software or to be made cinematically by filming thousands of incrementally different screens with a 'stop-frame' movie camera. This can involve several weeks of raw processing even using Silicon Graphics type workstations. LFA chose to regard each still as an entire 'scene' and impart the motion by panning and zooming a home video camera onto a white wall with the slide projected on it. By exploiting the camera's built-in fades and wipes, it was easy to connect the scenes in a logical sequence. A zoom-in to an exterior perspective dissolved slowly into the same view with the exterior wall suppressed to reveal the interior, and so forth. It was easy to create a ten minute walk-through with convincing apparent motion connecting each scene to the next.

Mixing sound and live footage

Another advantage of video was the ease with which live footage of the site could be mixed and faded with computer images and punctuated with realistic sound effects, music and a spoken commentary. LFA had very rapidly rolled over data from a CAD system, to a camera, to a slide projector and onto video without having to hot-wire in any of the three different technologies. In the event the Hospice Committee were sufficiently startled at being presented with a TV tour of the proposal that LFA were appointed as architects the very next day.

Shannon Airport fly-though

A few months later a proposal for an £80 million aircraft repair facility at Shannon Airport was put together equally rapidly. LFA used maps and aerial photographs to create a ModelShop terrain model 32 kilometres square, centred on the airport. A model of one of the client's new fleet of Boeing 767's was used as a live template for bending roof trusses to create a four-bay structure that the aircraft could roll through. This was a good example of three-dimensional dynamic analogue design. The object for which the design was intended became the principal design tool. Views could be set up from anywhere within this 'virtual reality'. LFA ported in the flight deck from the MicroSoft Flight Simulator and created a rolling series of cockpit views of flying down the Shannon Estuary, touching down on Runway 240 and taxiing through the facility.

Figures 11.13, 14, 15 & 16
Shannon Aerspace Facility, Ireland.
As the screen becomes the medium of choice, it creates a fourth dimension of motion, and change through time, impossible to simulate with lines on paper. CAD is now moving beyond the mere automation of routine chores. It is opening up new areas of activity and communication techniques impossible without the technology. The addition of sound and motion can mask the relative unsophistication of quick computer images

Colour cycling

The benefit of saving the Shannon views into Studio 8 was that they could be linked into a convincing semi-animation using the Gallery slide show utility. Colour cycling and slow dissolves were used to portray the sunrise over Shannon, the runway lights and homing beacons being switched on, and the winking of aircraft navigation lights. The client had Macs, and so the presentation was sent on disc. However, a videotape created in the same way as the Maidstone one was also sent. The video camera was bumped at the moment of touchdown. Irish pipes, seagull cries, revving jet engines and screaming tyres had all been dubbed over. Only four man-days had been required. The addition of sound and motion masked the relative unsophistication of the computer images.

Real-time computer animations

LFA now use 'true' animation software such as Studio One and MacroMind Director, both for our own projects such as for a recent Royal visit to the proposed V&A outstation at Lister's City, Bradford, and in support of other people's. LFA completed a 12-minute animated site history and 'fly-through' for the architects of Apple Computer's own manufacturing plant in Cork. A 15-minute video used by ARC Properties to market their Harlow Business Park was assembled in MacroMind Director from images generated in ModelShop and Swivel 3D. A great advantage of Director is that the background scene and foreground cast members can all derive from quite different programs. Typically, LFA use a conventional CAD package such as ArchiCAD, Architrion, Zoom or ModelShop to generate an architectural backdrop scene, which is brought to life with moving cars, people, helicopters or whatever in the foreground. These might be painted in Studio 8 or modelled and tweened in Swivel 3D. ModelShop's 'balsawood' can be combined with Swivel's 'plasticene'.

This approach suggests specialist hardware such as dual frequency video-boards and monitors, so that moving graphics can travel freely both ways by wire between video recorder and computer. MacroMind Director, along with supporting video editing software such as Media-Maker, is consolidating the microcomputer's pivotal role as the all purpose audiovisual presentation tool and editing deck of the future. LFA has already proved to itself that both effective on-screen design and affordable hyper-media presentation have been available for some time, with no more than a little lateral thinking.

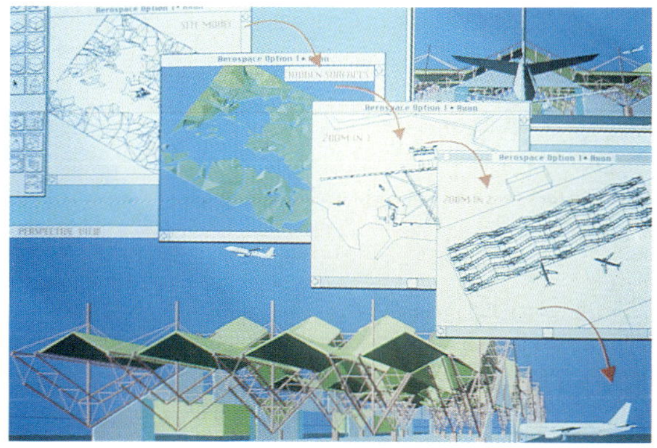

Conclusions

The impact of two-dimensional CAD on design thinking at LFA

After five years of running a drawingboardless studio the effect of the computers on initial conceptual design has been incremental. This reflects both the slow development of suitable software and the growth of computer skills within the firm. The indirect benefit of more design time as a result of automation of other office chores, was immediately apparent. Ease of deletion had an even greater impact than ease of draughting, as fear of commitment to ink evaporated. This led to much speedier iteration of ideas, a much larger range of options being investigated, and much speedier incorporation of changes. Two-dimensional 'object graphics' have led to clearer thinking at the detail design stage. The focus is now on manipulating grouped assemblies of structural components, and not

the lines that represent them. The advantage of layered drawings to ensure co-ordination is too well known to require comment.

The impact of three-dimensional CAD on design thinking at LFA

The fear is that the limitations of any particular modelling package will always constrain the creativity of the designer. The multi-program Mac approach lets one choose the tool that best suits the idea. The resolutions required at the three-dimensional conceptual stage, and the two-dimensional implementation stage are quite different. Ideas will evolve in the mind of the designer regardless of the tools at hand. So long as it is accepted that the three-dimensional sketching is only a fairly crude representation of the final product, no different from a cardboard model, limitations should not arise – indeed quite the opposite. When it comes to the closer representation required at the two-dimensional scale drawing stage, it is generally accepted that nothing that can be drawn by hand cannot now be more easily drawn on a computer.

Three-dimensional software as the key to sharing concepts

The epicentre of the design process, with or without CAD, remains the mind of the lead designer. The key advantage of sketch designing with three-dimensional software is the improvement in communication. Buildings arise as a collaboration between a large group of people including the client, the builder, the design team, the statutory authorities etc. Surprisingly few of even the professionals ever seem able to read a plan. Architects seldom have time, or even see the need, to render up fully by hand what is perfectly clear in their own mind's eye. Time and again, LFA's CAD-presented projects have benefited from crucial suggestions, ideas and observations that would never have come from committees squinting at two-dimensional blueprints. Early stage conceptual design with three-dimensional software allows the architect to share his spatial abilities painlessly with everyone most vitally concerned. Mistakes can be rectified long before they are set in concrete.

The impact of CAD on the practice profile

Automating the chores of producing the mountain of contractual documentation required to get a modern building up has made it much easier for smaller practices to compete with large ones. The number of meetings and amount of management time required to handle a small domestic extension is much the same as that for a multi-million pound project. It is in the number of junior draughtsmen and the drawingboards required that the principal difference lies. By operating a drawingboardless office LFA have found that the number of jobs that can be handled by the firm at any one time is strictly limited by how many people are available with the human skills to handle a client and run a project efficiently. The actual scale of the job is immaterial apart from the profitability aspect. Certainly CAD has major implications for the patterns of architectural training and employment in the future as staffing pyramids invert. In LFA there are no draughtsmen as such. The few 'Indians' are trainee 'chiefs' such as year-out students encouraged to run the smaller jobs.

The dangers of virtual reality

Both on-screen design presentation and multi-media may prove to be very short lived half-way houses on the road to tomorrow's dreamworld of user-definable 'virtual reality', hinted at by current groping with cyber helmets, see-through liquid crystal and sensory clothing. The 'peace dividend' will see sophisticated military head-up display and computer visualization technology seeking new applications. As the current vogue for role-playing fantasy games suggests, people's need to escape to self-defined alternative realities will grow in proportion to the grimness of an ecologically eroding world.

The walkmanization of information technology

The convergence of all electronic digital data technologies will allow an effective fusion of the computing, television, film, music, games, entertainment, education, training, design, graphics and publishing industries with political, social and cultural consequences as unimaginable for us as today's global TV and phone network would have been for the Victorians. Miniaturization and voice activation will overcome the desk-bound nature of personal computing. Mass markets opened up by 'idiot proofing' will create the hallucination in a headset. By the twenty-first century disco dancers will accompany themselves on 'virtual orchestras', lone joggers race themselves in 'virtual' marathons of all their previous performances, whilst would-be Rambos will zap any number of 'aliens' en route to the office.

The end of architecture

As an architect with a life expectancy into the 2040s, I can confidently look forward to walking my prospective clients through virtual realities of my own imagining, with both anticipation, and dread. The anticipation is of at last being able to convey design ideas fully without fear of misunderstanding. The dread is that the sensations, degree of control and unconstrained possibilities of the world within will so outshine those on the outside that events in the real world will start to lose their significance.

Current experiments with depth cue TV, holographic CAD libraries and even new Macintosh programs like Virtus Walkthrough, as well as the penchant of large corporations for commissioning prestige computer sculptures, all hint at a not too distant future where the medium might well replace the message. Such advanced means of design presentation would obviate the need for any real end-product. Reality may become the poor sister of simulation. Many human needs now catered for by travel, television, interior design, art and architecture may be more economically catered for by existential cyber-space. The consumer logic of executives being able individually to perceive the interior of their otherwise unadorned workshed as modern, classical, baroque or gothic, as a matter of taste, or even mood, is undeniable.

Computer-Aided Design Software to Augment the Creation of Form

Robert Aish
YRM Architects and Planners, London

The craft–design–CAD progression

We are witnessing an acceleration in the craft–design–CAD progression. In the craft process the user directly manipulates the form of object, allowing design intent and the object form to interact. Within limits this interaction is an ideal way to create form, but the craft process is recognized as being limited in scope and materials. Turning a craft material into an expressive medium depends on the acquisition of special hand–eye co-ordination skills. We should not underestimate the craft skills required in design and CAD.

Design is an abstraction of the craft process. The user balances competing requirements as a mental exercise and generates a design solution independent of its physical embodiment. This vastly extends the range of problems and solutions open for consideration. But the disadvantage of a conventional paper-and-pencil design process is that it uses multiple representations of both the design problem and the solution. These representations may be graphic, mathematical and textual, or indeed may use some craft processes to build particular design analogues. Co-ordinating these representations so that they consistently describe the same physical reality is a major problem and a source of many design errors.

Another disadvantage of conventional design is that the interaction between the designer and the form of the object is no longer dynamic. The creative processes may be further disrupted if the designer has to measure the design geometry in order to perform a formal engineering analysis of his proposed design solution.

The proposition is that CAD can provide a 'design environment' which can co-ordinate multiple representations of a design and can automate the evaluation process, thereby freeing the designer to focus on the 'form-giving' process.

Theoretical CAD

The theory of CAD is based on the following concepts:

- The design solution is not based on multiple independent representations, but on a single 'product definition' which can be viewed and manipulated by the designer via alternative graphic and non-graphic presentations.
- Computer graphics allows for the dynamic manipulation of geometry, which provides for the direct interaction between the designer and the object form. This was a valuable feature of the craft process that was lost during the progression to conventional design, but which is now potentially recovered by CAD.
- The design geometry can be directly measured by the CAD system and used as input into performances evaluation software. The integration of evaluation software allows the designer to balance configurational and performance issues more consciously.
- The CAD system is a comprehensive design environment, within which the complete design and documentation process can occur.
- The 'conceptual' designer directly uses the CAD system, since it is he who creates the form and must judge between the configurational and performance attributes of alternative design solutions.

CAD software development methodology

To implement the theoretical CAD system, we need a software engineering methodology. Typically this considers the following:

- The existing 'unaided' design process;
- The information flows between the design organization and other external organizations;
- How the design process can potentially be split between the designer (as a CAD user) and the CAD application;
- How the design process can be augmented by additional CAD functionality;
- What will be the resulting tasks for the designer and the skills he requires.

The CAD application designer must interpret these considerations and define two very precise types of software:

- How the CAD system will represent the objects being designed (both the geometrical and the behavioural aspect of the objects);
- What commands are required to create, manipulate and report these objects.

Pragmatic CAD

It can be argued that, whatever the theoretical basis for CAD, users will always take a pragmatic approach, exploiting some facilities and ignoring others, so that the 'pragmatic' CAD system diverges from the original theoretical intentions. However, the gap between the theoretical proposition for architectural CAD and the pragmatic use of CAD is so wide that it demands special attention, and hopefully some explanation.

Pragmatic CAD is characterized by the following features:

- It is used fragmentarily, as and when software is available and its use can be justified.
- Different application packages address different parts of the design cycle, each with their own representation of the design. Thus the concept of a single 'product definition' is lost and as a result co-ordination of the separate representation is still a major issue.
- There is little or no integration with evaluation software. This is particularly worrying because the integration of design models and evaluative software was originally projected as one of the main benefits of CAD. The current emphasis is on using CAD to create and present building form rather than to consider the interaction of building form and performance.
- The use of components (cells, blocks, subfigures etc.) forces the designer to consider detail design too early in the design process and artificially imposes the concept of 'assembly' of pre-defined components on the 'form-giving' process.
- The graphics are editable, but are often not dynamic.
- The systems are difficult to use. Users are preoccupied by the mechanics of using the system. Special 'craft' techniques evolve to make CAD work, and they distract the users from the primary concern, that of the design problem at hand.
- Pragmatic CAD systems are typically used for design documentation and are not often used by 'conceptual' designers who continue with conventional pencil-and-paper techniques.

Once a CAD system has been installed and used, the comment is often expressed in professional circles that 'CAD has not changed the way buildings are designed'. Either it really has not changed the design process or CAD has affected design but there is extreme reluctance to admit this within the profession. This comment is worrying since the whole intention of CAD was to have a very positive effect on design, in particular to augment human creativity.

Thus there is a fundamental difference between theoretical and pragmatic CAD:

- Theoretical CAD is based on the design decision process, starting with concept design and working through various evaluation and modification cycles to documentation and external communication (CAD is seen essentially as a medium of expression);
- Pragmatic CAD starts with the needs of communications, and allows that to dominate the upstream design process (CAD is seen essentially as a medium of communication).

Design documentation and communication are important, but instead of addressing the issue of how to communicate three-dimensional building models directly between the design and contracting organizations, the CAD industry (both vendors and users) has made the ultimate pragmatic response which is to do nothing and accept the existing architectural drawing convention as the communication medium.

Architectural drawing conventions: the burden of history

Architectural drawing conventions are a legitimate response to the problem of representing three-dimensional design information in two dimensions during the pencil-and-paper era of design. It is a two-dimensional shorthand intended to compensate for the difficulty of representing three-dimensional objects within the limitations of pencil-and-paper techniques. On further investigation we can see that architectural drawings often mix correct orthogonal projections of three-dimensional objects with symbolic graphics which are not true projections. This presentation process is further complicated because the same part of the building can be presented differently depending on the direction of view.

It is a legitimate requirement of CAD users that building design information needs to be represented and communicated in graphic and non-graphic form at different levels of approximation and detail. CAD offers the ability to represent three-dimensional objects accurately. Two arguments follow from this:

- Accurate three-dimensional representation substantially reduces the need for conventional drawing output;
- It is very difficult to derive conventional architectural drawings from such three-dimensional models because the derivation process mixes rules and value judgements which in turn are very difficult to encode in a CAD system.

In fact, the architectural drawing conventions are so complex and so ambiguous that few CAD vendors are interested in creating a system that can automate drawing extraction from a three-dimensional geometrical model which follows them. The software development effort could be more profitably used in developing applications for other user groups with more 'computable' requirements.

The CAD developer–CAD user 'stand-off'

It can be argued that the initial incompleteness of architectural CAD has led to the need to retain the

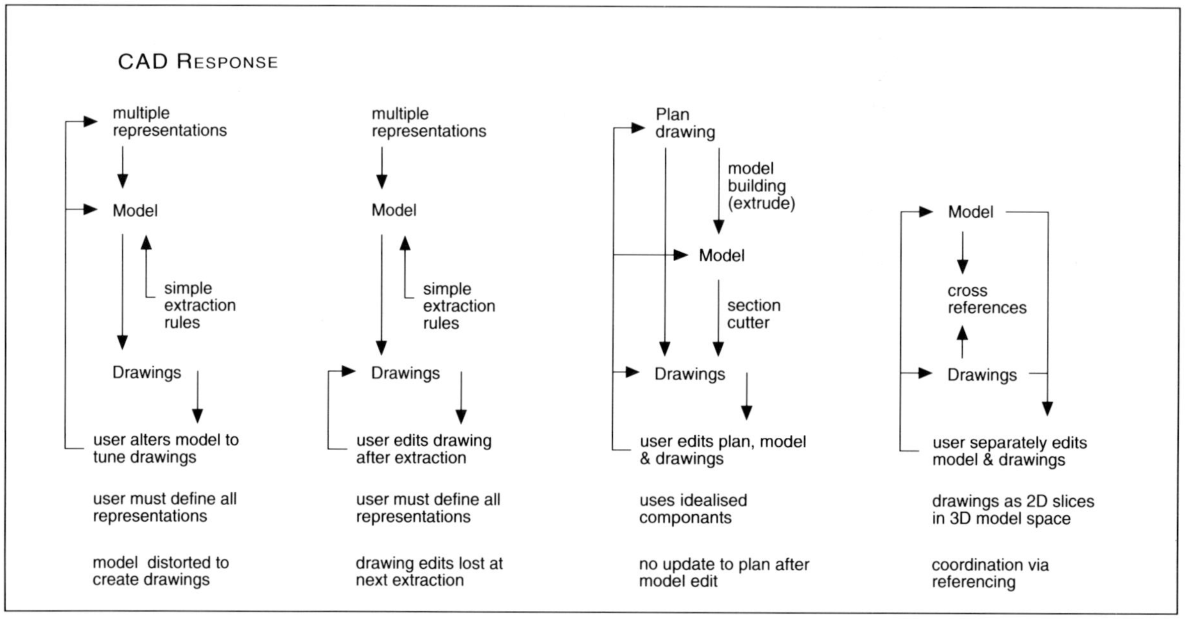

Figure 12.1
Three alternative approaches to architectural CAD and on the right, YRM's pragmatic CAD methodolgy. Any system which allows for multiple representations which can be directly edited by the users, but does not enforce consistancy between representations will inevitably create major management problems in the user organization

architectural drawing conventions, which in turn has led to the present stand-off between the CAD developers and users.

- A typical quote from a CAD application designer: 'the architectural drawing convention is a block to the development of architectural CAD'.
- A typical quote from a potential CAD user: 'the architectural drawing convention cannot be abandoned (if at all) until CAD offers a better alternative'.

The architectural CAD developers' response

Faced with this stand-off, a number of CAD software developers have attempted to design a special kind of hybrid CAD system which attempts to combine some aspects of three-dimensional modelling with some of the two-dimensional symbolic features of the architectural drawing convention. Phrases such as 'CAD system designed by architects for architects' come to mind.

It is worth considering these systems in passing (Figure 12.1) because they represent a stage in the evolution of CAD which absorbed substantial resources from many vendor and user organizations. Viewed with hindsight it is difficult to understand the attraction of these systems.

System A

'Components' are defined by the user with a number of representations, usually a three-dimensional form and various two-dimensional symbolic representations (plan, elevation and sections in various orientations). A three-dimensional model is built by placing instances of these multiply-defined components. When a drawing is required the representation of the component whose normal is nearest to the view direction is 'switched on'.

The problem with this approach is that these symbolic views are pre-defined by the user, not derived from the three-dimensional model, so that there is no way that the resulting drawings can respond to a particular juxtaposition of components, as would occur in a good conventional drawing. The user ends up artificially manipulating the model to give a drawing that looks correct. This leads to ambiguity. Is the model or the derived drawing the 'correct' representation of reality?

System B

System B is similar to system A, but in addition the user can modify the drawing after it has been derived from the model. Again we can ask whether the drawing or the model is the correct representation of reality. But there is an additional problem, in that each time the drawings are extracted from the model, they need to be hand-edited to incorporate the edits done to the previous drawing version.

System C

System C allows the user to draw a plan representation using special wall, door and window placement commands. This plan representation can be used with height parameters to extrude a three-dimensional building model. The user can edit the model away from the simple vertical extruded form, and various elevations and sections can be cut. However, edits to the model cannot update the original plan representation.

The problem with this system is that it is based on idealized components which have some useful functionality but which cannot be tailored to the user's specific needs.

The reader is invited to identify systems A, B and C. There are two general characteristics of these systems:

- Special architectural modelling features (such as doors in walls) are not sufficiently general to handle the full architectural design process. At some stage the user is forced to apply primitive graphics to complete the model, but for the subsequent user who wishes to edit the model it is practically impossible to distinguish between the special application entities and the primitive graphics.
- The drawing extraction rules are not sufficiently capable of producing 'correct' drawings from a 'correct' model and so the user is forced to manipulate the model or edit the drawings (derived data).

System D

System D is the YRM response to pragmatic CAD and avoids the use of special 'architectural' CAD applications with their attendant limitations. Separate three-dimensional models and two-dimensional drawings are defined. The two-dimensional drawings are effectively sections through the three-dimensional model space. Co-ordination between model and drawings is achieved by referencing the drawings to the model. Essentially, given a choice between limited application functionality and a general graphics system, we have opted for generality.

The recently completed Whitefriars Building (Figure 12.2) is an extremely successful application of pragmatic CAD. Support for the architectural design

Figure 12.2
The Whitefriars Building: A successful example of pragmatic CAD

Figure 12.3
Comparing CAD applications with other general purpose computing applications

CAD comparisons

CAD	equivalent general computer application	Comment
basic graphics	word processing	application has no knowledge of the problem domain
architectural application		idealised components may be restrictive
associative geometry	spreadsheet, relational database	application as a tool kit allows user to tailor to problem domain

process was provided by a number of three dimensional modelling, two-dimensional draughting and visualization applications developed by Intergraph. The craftsmanship with which these separate applications were used within the architectural design and documentation process was exemplary.

The results may look visually convincing, but we should be cautious and not claim too much for pragmatic CAD. The model is static. We cannot interrogate the model; we cannot play the type of 'what if' experiment which would be normal with an equivalent spreadsheet application. Consider the typical architectural edit request of the type 'what if we changed the column spacing' or 'what if we changed the floor-to-floor height'. This model could not respond to this type of normal architectural request.

In fact it is quite instructive to compare architectural CAD applications with other familiar computer applications (Figure 12.3). For example, a basic CAD graphics system is quite analogous to word-processing, in the sense that it is a useful aid to the user without having any knowledge of the user's application domain.

We shall come in a moment to the concept of 'associative geometry' which is analogous to a spreadsheet or database application. The important characteristics of these applications are that they do not directly address the user's requirements, but rather they provide a tool kit which allows the user to build his own application tailored to his own approach to the application domain.

What is significant is that there is no general computer software analogous to the existing set of architectural applications, and this is not really surprising since few other groups of users would accept applications which offer such fragmented functionality.

Return to CAD as a conceptual design tool

Two themes are converging: CAD users have exploited pragmatic CAD and are now interested in exploring CAD as a conceptual design tool; CAD developers have created 'object-oriented' software tool kits and are looking for potential application areas, particularly in conceptual design.

Associative geometry is an example of an 'object-oriented' CAD system which allows the user to define complex dependence relationships between geometry and algebraic objects. Based on the powerful associative geometry facilities available in the Intergraph Engineering Modelling System (I/EMS), users at YRM have been investigating how CAD can help explore underlying design relationships in complex structural systems.

The I/EMS associative geometry system consists of a set of geometry and parameter objects which can be formed into dependence relations. For example, lines can be defined as tangential to circles or parallel to other lines. Other geometrical relationships can be controlled by distance and angle parameters. A system of such dependent relations can be formed into a graph, so that a complex geometrical construction can be controlled by a number of root objects and/or parameters. Each of the graphical primitives and parameters is an object. The dependence relations between graphics and parameters are message channels between objects.

As we shall see, associative geometry can be used to model complex design relationships that would be difficult, if not impossible, to model intuitively. It is therefore worth considering a simple tutorial example (the 'penny farthing'), which both demonstrates associative geometry and is intuitive (Figure 12.4):

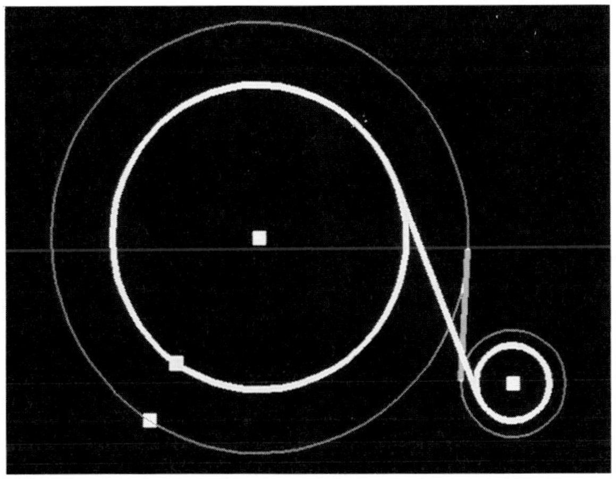

Figure 12.4
The 'penny-farthing' example: An intuitive demonstration of associated geometry

- Three 'root' points are defined.
- A parameter called 'big distance' is defined as the distance measured between the left two points.
- A circle is drawn centred on one of the points with a radius defined by the 'big distance' parameter. This forces the circumference of the circle to pass through the leftmost point
- A parameter called 'factor' is defined, whose value is 0.25.
- A parameter called 'small distance' is defined by the expression 'big distance factor'.
- Another circle is drawn, centred on the right point, with a radius defined by the 'small distance' parameter.
- A tangent is drawn between the two circles.

If the user now selects the leftmost point, the whole associative construction is displayed dynamically on the screen. As he/she moves the point interactively the parameter 'big distance' is remeasured from the graphics, the parameter 'small distance' is recalculated, the two circles are redrawn and the tangent is redrawn. The whole set of associative graphics acts like a dynamic geometrical mechanism (Figure 12.5).

The reader is invited to imagine what would happen if the other root points were moved, or if the value of the 'factor' parameter was changed.

The significance of this system is that the user can construct the network of objects by conventional interactive graphics, and can dynamically manipulate the associative graphics using conventional modification commands on the root objects. Modifications are transmitted through the network of graphical objects using 'message sends', with each object sending messages to its dependent objects so that prescribed geometrical relationships (tangency, parallelism etc.) are maintained.

Using associative geometry, the structural engineers YRM Anthony Hunt Associates have modelled the complex roof of the Channel Tunnel rail terminus at Waterloo Station, London. The architectural concept, designed by Nicholas Grimshaw & Partners, is for an arched roof which follows the curve of the railway and increases in span down the length of the station to accommodate the increase in the width of the platforms. The roof is supported by a series of three pin arches. Each arch and the related cladding are different as the roof changes width along the curved tracks. Rather than model each arch separately, a single associative model of an arch (Figure 12.6) was built which encoded the underlying design rules for the whole family of arches. The complete roof model is a series of 'instances' of this associative arch with a different value for the 'span' parameter (Figure 12.7).

Associative geometry allows the designer a choice of two manipulation techniques (Figure 12.8):

- Intuitive manipulation: associative geometry allows interactive experimentation with variation within a single geometrical configuration. Because an associative construct can be graphically dynamic, it can be manipulated in a plastic way. The user can move one of the roots and observe in real time the propagation of this modification through the associative construct.
- Strategic manipulation: associative geometry allows the user to change the values of key parameters and to observe the propagation of this change on the dependent expressions and hence the dependent geometry.

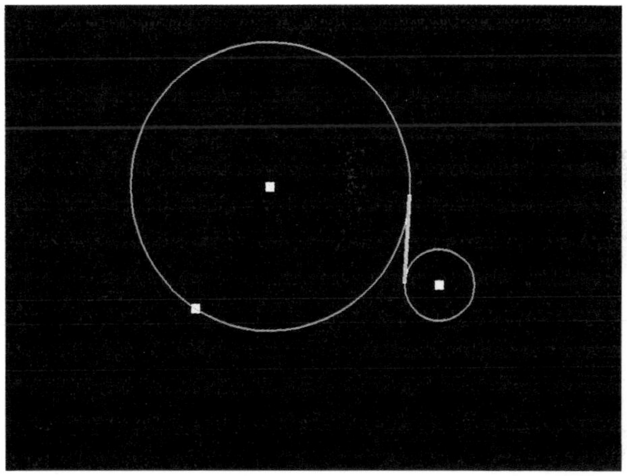

Figure 12.5
Dynamic interaction: the user moves a 'root' of the associative geometry construction and the dependent graphics update to maintain the defined relationships

Figure 12.6
The associative geometry for design relationships within the Waterloo Arch, with the construction geometry displayed

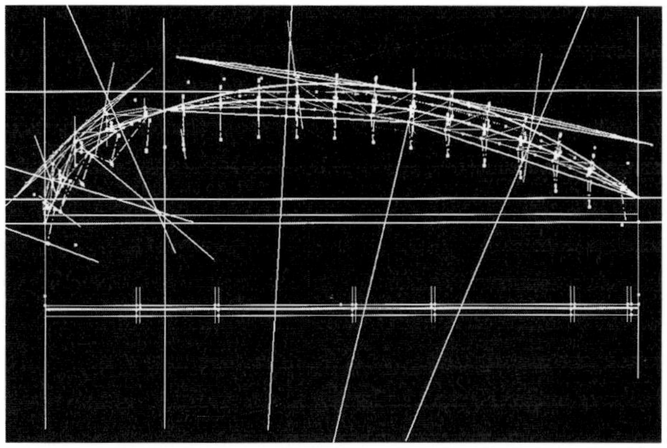

Figure 12.7
An interior view of the completed roof model, with the structure and cladding hung off the associative geometry

The dependences define how the construct responds to different manipulations. These dependences and the resulting responses may model the constraints of the design problem, the possible configuration of the design solution and the behaviour of a particular design mechanism within its operating environment.

We can compare associative and non-associative geometry. Non-associative geometry can represent only one design solution. To change that solution requires considerable editing skill. In the pragmatic use of CAD a conceptual designer will often employ a technician to perform this editing. The conceptual designer usually has no interest in the 'structure' of the geometry. Associative geometry represents not one design but a whole set of potential variations. Only the conceptual designer can anticipate the variations he wishes to explore, and construct and test the required dependences. Finally, the skill in the effective use of associative geometry is not just to create appropriate dependences but to provide useful and intuitive 'handles' with which to manipulate the geometry.

In summary, associative geometry encourages the plastic interaction with design form (as in the craft process), provides the geometrical accuracy (as in conventional CAD), allows for the exploration of variation, can be used to model underlying design relations and implies direct use of the CAD system by the conceptual designer.

Conclusions

CAD based on associative geometry is still at the research and development stage. Mature production systems offering a 'comprehensive' design and documentation environment will take some time to develop and will depend on adventurous vendors and users working together to explore how this potentially powerful technique can be applied to architectural design.

We should be cautious and not prematurely claim benefits which are not yet evident. However, we can anticipate one fundamental side-effect of associative geometry which is that a two-dimensional drawing cannot record or communicate the associative design relations. Therefore the two-dimensional drawing convention is a filter which may reject important design information and only transmit a simplified 'snapshot' of the design.

Associative geometry can be considered as a new medium for architectural expression, with the potential to augment human creativity. With this prospect in view, it is difficult to see how future users will be satisfied with two-dimensional drawings as a medium of design communication.

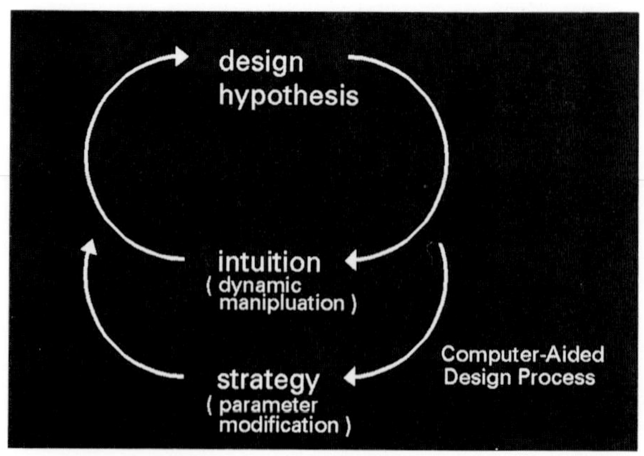

Figure 12.8
The CAD process: intuitive and strategic manipulation possibilities

Section 3: Future Developments

Introduction

William J. Mitchell

A crystal ball is a very unsatisfactory display device. You get a low-resolution image with lots of aliasing and, one suspects, a few ordering errors as well. The present unfolds in real time, of course, so you eventually get to see what lies ahead – but never quite fast enough for a prophet's purposes: just when you catch up with the future it transforms into the past. (Perhaps this is just as well: *Tristram Shandy* would not be nearly so amusing if you turned up the clock speed.) Undeterred by these technical limitations, the chapters in this part peer into the future for us anyway.

Patrick Purcell from Cambridge, Massachusetts, tells us of the current projects of MIT's Media laboratory. Convergence of previously distinct computational and media technologies is a central theme of work at the Media Laboratory. The chapter illustrates that theme with glimpses of current projects and suggestions about their implications for design. Other authors – Helen Mulligan, Giuseppe Mazzochi, Jean-Louis Schulmann, Earl Mark – focus on particular computational techniques that appear to hold promise for expanding the capabilities of CAD in new directions: object-oriented programming, interactive multimedia, formal grammars, computer animation and more. Paul Richens takes a broad view, and sketches the outlines of future integrated CAD systems and of the organizations that will use them. He builds a compelling case that increasingly highly integrated CAD systems will provide vertically integrated, multi disciplinary, design-and-construct organizations with an overwhelming competitive advantage.

It would be unfair of me to introduce the visions and predictions of my colleagues without risking a few of my own, so here goes. I think there will be a growing disparity between the rapidly evolving technical capabilities of CAD systems and the more slowly changing cultural frameworks that we use to comprehend and apply these capabilities. If we are able to meet and compare notes in ten years or so, I think we will indeed find that CAD systems are running on much faster platforms, providing real-time performance of many complex tasks as a matter of course, representing designs in very much more sophisticated ways, supporting wider ranges of functions and providing incomparably more fluid and natural user interfaces. But many of the applications in design practice will be severely constrained by metaphors that were once helpful but have long outlived their usefulness: we will still see operating systems disguised as desktops, geometrical databases layered like drawings, tools for manipulating bit-mapped images presented as paintbrushes and spraycans, solid modellers based on woodshop metaphors, nineteenth-century concepts of standardization and repetition in an era of CAD/CAM and construction robotics, image synthesis systems regarded as surrogate cameras, viewing parameters of animation systems treated like the controls of flying video cameras, and teachers of design who do not see any reason to doubt that the way they were taught is the way that their students should be taught. You cannot buy the right new metaphors in shrinkwrapped packages; you have to struggle for them.

Programming in Pictures

Simon Ruffle and Helen Mulligan
Cambridge Architectural Research Limited, Cambridge

The background

In the late 1970s, if you switched on one of the brand new Apple II computers you would find yourself deposited into a BASIC programming environment from which there was no escape. At that time 8-bit microcomputers like the Apple were shipped with no application software apart from a few extremely simple games. There was no disc operating system as such, disc commands being part of the BASIC environment, and there was little off-the-shelf software. This established the culture of the personal computer (PC). In the early days you were expected to be a programmer, and BASIC, despite its numerous drawbacks, did offer a simple programming language that allowed many non-specialist people, albeit enthusiasts, to get into computing and lay the foundations for the PC boom of the 1980s.

By the time the IBM PC appeared in 1982 the idea was established that the user should be able to program even if some professionally coded off-the-shelf software was used as well. The PC's operating system DOS was a simple language in its own right that allowed users to streamline the otherwise unfriendly PC. The assumption of any PC user was that it was not a machine that could be used without at least thinking like a programmer even if no programming was done. The 'casual programmer' emerged, a person who was not a professional computer scientist yet felt comfortable writing simple programs on PCs. He or she might put together a BASIC program, or write a DOS batch file, or perhaps extend to Turbo Pascal. The important point about this kind of person, compared with a professional computer programmer, is that they were application oriented and likely to be innovative in their own particular field. They would not write production code that was fully commented and tested (and how this annoyed the professionals!) but they could, and did, break new ground.

The Apple Macintosh first appeared in 1984. Once you had assimilated the novelty of its visual direct manipulation user interface it was obvious that it had no equivalent of BASIC, nor a line oriented operating system command language like the PC's DOS, nor any means to customize it in the traditional sense. The essential point about the Mac was that it was a computer to use rather than to program. The Mac took some time to become popular because it had to appeal to a new market, those who wanted to get on with a task without having to think like a programmer.

For those who wanted to write programs for the Macintosh a shock awaited. Whereas a simple PC program could be put together quickly in, say, BASIC or Turbo Pascal, a program for the Macintosh took pages and pages of complex program code before even the simplest thing could be achieved. The problem was that programs that ran within the direct manipulation user interface style were many times more complex than a PC program. Consequently the 'casual programmer' was initially put off the Mac. Since 1984 there have been a number of attempts to provide casual programming facilities on the Macintosh. By far the most well known of these is HyperCard.

HyperCard to the rescue

When Bill Atkinson was formulating HyperCard it was the casual programmer that he was trying to woo onto the Macintosh. He asked himself what this kind of person wanted to do with a computer, and it appeared

Figure 13.1
Screen from the Office Users' Questionnaire: respondents are invited to state a preference between images of two office buildings

that it was three things. *Customizing* means taking generic programs such as spreadsheets and databases and making them do tasks specifically moulded to a particular user or group of users. *Integrating* means taking a collection of different applications and data and bringing them together into a coherent and synthesized whole. *Prototyping* is quickly putting together simple programs to try out ideas that may be readily altered to suit changing needs but are not guaranteed to be fully documented or tested as an off-the-shelf package must be. Furthermore, a programming language to do all these things on the Macintosh had to be in the direct manipulation style and have a visual metaphor, and relieve the programmer from the complex task of programming the windowing environment.

At Cambridge Architectural Research Limited (CAR) we have embraced HyperCard, and similar products Supercard (offers full colour and multi-windowing) and ToolBook (for the PC). We have found the HyperCard approach very effective as an application development environment in the hands of both casual and professional programmers. We find that Bill Atkinson's objectives have been largely met, and HyperCard produces a surprisingly diverse range of results, as the examples in this chapter indicate.

Project 1: The office users' questionnaire

One of CAR's first applications of HyperCard techniques was the Office Users' Questionnaire. This project was carried out for a property developer who was interested in researching into the attitudes and opinions of staff in office buildings. Respondents were asked their opinions on their office environment, their attitude to certain key issues such as car parking, and finally to express preferences between pairs of images of recent high-tech office developments. Various techniques were used including picking keywords like 'warm', 'crowded', 'spacious' from screens, responding on a five-point scale from 'agree' to 'disagree' in response to statements, and choosing from a four-point scale in response to pairs of images of buildings (Figure 13.1). Eleven surveys have now been carried out in a number of company's office buildings using two Macintosh II computers.

Respondents were enthusiastic about the questionnaire. Even participants who were unfamiliar with computers found very little difficulty driving the system. Many commented that they enjoyed the experience and were surprised to find how long (average 35 minutes) they had spent at the computer. There were no uncompleted surveys; no one lost interest or refused to continue. In all cases supervisors were on hand but they answered queries mostly about the meaning of particular questions rather than the use of the computer. One particular benefit of the approach was that data were complete because the respondents could not omit questions. Surprisingly respondents expected the survey to be more sophisticated than it really was, with branching on the results of questions and so on.

The system was constructed in Supercard and employed an arrangement of one card per question. Cards were arranged into five groups or *stacks* reflecting the five parts of the survey: introduction, attitudes, words, features and images. In general the user progressed through the survey by clicking on a 'go to next card in the stack' button, though refinements were built in to ensure that users at least gave a few seconds' thought to each question. Being one of our first forays into Hyper techniques the system became rather complex. Results for each stack were stored on the front card of each stack, and then at the end of the survey the results were written to a company stack where one card per respondent recorded the overall results. The company stack therefore represented the survey for one group of respondents. This was then written out as a whole on an Excel spreadsheet for subsequent detailed analysis.

We learnt some lessons from this project. It established the idea of using HyperCard techniques as a front-end for another application, in this case Excel. It also showed how complex the programming can get if you approach Hyper programming as if it were a traditional programming language. In trying to emulate traditional sequential programming we set up control cards that directed how the question cards were to appear, but in retrospect it would have been better if we had let each card control itself. We stored data in temporary holding areas when perhaps we should have simply left the data on the question cards themselves.

HyperCard and Pascal compared

It has become evident to us that the HyperCard approach is more than a card index or a Hypertext tool. The more we use it and realize its potential the more we have become convinced that this approach, as exemplified by HyperCard, Supercard and ToolBook, is a valiant, yet incomplete, attempt at a visual programming language. When viewed in these terms it is possible to see what it is trying to do, what it has achieved and where it is lacking. To find out how much of a programming language the HyperCard approach is, it is worth comparing it with a familiar traditional language such as Pascal.

The fundamental element of the HyperCard approach is the card. A card can have on it various types of graphical device such as buttons, fields and pictures. What is interesting is that each of these devices loosely corresponds to a *type* in the Pascal language. For example, a HyperCard radiobutton, which offers a single choice from a set of defined keywords, is very similar to a Pascal enumerated type which allows the choice of a single value from a predefined list. This analogy can be continued with a number of the basic HyperCard graphic devices, as Figure 13.2 shows.

Figure 13.2
Types of graphical elements that can reside on a card. On the right are the equivalent Pascal types

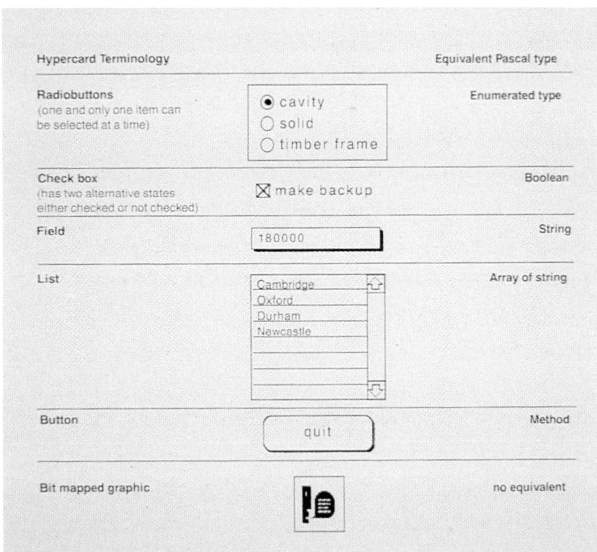

It is interesting to examine where this analogy does not quite work. Some Pascal data types do not have equivalents in HyperCard. Yet they could. A pointer, for example, would be very useful in HyperCard because

Figure 13.3
Property developer's Sales Database: site card

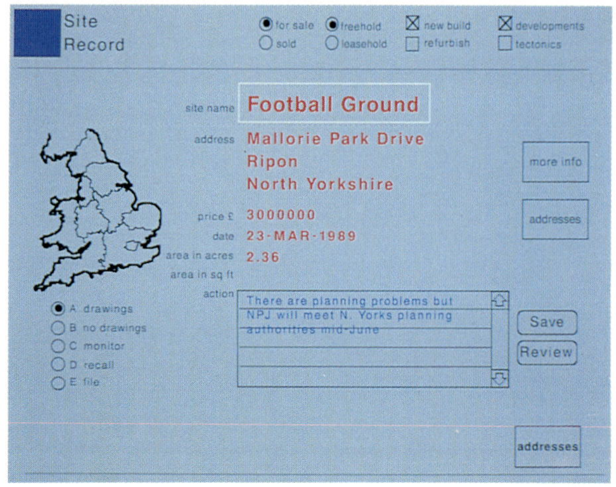

it could link you straight to another card, which is not possible (visually) at present. A Pascal set could be an interesting Venn Diagram type element in HyperCard. More strongly typed fields (integer, real and so on) would be useful. On the other hand, Pascal does not have equivalents to HyperCard's graphics. Again, there could quite feasibly be equivalents, and probably future Pascals will have them. So, in theory at least, HyperCard shows many signs of having the data structures of a traditional programming language. In some areas, like graphics handling, it is more advanced, and in other areas, like variable typecasting, it is less complete.

Project 2: The Sales Database

Whereas the earlier example of the Office Users' Questionnaire was essentially stacks of simple cards, a more recent CAR project employs the full range of HyperCard graphic elements and each card becomes correspondingly more complex. The Sales Database was developed for a property developer client to track potential tenants and match them with buildings owned, projects on site and sites as yet unpurchased. Supercard was used, with seven stacks each storing particular sets of data. Conceptually each card in the stack stores an individual record, but in practice records are stored in an Oracle for Macintosh database and the Hyper techniques are just used as a front-end. Each stack represents a table in the Oracle database. Figure 13.3 shows one of the record cards, that of a site record, which carries the full range of HyperCard graphic devices and includes a set of radiobuttons disguised as a map of England.

Compared with a typical database application the Sales Database is very easy to use. The HyperCard front-end is significantly more productive than databases we have programmed using the same Oracle database on the PC using a traditional forms package.

In the software design on this project we tried to apply the lessons learnt from the Office Users' Questionnaire and simplify the concepts. We found that bringing together the functionality to do with each card into the card stack itself helped rationalize things enormously. For example, for every card there is a 'validate yourself' function, which is in fact a hidden button on the card background called 'validate'. Thus the data, and the code to validate those data, both reside within the same stack. A number of stack functions such as new card, delete card, find card were imple-mented in this way. We gave up trying to control the system centrally and became more event oriented, realizing that buttons and menu items are the key initiators of actions in this sort of programming. Perhaps the most important realization was that the HyperCard approach is *object-oriented*.

HyperCard as an object-oriented language

There is great enthusiasm in computing circles for object-oriented programming. It is a technique of structuring that encapsulates data, together with the procedures and functions that manipulate them, to form a new data type called an object. It makes programs easier to understand, maintain and extend by bringing related things together. It is sometimes claimed that it is easier for a non-programmer to understand object-oriented programs because objects reflect real-life concepts. HyperCard is object oriented, and to prove it we can express pieces of visual HyperCard in a written object-oriented language.

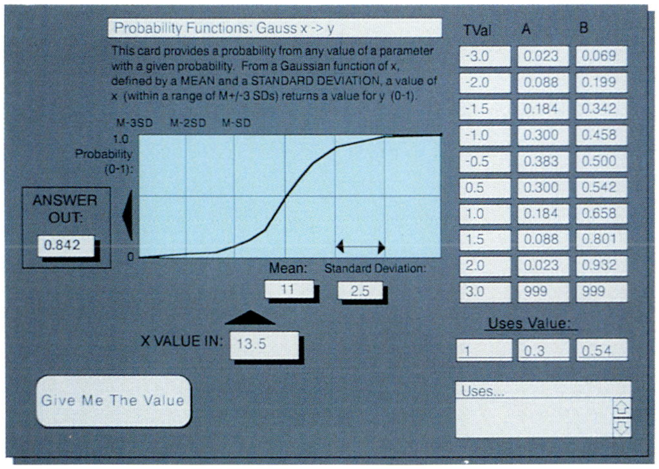

Figure 13.4
Gaussian Function, an example of object-oriented programming

In Figure 13.2, an analogy was drawn between graphic elements from HyperCard and Pascal data types. Buttons, which are so important in the HyperCard approach, do not have an equivalent type in regular Pascal, yet they do in object-oriented Pascal. A record, or more properly an object, can carry a procedure or function header called a *method* within the object template. This is analogous to a button on a HyperCard card. And, just as with HyperCard, if the object-oriented model is followed properly in Pascal, then the majority of programming consists of setting up the methods (buttons) to manipulate the data residing within the object (card). The following code shows how the card in Figure 13.3 could be equivalently declared in object-oriented Pascal.

```
type
   site_record = object
         { The straightforward fields...}
         site_name , action: string;
         address_line_1, address_line_2,
         address_line_3: string;
         price, area_acres, area_ft : integer;
         date : date;

         { The radiobuttons...}
         status : ( sold, for_sale );
         holding : (freehold, leasehold);
         site_location : (SE, London, SW, N,
               NE,NW,Midlands,West_Midlands,
               Wales,Scotland);
         info_level : ( drawings,no_drawings
               ,monitor, recall, file);
         {The check boxes ...}
         new_build, refurbish,developments,
               tectonics : boolean;
         {The buttons...}
         procedure save;
         procedure review;
         procedure more_info;
         procedure addresses;
         function validate: boolean;
   end;
```

Project 3: Gaussian Function

The Gaussian Function is a small part of a larger Supercard prototype system for seismic monitoring and damage estimation developed for a Japanese manufacturer of seismic instruments (Figure 13.4). The card carries internal (private) data constants, input variables, output variables, visual comments in the form of the graph and accompanying text, and finally the button which executes the function code itself. You can put the card on the screen, put values in the input fields and click the button to see your answer – great for development and debugging. When you want to use this function from within a larger program you send messages to it, to fill the input fields with values, to the button to click itself, and then for the answer to be read out of the output field.

This is the most object oriented of the HyperCard-type programming that we have done. What is interesting is that despite object-oriented programming being perceived as an advanced programming technique, casual programmers found it easier to understand this HyperCard function than a function declaration in a traditional programming language. In addition, professional programmers find object orientation the only way to keep a complex HyperCard-type application maintainable.

The problem of HyperTalk

HyperTalk (or SuperTalk in Supercard or Openscript in ToolBook they are almost identical) is a line-oriented text-based language that is essential for developing the procedural part of any HyperCard-type application. It is quite friendly and elegant but is most definitely not visual, and HyperTalk is where HyperCard falls down because it has all the inherent disadvantages of a traditional programming language actually made worse by being connected into the visual system. We have found that maintaining and debugging in HyperCard can be tortuous because the HyperTalk is invisible and can be hidden away in all sorts of corners of the system, although adopting object-oriented thinking helps a lot. There is no equivalent of listing out a program in one long sequence.

Nothing can get away from the underlying problem that, despite the visual approach, in HyperCard you still need to spend a lot of time writing in a text language. To go all the way to being a visual programming language HyperCard would need to replace HyperTalk with something visual.

This is an example of a HyperTalk script. It is the button script for the right-hand arrow button of the card shown in Figure 13.1.

```
– Mouse button-up handler
on mouseUp
   – turn on the hourglass cursor
   set the cursor to 4

   – check we are not looking at the first
   card of the stack
   if the short name of this card is not
   "Section 4 Help" then
         – See how long it took the
         respondent to respond
         put check_time() into time

         put ( the number of this card )
         - 1 into line_no
         – now record the response along
         with the time taken
         – The 4 is the section number and
         the 2 is the response.
         put "4,2," & time into line line_no
         of card field
"Section  Response" of card "Section 4 Help"
   end if
         – Go to the next question
         go to next card
   end mouseUp
```

Conclusion

As a company writing software for applications in architecture and the construction industry we have embraced HyperCard and its family as useful computer programming tools. Yet we still use Pascal and C on both PC and Macintosh for serious programming work. We feel this is a pity as visual programming is quicker and more enjoyable.

Although we are very pleased with what we have achieved with HyperCard, the more we use it the more apparent it has become that it only goes part way towards providing a full visual programming environment. HyperCard only implements data structures visually, and leaves the procedural parts to the line-oriented language HyperTalk. Furthermore, we have the feeling that it lacks the discipline of a traditional language, for example, in the area of data typing. If these issues could be addressed we may be close to our ideal, to be able to write serious computer programs using an entirely visual technique. In fact, what we really need is a visual compiler for an established language such as Pascal, that uses the HyperCard approach for its data structures and goes on to provide visual tools for loops, of statements and the rest.

Buildings as Artificial Reality Objects

G. Mazzochi, M. Locatelli and R. Morandi
University of Milan

Object-oriented artificial reality

Artificial reality is a sort of computer lens, which shows the world on a computer screen. It gives the user the ability to move in the artificial world just as in reality Krueger, 1983; Degli/Antoni, 1989a, b. This necessitates building a suitable model of the reality we want to explore, reminding us that the user needs to be familiar with the model.

We use an object-oriented approach because we can easily view the real world as constituted of classes of entities which share a common behaviour. In this way we can build a common model for all the entities, and then we can view this artificial world in a standard way.

When we look for information about an entity, we do it in a particular context. In fact we look for a subset of the knowledge available for the entity. For example, we can view computers in terms of space tradings, rather than processor speed and memory size or power consumption. In other words, we use different lenses to glean different types of information.

Now we can give a preliminary definition of our work: the *context function*. A context defines a function f_c dependent on the given context and defined over all entities. When it is applied to an entity it extracts a *subset of information relevant to that context.* Therefore, a context defines a relevant set of information governing all entities. The context function can give an empty result: for example, what do we expect when we look at a book in the context of processor speed?

A context also defines a language L_c by which knowledge is expressed. The context function result is of course expressed in this language. A context language has an external representation which is humanly comprehensible.

Thus a context is a relationship $C = <f_c, L_c>$.

Next we note that we can quickly jump from one context to another by simply following mental associations. These associations correspond to links in hypertexts. The links we follow can be defined explicitly or implicitly. Links are generally suggested by the environment surrounding the entity that we are examining.

Two other definitions are needed to represent this concept: the first states that an entity has *direct information*. This is the knowledge it can give as distinct from the world. Next, an entity has *indirect information*, deriving from the environment in which it is inserted (Figure 14.1). Rewriting the definition of the context function, we can say that its argument is the *direct information* of an entity, and the result is a phrase of L_c.

For our purposes, the world can also be considered as composed of entities, each related to another, that can be viewed in different contexts. One such relation between two entities is the *structural relation*; i.e. any given entity includes a reference to another as part of its definition. This relation imposes another distinction on the type of information provided by an entity: it is composed of *analytical* and *synthetic* information. The former is the information we can reach directly in the definition of an entity. The latter can be reached only by de-referencing some structural relations.

Another important kind of relation is the *context based* relation, which connects two entities which have non-empty results to a context function: if a context function gives a non-empty result when computed on two entities, then they are *context related.* To overcome the problem of the representation of these concepts in a model suitable for a programming language a graph can be used to represent a world made of structure-related entities.

Figure 14.1
Entities are made up of direct and indirect information

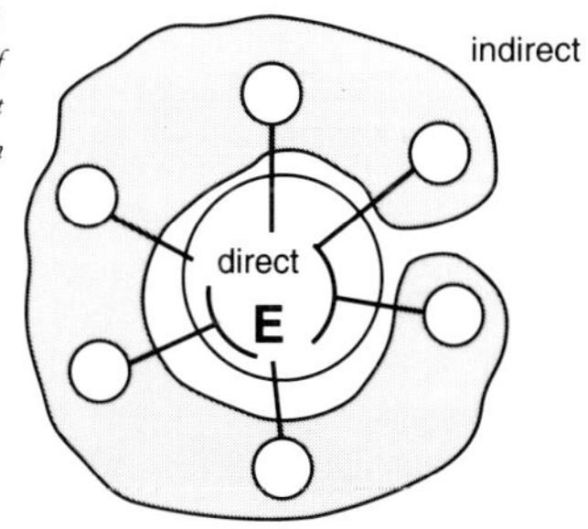

Figure 14.2
Directed acyclic graph

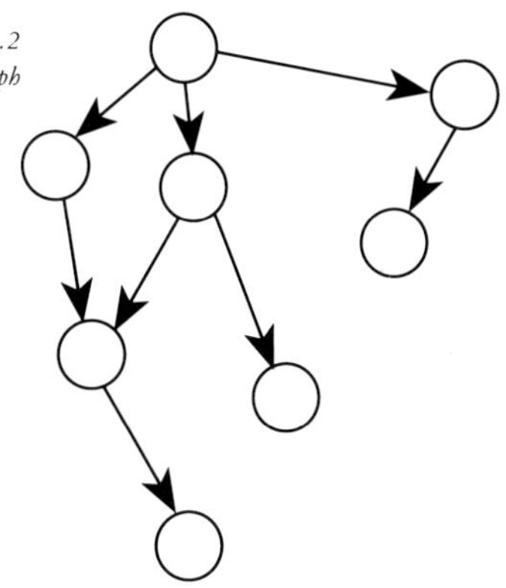

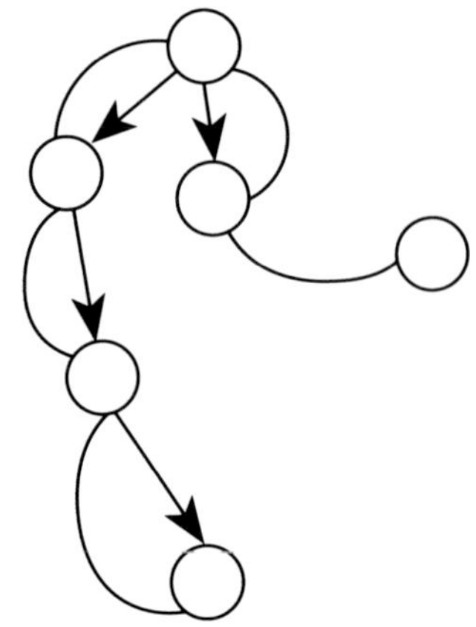

Figure 14.3
Structural relations of the model

The entities are represented by nodes and the relations by arcs. Previously exposed concepts can now be identified. In fact, the analytical information of an entity is the node itself, while the synthetic information is represented by the nodes reached by arrows. These arcs are directed, and a node cannot be a component of itself, either directly or indirectly. So Figure 14.2 is a directed acyclic graph, and we can only follow hierarchical paths. It is not very important to add transverse paths, because we have not specified classes of objects or levels of hierarchy yet. By examining this model we can analyse the components of entities in depth, focusing on a single component at a time.

When we look at the graph in a particular context, we are effectively using a context function to identify the nodes that carry relevant information for that context. Few nodes can survive, and an implicit relation (i.e. context-based) connects them. As seen in Figure 14.3 the structural relations define an explicit graph which never changes its shape during the exploration of the model. But a strange thing happens when we change the context in which we are looking at the artificial world: the graph consisting of the context-related entities changes, showing other possible paths to walk through. The browsing action now involves following associations among entities.

We can use different approaches to build a model suitable for a programming language. The most appropriate is the object-oriented approach.

Object-oriented programming is an evolutionary approach (Cox, 1988) by which we define classes of objects. A class declaration is generally composed of two parts: the interface and the implementation. The first specifies the structure of a generic instance of the class and the operations a user can do with it. The second is generally hidden to the user and implements the declarations given in the interface part. An instance of a class is called an object.

An object belonging to a class has a specific behaviour, defined by the class itself. The behaviour is specified by the operations declared in the interface part. The operations are generally called methods. The user of an object can communicate with it by sending a message, composed of a verb and an array of arguments. The verb is then decoded and the proper method is performed.

A class can have descendants, which inherit or override the behaviour specified by the parent. For example, if we define the class of the geometric entities, we can state that they have a common operator, i.e. draw, that causes a shape to be drawn on the screen. We have not specified yet how the operation is performed. Now we can say that the lines and the arcs are descendant classes of the geometric class. Therefore, they inherit the draw operator and specify how lines and arcs are to be drawn.

A set of object-oriented languages and tools have been developed, starting from Simula to SmallTalk, LOOPS, Eiffel, Actor, Objective C and C++. An example of work already developed in an object-oriented fashion and using C++ as the host language is as follows:

```
class Entity {
   someInfo directInformation;
   someInfo *indirectInformation[];
public:
   void browse(void);
};
class Context {
   someStuff theContextLanguage;
public:
   aPhrase *contextFunction( Entity
&anEntity );
   Graph *contextFunction( Graph &aWorld );
};
class ArtificialWorld : public Entity {
   Set  AlltheEntities;
   Set  AlltheContexts;
public:
   void browse(void);
};
```

We have not specified the exact meaning of some terms. In fact it is not necessary to know how the context language is implemented, nor the implementation of a graph. We only have to know that we can communicate with an instance of a context simply specifying aContext.contextFunction(anEntity).

The artificial world is composed of entities and contexts but, above all, it is itself an entity subjected to the rules defined above. That is, we can enter the artificial world by simply applying a context function to the single instance of the class ArtificialWorld. A phrase of the context language is obtained, and it can be represented by using a visual convention.

In order to complete the description of the artificial reality metaphor in an object-oriented way, we must give a meaning to the function *browse*. Its purpose is to enable the user to 'walk' through the graph currently displayed on the screen in some implicit form, changing the context whenever he or she wishes. Care must be taken in establishing a common convention to represent the phrase resulting from the evaluation of a context function over an entity.

In this scenario, hypertext and its derivatives can be useful tools to organize and demonstrate the knowledge. HyperCard (Apple Computer, 1988a), for example, allows the user to integrate text, graphics and sound in a single hypermedia document. It also provides buttons, fields and advanced concepts such as backgrounds to take full advantage of its message-driven architecture. HyperTalk (Apple Computer, 1988b), the embedded programming language, gives the user the ability to perform complex operations responding to specific messages.

We have described the theory and the tools. Now we need an example.

Intelligent buildings

Intelligent Buildings (IBs) are a possible field of application for the theory described above. First we have to state a common definition for an IB. In our approach, an IB is a building in which everything is projected, designed and implemented using, possibly electronic, intelligence. That is, CAD, facility management, real-time inventory, work-of-the-day scheduling and checking, and as many other things as one can imagine are all part of the IB world.

An IB can be viewed as a set of co-operating parts, communicating through channels that transport everything the building needs: water, heat, air, electricity, data and so on. In order to use IBs as an

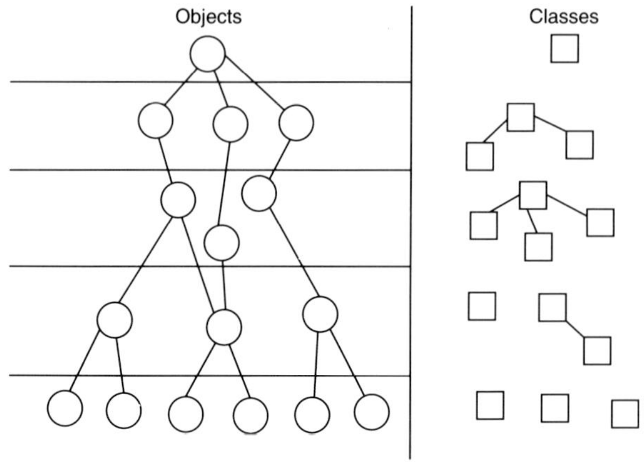

Figure 14.4
Example of a building model split into five hierarchical levels

example of an application of the artificial reality metaphor, we have to identify the contexts by which we want to look at the IB, and then we have to implement the browsing and presentation tools.

Building product models

Building product models classify a building in a five-level hierarchy. The levels, from the lowest up are components, parts, subsystems, systems and building.

Each level contains objects. The building level objects contain information about the site, the climate, the total cost, the type of building and so on. In the system level objects we can find information about the systems that together constitute the building: heating, power, communication network, spaces. The subsystem level objects are functional parts of the previous level objects. We can find floors, offices and so on. A set of partly overlapping subsystem objects constitutes a system. The part and detail levels contain objects that are usually tangible objects, generally related by structural relations as defined before.

The objects in the five levels are structure related as explained above. A possible (partial) graph of the objects is shown in Figure 14.4. Most of the data pertaining to objects can reside in remote databases, and so the browsing of a node of the graph is translated into a query to the proper database.

Buildings and artificial reality

Using the conceptual tools introduced in the first section of the chapter, we can represent a building, an IB as an artificial reality object. We have to map concepts like contexts into a real-world model. In other words, we must identify in our model the entities that play a role in the context.

A possible answer to this problem can be found using building product models. We can merely identify contexts as systems. So we have the data network context, the HVAC context and so on. But we can also think of many other contexts, such as the legal, the real-time inventory, the work-of-the-day, as developed below.

The legal system contains paths from the building to the rules that are relevant for its design, the life of its workers, fire prevention, building regulations and so on. The aim is to provide the user with access for consultation of all these laws, interactively verifying whether the building complies with them.

The real-time inventory makes a direct connection between the model and the reality. Its purpose is to monitor the state of each entity in a database inventory list. We can imagine that each entity is connected to a sensor, which in turn belongs to a data-collecting network. Every time the sensor detects a change in the state of the entity that it is monitoring, the data-collecting network can send a message to the database administrator. In this way we can quickly update the database without a lot of paperwork.

The work-of-the-day system is a tool to plan the work that should be carried out by people in the building. It is heavily based on computer networks and co-operating environments. We can imagine someone needing an authorization. Normally that means filling a module and sending it hierarchically to the top. The module then has to follow the reverse path. We can automate all this work by writing a computer-based procedure which explains the actions which are to be done in order to complete the job. Upon activation, the procedure brings the document, possibly in electronic form, and schedules all the work to be done. It can also

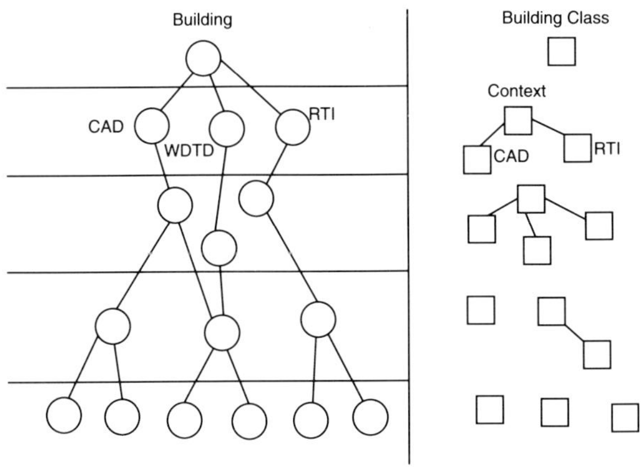

Figure 14.5
Building product model

verify that the work has been completed in a fixed amount of time. The result is an overall performance increase.

All these systems have to be explored by the user in a natural way, looking at them and feeling as if he was in the real world. A common way for the computer screen is a geometrical two-dimensional view of the model. So we have to add a system to the list: the CAD system. This is not only for presentation purposes but can also be used to design and project the building itself. The CAD system is to be integrated with the legal system in order to highlight potential problems with the law or building regulations.

The graph representing our example of a building product model becomes like Figure 14.5. The contexts we shall use to browse the graph are CAD, work-of-the-day and real-time inventory. Below follow some of the implementation details.

A HyperCard 2.0-based prototype

We need to build a prototype based on the ideas developed earlier. Our choice for the software platform to use is based on many factors. Some of the requirements are ease of use, hypertext and hypermedia support, object-oriented programming capability and fast prototyping. All these requirements lead us to Hyper-Card 2.0, currently available from Apple. It includes all the features originally contained in Hyper-card 1.2 and an extension to allow the use of external windows. Here we present a short description of the features used to implement a system based on artificial reality.

Buttons are screen regions sensible to mouse actions. A button responds to an event by executing a script. It can be represented in many ways: by icons or a box or a combination of these and other methods. Normally we use buttons as representative of actions, such as context change, object manipulations, fixed path browsing. The script is a procedural attachment needed to carry out some jobs, such as showing the list of available contexts.

Fields are text containers. They can be made visible under script control. They also have many formats, with or without editing capabilities. We use them to store and show information about entities. They also have scripting capabilities which are generally used to help the user to fill them in.

XCMDs (eXternal CoMmanDs) and ***XFCNs*** (eXternal FunCtioNs) are stand-alone code segments that can be executed under script control. They are usually used to perform number crunching or time-consuming tasks.

The prototype is still under development, but it already implements some of the concepts expressed here. It is derived from ARSAD, the application presented at Europia 90 (Bianchi *et al.*, 1990).

XCMDs play the major role in this prototype: they are used to represent classes of objects. Whenever the user interacts with an entity on the screen, an XCMD is invoked, with the parameters set to carry out the required tasks.

The context implementation is based on external windows. They are created and managed by special XCMDs. When a context is applied to a node of the graph an XCMD computes its function, obtaining the relevant information set. It then shows the results in the window by using a graphical convention built into the window type. For example, we can use a CAD window to show some graphics, while we use a document window to present legal information. Changing a context means changing the front window.

The main context window is a CAD window. In fact we can read DXF files coming from Autocad, Radar-CH and so on. So we can show a geometrical view of the building. Next we can recognize rooms and browse the structural links of the building while we are in CAD context. That is, we can zoom in on a room, showing its details.

Once in a room we can add furniture, and move it around according to given criteria (e.g. a desk cannot be placed on top of another desk). All these actions update a database on a remote host. Clearly we can also simulate a walk at room level, or search for a particular office and so on.

Currently we plan to integrate a legal system within the prototype, possibly using a CD-ROM containing all the building regulations. The next step will be the automated control of the building, including the work-of-the-day function.

Conclusions

The analysis above can be a good way to approach artificial reality. In the case of IBs it can be readily implemented. The time-consuming work is to code all the object classes which implement the entities of the domain and the contexts. Many technical problems can arise using external stand alone code instead of coding the prototype from scratch, but the trade-off is the fast prototyping capability given by HyperCard.

This study is, in part, the subject of a thesis at the University of Milan. The authors want to thank Professor G. Degli Antoni for his continuous assistance.

References

Apple Computer (1988a) *HyperCard User Manual.* Addison-Wesley, New York.

Apple Computer (1988b) *HyperCard Script Language Guide: The HyperTalk Language.* Addison-Wesley, Reading, MA.

Bianchi, D. *et al.* (1990) Artificial reality spreadsheet for architectural design. *Proceedings of EUROPIA 90.* Editions Hermès, Paris, p.148.

Björk, B.C. (1989) Basic structure of a proposed building product model, *Computer Aided Design*, 21(2), 71–8.

Björk, B.C. (1990) Issues in the development of a building product model standard. *Proceedings of EUROPIA 90.* Editions Hermès, Paris, p.372.

Cox, B.J. (1988) *Object Oriented Programming: an Evolutionary Approach.* Addison-Wesley, Reading, MA.

Degli Antoni, G. (1989a) Artificial reality: making knowledge live with computers, *Time Magazine,* 3 October.

Degli Antoni, G. (1989b) From reality to hypermedia through artificial reality, *Educational Media Technology,* 26 (3).

Krueger, M.W. (1983) *Artificial Reality.* Addison-Wesley, New York.

Planar Tessellations using Parallel Grammars

Jean-Louis Schulmann
Image Digitale, Paris

Introduction

The development of the theory of computation and complexity is based on the study of formal systems as a representation of languages; from Turing to Chomsky, we can follow the research path that has led computer theory to its present state (Hopcroft and Ullman, 1979). One of the fundamental theorems in formal systems theory proves the equivalence between acceptance and generation of strings belonging to a language by an automaton.

In 1968, Aristides Lindenmayer introduced L-systems, which provided a mathematical formalism for parallel grammars well adapted to the modelling of growth phenomena (Lindenmayer and Prusinkiewicz, 1989). While computer scientists were investigating L-systems from a theoretical point of view, researchers of other fields such as biology, embryogenesis, computer vision, etc. started to show interest in this model.

In 1984, Alvy Ray Smith, a computer graphics researcher with a sound background in formal systems theory, showed how L-systems could be used to synthesize realistic images. He also pointed out the relationship between the concept of fractals, introduced by Benoit Mandelbrot, and L-systems (Smith, 1984).

Since 1986 Przemyslaw Prusinkiewicz, now at the University of Regina (Canada), has been working consistently with his team and the Lindenmayer group on extending previous work and providing formalisms that could allow L-systems to be used to generate plants with or without inflorescence, cell growth and geo-metric patterns such as Indian kolams or mathe-matical 'monsters' such as the Von Koch or Hilbert curves. In the concluding chapters of a recent publi-cation where all these results are documented (Prusinkiewicz *et al.*, 1989), we find the following statement:

> Many geometric patterns and tilings can be generated using L-systems.... The problem of describing patterns and tilings using L-systems is a largely unexplored one ...

In 1988, Mark Friedell and Jean-Louis Schulmann at Harvard University developed a prototype for the automatic generation of architectural scenes. This prototype was based on the more powerful formalism of shape-grammars, and although it led to some interesting results (Friedell and Schulmann, 1990) it appeared that soundness and completeness of the languages described by various grammars could not be proven. It was then decided to focus on grammars. Taking advantage of the C code given in the appendix of the publication by Prusinkiewicz *et al.*, (1989) a program was written for the Macintosh which would allow the infinite range of forms that can be generated using the L-system formalism to be explored.

In order to understand the behaviour of grammar-based systems, it was decided to try to write grammars that could encapsulate the properties of the 17 groups of symmetry in the plane. After some blind searching, a standard method appeared, a *meta-grammar*. The general method is as follows.

One set of rules (in the simplest examples, only one rule) describes *the pattern* to be repeated. Another rule describes the *expansion* of the pattern through translations and a third rule describes the *rotational symmetries*. Using this basic structure, all symmetry groups can be described easily using the same grammar skeleton.

Strangely enough, a close look at the expansion rule shows that planar tessellations are self-similar; the structure of the plane can always be refined to a smaller scale with identical isometric properties. (This is visible in the reciprocally recursive rules for 'X' and 'C' in the examples given).

Introducing mirror symmetry is trivial, as the mirror groups can be seen as subsets of the rotational groups, where each pattern would be composed of the basic pattern and its mirror image along any axis of mirror symmetry (e.g. R632 Sym Helix).

It is noteworthy that all grammars are context free for all symmetry groups. Other patterns can be generated using context-sensitive rules.

Presentation of parallel grammars

The formalism used is the 0L systems formalism (Ehrig *et al.*,1987) summarized as follows.

Let V denote an alphabet of symbols, V* the set of words over V and V+ the set of all non-empty words over V. An 0L system is an ordered triplet G = (V, w, P) where V is the alphabet of symbols, w Œ V+ is a non-empty string of symbols called an axiom and is the 'seed' from which the genotype is expanded and P Œ V x V* is a finite set of production rules. Each rule specifies a replacement scheme for the symbols found in the expanding phenotype. The structure of the rule is as follows:

left context < symbol > right context -->
replacement string

where left and right context are sub string patterns to be matched for the production rule to apply to the symbol. If a match is found, the symbol is replaced by the replacement string.

Application of parallel grammars to planar tessellation

Included in V is a set of special symbols that will be used for the graphic interpretation of the string generated by the OL system (see Prusinkiewicz and Hanan (1989) for more details):

F move forward, pen down
f move forward, pen up
+ turn right
- turn left
| half-turn
[save current turtle position
] restore previously saved turtle position
* null symbol (used to specify context-free grammars)

Simple example with translations only: Ro

axiom: PX	**Pattern and expansion**
* < P > * —> [FF+F]	**The Pattern**
* < U > * —> fff	**Translation** up
* < D > * —> fff+fff-	**Translation** in diagonal
* < R > * —> +fff-	**Translation** to the right
* < X > * —> X[UPX][DPX][RPX]	**The expansion rule: Place the expansion symbol**
* < f > * —> ff	**Scaling** the configuration by 2

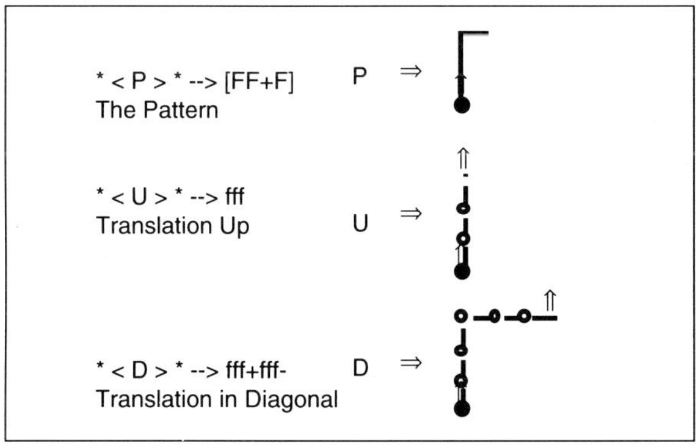

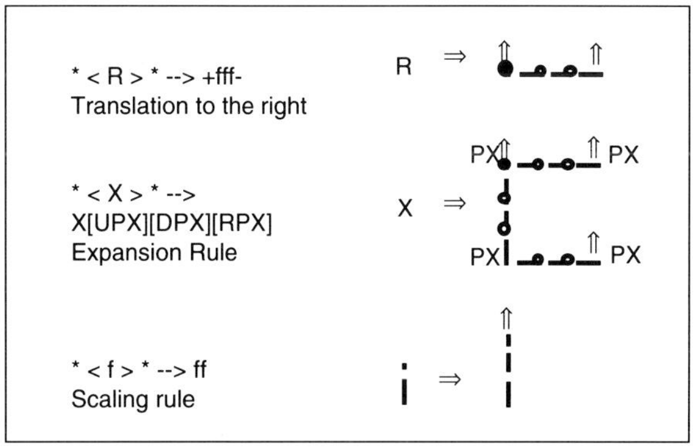

A more complex example: sixfold with mirror symmetry

axiom: PX — Same as above

* < P > * —> [+F+F+F][-F-F-F] — The mirror symmetry is encapsulated in the description of the pattern itself. It could be specified in a rule of its own if we wanted to be fully formal. They are grouped for reasons of efficiency .

* < U > * —> ++ff— — Same as above

* < D > * —> ++ff++ff—— — Same as above

* < R > * —> ++++ff—— — Same as above

* < X > * —> CX[UCX][DCX][RCX] — Same as above with introduction of C

* < f > * —> ff — Same as above

*** < C > * —> P[++P][++++P][lP][——P][—P]** C: sixfold rotation rule:

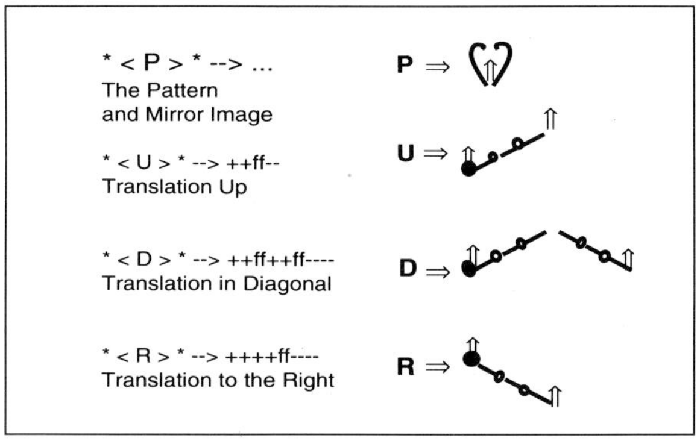

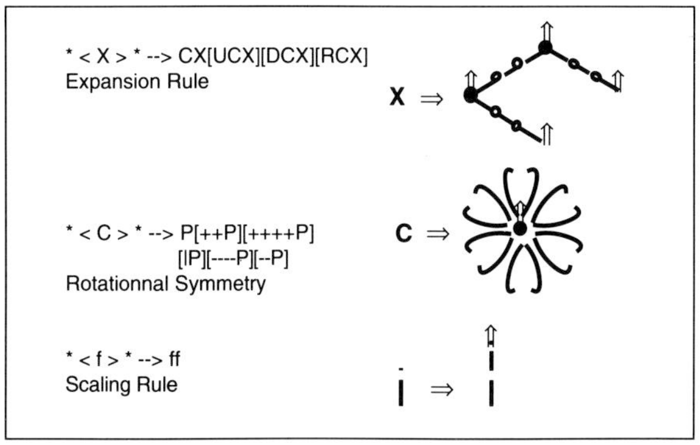

Examples of Tessellations

```
axiom: PX
* < P > * --> [F+F]
* < X > * --> CX[UCX][DCX][RCX
* < C > * --> P[++P][--P]
* < f > * --> ff
* < U > * --> +f-
* < D > * --> +f+f--
* < R > * --> ++f--
```

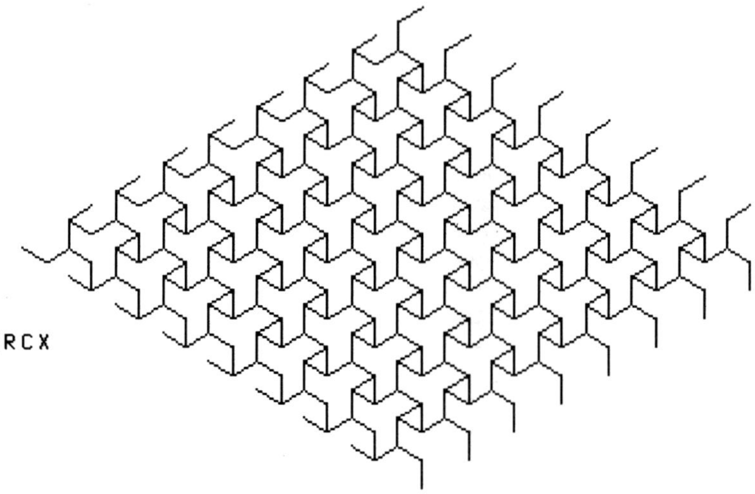

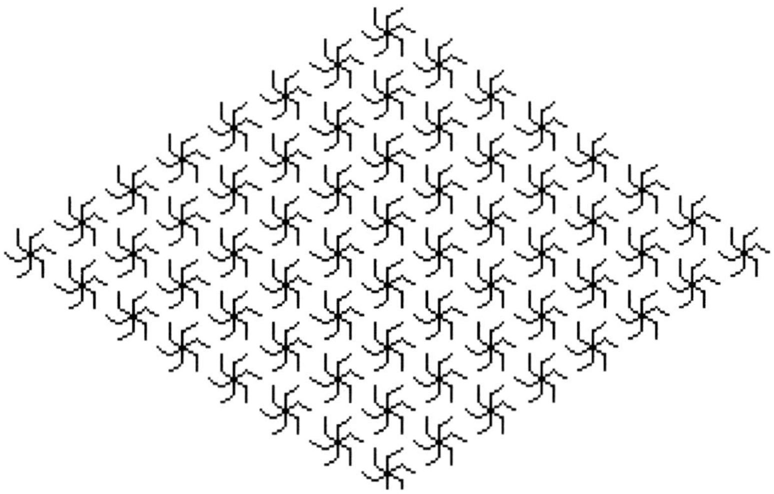

```
axiom: PX
* < P > * --> [F+F]
* < X > * --> CX[UCX][DCX][RCX]
* < C > * --> P[+P][++P][|P][--P][
* < f > * --> ff
* < U > * --> +ff-
* < D > * --> +ff+ff--
* < R > * --> ++ff--
```

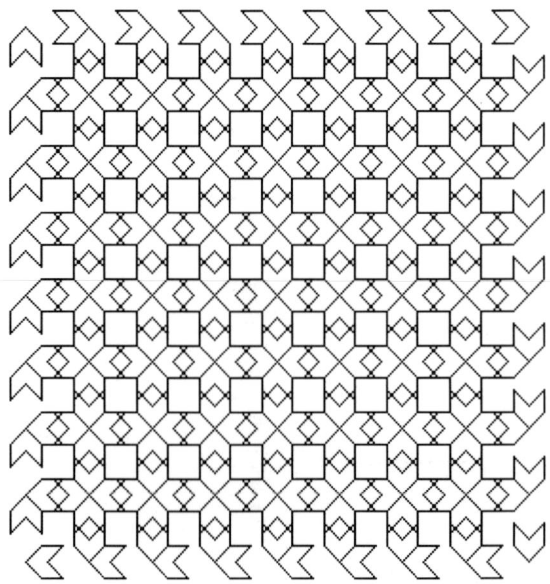

```
axiom: PX
* < P > * --> [+F+F+++F--F+++F+F]
* < X > * --> X[UPX][DPX][RPX]
* < f > * --> ff
* < U > * --> fff++
* < D > * --> fff++fff++
* < R > * --> ++fff++++
```

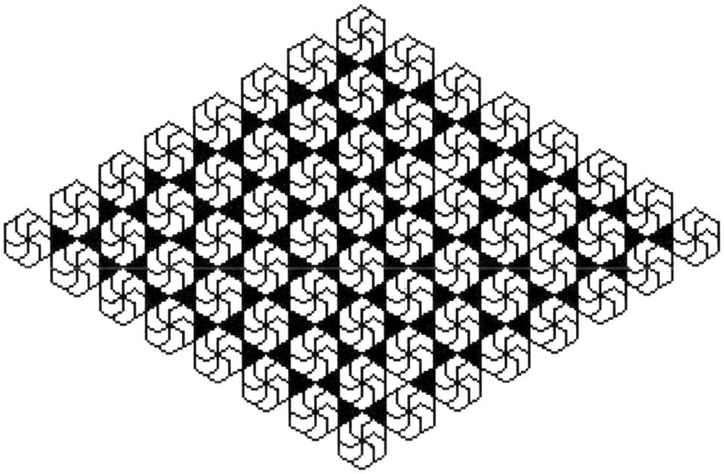

```
axiom: PX
ignore: +-F
* < P > * --> [F+F+F+F]
* < X > * --> CX[UCX][DCX][RCX]
* < C > * --> P[+P][++P][|P][--P][-P]
* < f > * --> ff
* < U > * --> +ff-
* < D > * --> +ff+ff--
* < R > * --> ++ff--
```

```
axiom: PX
* < P > * --> [+F+F+F][-F-F-F]
* < X > * --> CX[UCX][DCX][RCX]
* < C > * --> P[++P][++++P][|P][----P][--P]
* < f > * --> ff
* < U > * --> ++ff--
* < D > * --> ++ff++ff----
* < R > * --> ++++ff----
```

```
axiom: PX
* < P > * --> [F+F+++F--F+++F+F]
* < X > * --> X[UPX][DPX][RPX]
* < f > * --> ff
* < U > * --> ffff++
* < D > * --> ffff++ffff++
* < R > * --> ++ffff++++
```

Future developments

The first step of this research is now completed. Experimenting with this prototype has led to several conclusions.

The formalism of grammars used to describe complex forms is a very powerful one but grammar-generated forms are extremely unstable. The smallest change in the description of a grammar rule can trigger drastic changes in the resulting form. Together with other researchers working in the field of artificial life (Langton, 1989) we have to accept the apparent hiatus between genotype and phenotype.

By using meta-grammars, it is possible to gain more control on the morphogenetic process. In order to explore further that fascinating universe, we have to give ourselves tools that are commensurate with our goals. If we consider ourselves as the geneticists of artificial forms, we need to build a **synthetic morphogenesis laboratory** – a computer environment that will allow systematic exploration of grammars, where interaction will be the key to understanding the behaviour of phenomena. If writing grammars can be seen as the programming of forms, we need to design the morphogenetic equivalents of editors, debuggers etc. With a better understanding of the behaviour of grammar-based systems, we are ready to tackle the more general problem of the automatic generation of architectural landscapes as described in a previous paper (Friedell and Schulmann, 1990). The ultimate goal of this research is the development of a grammar-based system that will allow the automatic generation of architectural landscapes in accordance with pre-imposed constraints (Schulmann, 1988).

References

Abelson, H. and diSessa, A. (1982) *Turtle Geometry*. MIT Press, Cambridge, MA.

Ehrig, H., Nagel, M., Rozenfeld, A. and Rozenberg, G. (eds) (1987). *Graph Grammars and their Application to Computer Science*, Third International Workshop, December 1986. Springer-Verlag, Berlin.

Friedell, M. and Schulmann, J.L. (1990) *Constrained, Grammar Directed Generation of Landscapes,* Proceedings of Graphics Interface–Vision Interface, pp. 244-51.

Hopcroft, J. and Ullman, J. (1979) *Introduction to Automata Theory, Languages and Computation.* Addison-Wesley, Redwood City, CA.

Langton, C.G. (ed.) (1989) *Artificial Life,* Proceedings of Workshop on the Synthesis and Simulation of Living systems, September 1987, Los Alamos, New Mexico. Addison-Wesley, New York, Vol. IV.

Lindenmayer, A. (1987) An introduction to parallel map generating systems. In H.Ehrig, M. Nagl, A. Rozenfeld and G. Rozenberg (eds), *Graph Grammars and their application to Computer Science,* Third International Workshop, December 1986. Springer-Verlag, Berlin, pp. 27–40.

Lindenmayer, A. and Prusinkiewicz, P. (1989) Developmental models of multicellular organisms: a computer graphics perspective. In C.Langton (ed.) *Artificial Life*. Addison-Wesley, Redwood City, CA, pp. 221–249.

Mitchell, M.J. (1990) *The Logic of Architecture. Design; Computation, and Cognition*. MIT Press, Cambridge, MA.

Mandelbrot, B. (1982) *The Fractal Geometry of Nature.* W.H. Freeman, San Francisco, CA.

Prusinkiewicz, P., Hanan, J. and Lindenmayer, A. (1989) *Systems, Fractals and Plants.* Lecture Notes in Biomathematics. Springer-Verlag, New York .

Schulmann, J.L. (1988) LandMark; automatic generation of urban landscapes, Technical Report, Harvard University.

Smith, A.R. (1984) Plants, fractals and formal languages, *ACM Computer Graphics* 18(3), 1–10, *Siggraph '84 Proceedings.*

Thompson, d'Arcy W. (1917) *On Growth and Form.* Cambridge University Press, Cambridge.

Architecture in Motion

Earl Mark
School of Architecture and Planning,
Massachusetts Institute of Technology

Architecture in motion refers to the appearance of change in the visual image of a building when it is observed in real time. For example, it may change when observed from a moving vantage point, when light varies, when use varies or when parts of a building are physically relocated or transformed.[1] A motion picture recording or computer graphics animation may seem to visualize these changes to the appearance of a building realistically. However, people can be trained to recognize ways in which apparent motion in a movie may be different from the everyday experience of observing real motion (Goodman, 1978). Still, movies may provide a good characterization of architecture in motion, but not as strong a characterization of other aspects of architecture, such as the boundaries of a floor plan, the juxtaposition of its objects or the proportions of its spaces (Mark, 1990). In this chapter we refer to some work in which the cognitive role of moviemaking was considered. It is proposed that change to the appearance of architecture in real time may serve as the aesthetic basis for using movies as a design tool.

Traditional drawing media within the paper-based architectural design studio are similar to moviemaking media in the sense that they do not necessarily replicate everyday visual experience. For example, a sectional drawing of a building may be used to represent how a building is subdivided, yet it does not replicate anything a person would typically see. A thumbnail sketch of a proposed design may seem to simulate what a person sees, but it also smuggles in acquired ways of characterizing visual perception, such as the conventions of Western perspective drawing. Not all peoples are automatically able to interpret Western perspective drawing, and even if they were, there may only be a narrow connection to everyday visual experience (Goodman, 1985). The philosopher Nelson Goodman writes that to view the world in Western perspective amounts to establishing a convention whereby we must look through the pinhole of a camera with a fixed eye. Goodman writes that Western perspective gives us only a way of 'catching a likeness', rather than duplicating direct visual experience.

A method of sketching

Students were encouraged to reproduce, analyse and conceive of architectural form by means of moviemaking.[2] They were encouraged to express a personal style of working with the media. They used motion pictures to a 'catch a likeness' that might serve to put into focus a key aspect of a design proposal, rather than trying to simulate everything a person would experience when visiting a building. Short motion picture sequences were produced on videotape, analogous to a series of thumbnail sketches on traditional paper based media. For example, each motion picture recording may provide an interim view of a design work in progress. This 'checkpoint' may be used to verify and further stimulate design thinking.[3]

At 30 frames per second, the motion picture recording might seem to overwhelm a designer with too much information.[4] The threshold of human perception of still pictures in a movie may average about 15 frames per second.[5] Even at the rate of 15 frames per second, however, it still does not seem likely that architecture students could think through a design proposal with such a rapid speed of conceptualizing images.

Alternatively, a motion picture sequence does not need to be conceptualized at 30 frames per second. For example, a film director may try out a particular

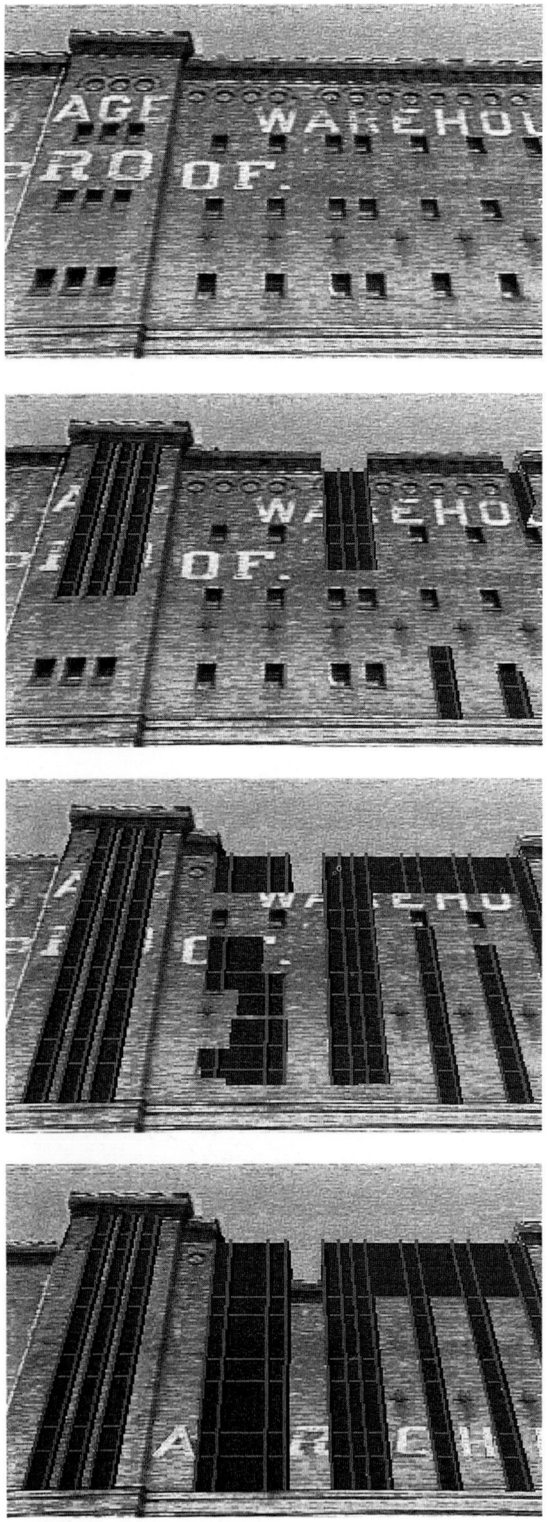

Figure 16.1
Burke and Gipstein Movie about their design and renovation of warehouse into a new home for the Dept of Architecture at M.I.T.

juxtaposition of actors and objects and then do a test recording of the scene. The test recording is reviewed by the director and crew for possible flaws. The characters, props, light sources and camera movement paths may be reconsidered before the final 'take' of the scene is recorded.

Similarly, a model of a design proposal can be recorded in computer animation or on film/video media (see Figure 16.1 from a final design proposal).[6] The motion picture recording is then screened for an 'in progress' review of the design proposal. The design proposal may then be modified. The approach to making the movie of the design proposal may also be modified. This process of screening and modification is repeated until the final revision to the design proposal is accepted.

Cell animation is a technique of using a transparent layer to draw over the frames generated in the movie (see Figures 16.2 and 16.3 from an exercise on lighting).[7] With this technique, the movie can be recomposed one frame at a time. At this rate, the pace of production of individual frames seems well within the architect's conceptual control and threshold of perception. The use of the transparent layer allows the architect to render each successive frame in the movie without having to redraw the parts of the image that do not need to be changed. This significantly reduces the amount of effort needed to produce an animation. A skilled architectural animator can therefore draw a rapid succession of images in a spontaneous process that is similar to sketching.

Similar to the experience of working with traditional paper-based media, architects may accumulate practice and develop judgement as to what ideas represented in the movie are good architectural ideas. In particular, some architects may be able to develop a sense of 'rightness of fit' of an architectural space according to the rate of change of its appearance in a movie over time. However, the bad ideas we have about architecture in motion may not show up very strongly in traditional paper-based media. In using paper based representations, we do perhaps talk about variable lighting, about sequences of views and about people moving through architectural space. We may represent change to the appearance of an architectural space over time by making a series of drawings. A traditional rendering, however, does not seem to provide a formal way of directly varying the rate of change over time. For example, in movies, it is possible to slow down the motion of the viewpoint as it goes past a particular space in the building where there is an important view.

The dimension of time

In some computer animations of architectural space, the rate of change over time seems to be ignored. Many of these productions incorporate the same basic camera motion, position and angle, such as that provided by a viewpoint moving perpendicularly towards the front elevation of a building at an unvarying speed. Yet, the pace of movement about a building is not a constant in everyday experience, but may be modified at the threshold to an interior space, or when a good view is encountered (see Figure 16.4, a design as viewed from a car moving at different speeds around a site location).[8] From any location, the rate of change in direction and angle of a view may also be varied over time.

Designing a building for how people move and view architectural space may require some sophistication.

Figure 16.2
Burke Animation of lighting over 24 hours

The sophistication is not necessarily the type provided by a tenable theory about visual perception, but rather the skill to be able to work with architecture in motion as in the art and aesthetics of professional moviemaking. The psychologist of art, Rudolf Arnheim, attributes the success of Italian film directors of the 1930s to many years of schooling and sophistication in the use of the medium (Arnheim, 1957). Similarly, architects might also be at an advantage if they were to engage in explicit exercises and representations of architecture in motion.

The motion picture exercises can be based upon (a) light changing over time, (b) the dynamics of spatial juxtapositions as the viewpoint moves through a sequence of spaces, (c) the appearance of people and objects as they move through a space, (d) the real-time transformation of an architectural form and (e) a montage of motion picture images that reveals the overall aesthetic intention and spirit of a design proposal. The five sets of figures (Figures 16.5(a) – 16.5(e)) are reproduced from student movies developed along these ideas.[9]

The artifice of making movies about architecture

In each of the five types of exercises, motion picture imagery can be used deliberately to mislead about the real character of a place as well as to inform. In some instances, the most compelling cinematic treatment may provide an unfaithful view of the actual character of a work of architecture. The technique of editing together two scenes in a movie, for example, may be used to join two spaces in time which are otherwise separate physically. In his diary for the making of the film *Beauty and The Beast,* Jean Cocteau reports on a number of such instances of fabricating architectural space cinematically by means of editing together two separate pieces of film (Cocteau, 1972). The distortion of reality may also be achieved by the use of lighting. For example, the Vienna depicted in the movie *The Third Man* may seem to be a more dramatic setting than would be directly provided by the actual site locations in the city that were used (Balter, 1990). Such a movie may legitimately inspire design thinking by transforming the image of a mundane place into a suggestion of what it could be like.

Artifice in the cinematic treatment of space – time may be a source of disagreement among moviemakers. The film director Eisenstein exhorted his students to be very exact in planning how scenes should be architecturally arranged (Nizhnii, 1979). He would describe a scene from a play and then call upon his students to propose a cinematic treatment. They were expected to plan the positions of the camera and actors carefully, and to order the sequence of shots relative to the architecture in just the correct way so as to reveal the nature of the story most appropriately . If the student movie director made the wrong judgement about the depiction of the action in an architectural space, then, according to Eisenstein, the whole plot could be distorted or break down. Each symbolic and aesthetic gesture to be conveyed within the movie was very meticulously planned.

Such a careful predisposition to the production of a movie is at odds with another school of moviemaking. The freedom to look at the world through a camera, for all that it may offer to those who love to depict the world cinematically, may have been overly constrained by the predetermined construction of carefully scripted

Figure 16.3
Ying Animation of lighting over 24 hours

Figure 16.4
Finch and Goore Movie depicting views of design proposal from automobile in motion

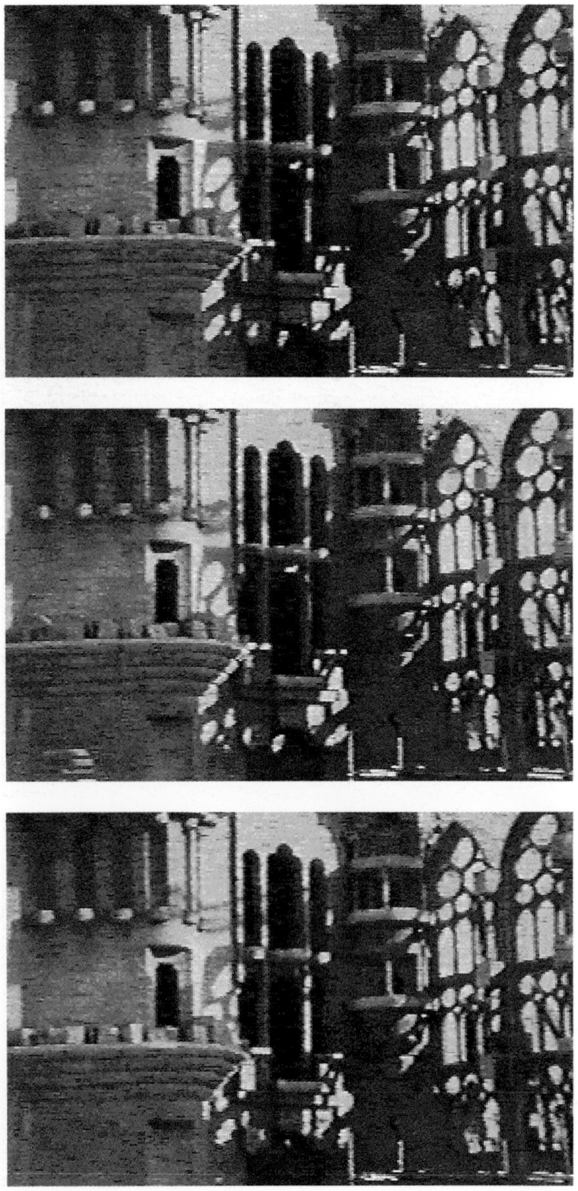

Figure 16.5a)
Mark Time lapse of lighting at the Sagrada Familia Temple

camera movements and scenes. The motion picture is constructed from predefined notions rather than directly explored. By comparison, the *cinéma vérité* approach is less predetermined. Emphasis is put on the discoveries that might be gained while in the act of shooting the movie. To be open to making such discoveries, a *cinéma vérité* moviemaker is constrained by different guidelines than those taught by Eisenstein. In particular, *cinéma vérité* imposes anthropological-like constraints upon moviemaking. The moviemaker does not plan or force events to occur in a way that guarantees the outcome of what is captured on camera. Rather, he or she hopes to be sufficiently knowledgeable about the subject matter to be able to recognize the important events which unfold before the camera. This may in effect mean that the moviemaker is somewhat predisposed to how the subject is captured on camera, but not in the extreme manner advocated by Eisenstein. Ricky Leacock, a pioneer of the *Cinéma Vérité* movement, encouraged an informed sort of free association with the camera.[10] Eisenstein's approach was so prohibitive of this that Leacock referred to it in a paper as 'guilt by association'.

The two schools of moviemaking may be relevant to different stages in the design process. The Eisenstein approach is similar to the planning for a final architectural rendering, where the location of each detail in the drawing is predetermined by convention. The *cinéma vérité* approach is similar to the free association process of making a thumbnail sketch of a proposed design. The form of the movie can be developed freely without fear of upsetting a predetermined order, similar to how an architect may discover 'emergent form' in the fleeting moments of making a rapid sketch. On the other hand, Eisenstein might have objected that the *cinéma vérité* approach is too indeterminate with regard to the intentions of each production. He may claim that the movie is based only on the immediate reactions of the architect, but lacks the basis for an overall coherent direction.

Regardless of the school of thought, however, the intended purpose of a movie may provide a basis for critically developing its methodology. Is the intention of an architectural movie to convey what it is like to move around freely in an architectural place, and does the moviemaker therefore hope to recreate an aspect of that experience by spontaneously moving around and shooting the camera? Is it to offer a visual essay on the sculptural juxtapositions of three-dimensional form that the architect had intended, and therefore do the camera movements need to be planned in a precise manner to get the exact angles and transitions that the architect wanted to be seen? Or, is the intention to produce a comprehensive presentation of all the interior spaces of a building for the client, where the spaces may be ordered very systematically in the movie rather than being visited from a particular aesthetic vantage point? After considerable testing and speculation, the moviemaker may decide on what method or combination of methods most directly relates to the architectural subject, even if this involves mixing some of the ideas of Eisenstein with *cinéma vérité*.

Architectural aesthetics realized by the style of moviemaking

The techniques used in the final production of a movie may determine its aesthetic orientation to architecture. Some of the initial decisions about technique are likely to be tested and then rejected by the time that the architect develops the final form of the movie. To put

Figure 16.5b)
Buchanan & Hemenway Dynamics of spatial juxtapositions

together a movie about architecture is something which even an experienced moviemaker may finish with quite an uneasy feeling. There is no dramatic story to provide thematic continuity as in a conventional feature film.

The theme of the movie may be evident in its style. For example, a movie style can be sympathetic to the theme of rhythm and symmetry. The way to describe the rhythms and symmetries of a classical colonnade on the Parthenon may be to produce a realtime animation in the following way. The camera could point perpendicularly towards the colonnade but move in a direction parallel to it. The continuous movement of the camera would not be broken by edits that may disrupt the continuity of seeing the rhythm of the colonnade. With respect to the architect Gaudi, however, realtime movement in a parallel direction to one of his colonnades at the Sagrada Familia Temple may be of secondary interest. The movement of sunlight may provide a more interesting orientation (Figure 16.5(a)).[11] In the first example, rhythm and symmetry may be important to the way in which the classical column was conceived. Yet, in the second example, the movement of shadows may be a more significant feature of Gaudi's columns at the Sagrada Familia Temple. Developing the stylistic orientation that fits best may be helpful, not just for the purpose of making the movie coherent, but for unravelling the aesthetic nature of the architectural subject. Sensitivity to the aesthetics of movies may reflect or even be used to develop sensitivity to the aesthetics of architecture in motion.

The stylistic orientation of a movie may be evident in the camera work, the composition of scenes and editing. As noted before, Eisenstein might specify the method of making the movie in meticulous pre-production planning, whereas a *cinéma vérité* moviemaker might develop it in the spontaneous process of actually shooting the camera. Filmmaker Ricky Leacock, who was Chairman of the Film–Video Section at MIT, encouraged students to develop a style of moviemaking that responded to the unique problems of making its themes clear. His own style within the *cinéma vérité* school is quite distinct from others within that genre. For example, his camera movements are deliberate and exact, whereas those of D.A. Pennebacker consist of quick wide-angle pans from stationary shot to stationary shot.[12] Yet, some of Leacock's work is characterized by quick camera movements from shot to shot, as when he followed presidential candidate John Kennedy to the podium in the movie *'Primary'*. These varieties in style suggest that there are no ready-made solutions to making the themes of a movie clear. In particular, a solution to an architectural movie may be found by finding a stylistic approach that is sympathetic to the architecture in such a way that it can convey its aesthetic attributes directly, coherently and concisely.

In the process of developing the style of a movie, it is not always clear from the outset (a) what are the most important themes, (b) what are the most important moviemaking production strategies that can provide sufficient material to support those themes, and (c) what are the editing strategies that will make the significance of that material clear. It takes months and sometimes years to find a production solution for a particular movie. Architects typically do not have that many months to develop a design proposal. They therefore might be tempted to make a series of stylistically similar movies for many separate design projects.

Motion picture renderings of architecture could take the form of standard sequences. This would be

Figure 16.5c)
Xi, Das Gupta and Fruet Time lapse of people moving through architectural space

Figure 16.5d)
Burke and Gipstei Transformation of architecture

comparable with the section, plan and elevation drawings made on paper-based media. These conventional drawings are informative about the proportions of spaces and locations of objects within a design proposal, if a little disengaged from its aesthetics. Issues of the draughtsman's style may be relatively unimportant to interpreting the drawings. Yet, these drawings may fail to clarify the inspiration and the selective focus on particular ideas which an architect considered in the design of the building. Such clarification and focus may be more evident within the architect's thumbnail sketches.

Similarly, moviemaking could be used to present the main circulation paths, the key flyovers and cardinal views in a style that does not vary from project to project. A professional camera operator could handle the entire production according to a standard formula of sequences, similar to how a draughtsman is charged with fulfilling the conventional requirements of plan, section and elevation drawings. Alternatively, the architect can choose to pay greater attention to some aspects of moviemaking, even if there is not enough time to make a whole movie. For example, the architect can focus on real-time movement around a building in a way that reveals rhythm and symmetry. Or, the architect can emphasize the important transitions in the geometry of a column. In such cases, discovering the style that is to become the basis of the movie can be used by the architect to speculate on the aesthetics to be developed within a design proposal.

References

Arnheim, R. (1957) *Film As Art.* Los Angeles University of California Press, Los Angeles, CA, p. 7.

Balter, M. (1990) *The Third Man, International Herald Tribune*, Zürich, 13 July, p. 9.

Cocteau, J. (1972) *Beauty and the Beast: Diary of a Film.* Dover Publications, New York, p. 47.

Goodman, N. (1978) *Ways of Worldmaking.* Hackett, Indianapolis, IN.

Goodman, N. (1985) *Languages of Art.* Hackett, Indianapolis, IN. Vol 1 pp. 12–18.

Mark, E. (1990) *Case studies in moviemaking and computer aided design.* In M. McCullough, W.J. Mitchell and P. Purcell (eds), *The Electronic Design Studio.* MIT Press, Cambridge, MA.

Nizhnii, V B. (1979) *Lessons With Eisenstein.* Da Capo Press, New York

Notes

[1] *by William Mitchell during his computer aided design studio review at the Harvard Graduate School of Design, May 1990.*

[2] *I taught a subject called 'Moviemaking and Computer Aided Architectural Design' simultaneously at the MIT School of Architecture and Planning and the Harvard Graduate School of Design, Spring 1990. The Harvard subject was offered in conjunction with a design studio that was taught by Professor William Mitchell. The MIT subject was taught independently from a design studio and focused on the use of moviemaking to examine existing works of architecture.*

[3] *The idea of the medium serving as a 'checkpoint' was suggested by David Gipstein, one of the students involved in this process.*

[4] *Videotape speed is at 30 frames per second. According to Morris Smith, a senior studio instructor at MIT, the medium of moviemaking may overwhelm the architect with too many images. He stated this to me informally during a faculty meeting in April 1989.*

[5] *This will vary from person to person. This figure is based on an informal experiment within an 'Introduction to Moviemaking' subject at MIT, Film/Video Section, October 1981.*

[6] *Burke, S., and Gipstein, D. MIT, School of Architecture and Planning, 1990.*

[7] *Burke, S. MIT, School of Architecture and Planning, 1990, and Ying, C. MIT, School of Architecture and Planning, 1990.*

[8] *Finch, A. and Goore, N. Harvard University, Graduate School of Design, 1990.*

[9] *These figures were produced by (a) Mark, E. MIT, School of Architecture and Planning, 1983; (b) Buchanan, M. and Hemenway, N. MIT, School of Architecture and Planning, 1990, (c) Xi, Lei, Das Gupta, A. and Fruet, G. MIT, School of Architecture and Planning, 1989, (d) Burke, S. and Gipstein, D. MIT, School of Architecture and Planning, 1990, and (e) Shih, J. MIT, School of Architecture and Planning, 1990 (produced at MIT in my subject for William Mitchell's CAD studio at Harvard).*

[10] *Ricky Leacock was my teacher at MIT from 1981 until 1983.*

[11] *This orientation was the focus of 'The Sagrada Familia Videodisc Project', an 'interactive' movie which was based on the work of the architect Gaudi, which I completed with support from the MIT Council for the Arts and Computervision Corporation in 1985.*

[12] *Reference to Leacock's camerawork in the film he directed for the Muncie Indiana PBS Series in 1983, comparing it with D. A. Pennebacker's movie 'Daybreak Express'.*

Figure 16.5e)
Shih Montage on spirit of a design proposal for studio

Integrating Media: a New Venue for Design Techniques

Patrick Purcell
MIT Media Laboratory, Cambridge, MA

Introduction

The role of computers in architecture, and in the design of the built environment generally, has had a long and varied history. Most sources identify over 50 applications for the use of computation in every part of the spectrum of activity spanning the full design process from the first embryonic ideas to the final details of the fully articulated building design. A new conspectus in this field indicates that new technology is significantly adding to this list of design applications. A major factor in this situation has resulted from the way in which a number of previously discrete electronic techniques are coming together to form a new composite technology. In this chapter we look at some of the ways in which this composite technology is generating new applications for design. In particular we consider the human interface issues and associated problems in electronic imaging that form part of these developments.

For example, the development of advanced computer graphics, digital audio and digital video, together with transmission media, has opened up a range of design applications such as electronic image libraries, three-dimensional spatial imaging and design applications using video mail. Also, the intersection of advanced computer animation (Zeltzer *et al.,* 1989) and new forms of gestural modelling (Russo *et al.,* 1990) is providing a new interface to the technology of 'virtual reality' (Purcell, 1990).

One aim of this chapter, then, is to give examples of technology convergence and present some case studies in this area that relate to the design process, as a set of new design facilities. The chapter presents other design-related research that connects the designer's workstation with both telecommunications and optical laser storage technology, giving rise to new visual information systems. The common ground that links all these diverse sets of issues and techniques is called media technology. An example of a research programme of this kind operates in the MIT Media Laboratory (Negroponte, 1985).

This composite new area for research requires its own special academic syllabus, which embraces the very wide spectrum of topics which together make up the interdisciplinary framework of media technology – topics as diverse as signal processing and the principles of musical composition. Basically, media technology is a forum for the advanced study and research of a cluster of previously discrete information technologies, mainly the technologies which touch people directly at the human–computer interface.

The application of this new integrated technology in a variety of topics, such as primary education, movies and television, music (including performance, composition and comprehension), telephony and electronic publishing, design and information display and human and machine vision, forms an important part of the research agenda of the Media Laboratory. The most significant aspects of that research agenda are the many interconnections and collaborations that occur between these aforementioned constituent research groups and projects. As an example, current work in the Spatial Imaging Group, (the title given to synthetic holography research), in addition to the physics and optics of holography, also extensively employs digital modelling, computer graphics and animation techniques (Benton, 1988).

Figure 17.2
A CAD model (the Robie House) being developed on a CAD system for input to a synthetic holographic process

Figure 17.3
Design hardcopy of the future: the CAD model of the Robie House generated as a synthetic hologram from the previous CAD model. (Courtesy MIT Spatial Imaging Group)

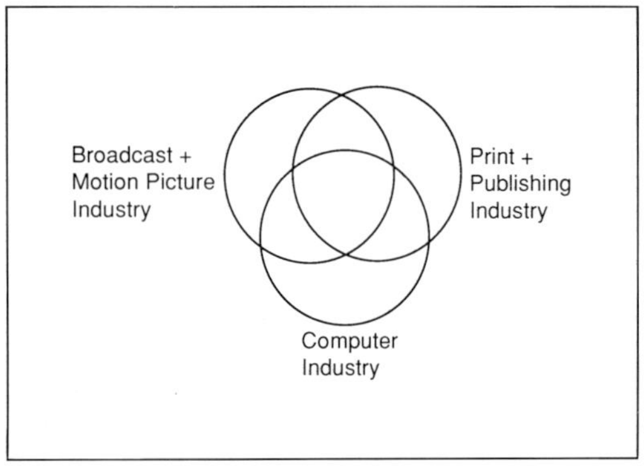

Figure 17.1
Media technology sponsorship represented as a trefoil, portraying the intersection of the media industries (publishing, printing, broadcasting and film) with computers and electronics

Media arts and sciences

The Media Laboratory's academic programme, called 'Media Arts and Sciences', also reflects, by its title, a broadly based syllabus of subjects and techniques, all of which are relevant to the research programme in media technology. The link between teaching and research is complementary, in that, while the topics in the syllabus support the research activity, the new techniques and knowledge being distilled from the research programme continuously update the syllabus.

Many of the disciplines represented in the Media Laboratory's programme, such as holography, digital audio electronic imaging, have traditionally been treated as discrete single topics in university research. The process of invention has occurred in many of these new media as isolated advances, isolated, that is, from concurrent developments in other related technologies. An important mission of the Media Laboratory is to provide a matrix of interrelated technologies as an integrated background or context to these individual advances.

Broad diversity is an attribute of the agencies who form the sponsoring community of the Media Laboratory (Figure 17.1). The sponsors come from computers and electronics, printing, publishing and broadcasting, and in recent years from the telecommunications industry.

The term 'media' has several connotations in its day-to-day usage. One such connotation is that of impersonal one-way channels of communication, with implications of admass taste and low intellectual standards. The mission of the Media Laboratory is to contest these preconceptions. It aims for a new personalized era of media which offers opportunities for individual choice from a rich and varied matrix of options. In the Media Laboratory the term 'media', also conveys an element of mediation – envisaging a technical interface which acts positively and beneficially as a mediating agency between users and an increasingly complex information environment with which those users have to contend. The issue of mediation applies equally, for example, to the children in the 'School of the Future' programme, and to a professional composer in the 'Music and Cognition' programme, both current programmes in the Media Laboratory.

Researchers in media technology are usually impelled by one of two complementary motivations. Motivation may take the form of either an application imperative, fuelled by an interest in one or more of the many areas of application (such as movies, music, animation, or a technical imperative, fuelled by a deep commitment to the technology of media.

Implications for design and designing

The current research agenda in media technology has a number of important implications for the future development of tools and techniques for designing in both the natural environment and the built environment. For example, in the work of the Vision and Modelling Group, the development of complex digital models has obvious application in the form-giving process of design.

In a similar vein, achievements in the Spatial Imaging Group seek to enhance the visualization capabilities of the digital model. In addition to medical imaging and electron microscopy, this programme has generated visually powerful three-dimensional images in both automobile and architectural design (Purcell,

Figure 17.4
The Visible Language Workshop of the MIT Media Laboratory.
(Courtesy Visible Language Workshop MIT)

Figure 17.5
A multi screen CAD system on a single HP advanced graphics workstation.
(Courtesy Visible Language Workshop MIT)

and Plesniak, 1988). The holographic image of the Robie House (Figures 17.2 and 17.3) is generated from a digital model of this house, assembled on a CAD system. In a similar vein, the Visible Language Workshop (Figure 17.4) is using parallel processing technology to simulate very subtle visual effects (such as transparency, translucency and colour diffusion). A further significant thrust of the workshop is the development of knowledge-based techniques to assist the design processes (Figure 17.5) particularly in graphical layout and in multi media information display. This group is also actively involved in the development of interactive systems for image retrieval from local and remote image banks.

The Interactive Cinema Group is investigating the potential of interactive video technology (linked to video disc and CD) to create multi media educational systems, with applications in both the natural and the built environment.

The history of human–computer interaction has been based on a limited set of input–output devices (restricted to the keyboard, mouse, joystick, stylus or light pen). The work of the Advanced Human Interface Group has been directed at augmenting the modes of man–machine interaction using speech, gesture, eye-tracking and touch (Bolt, 1987). The development of speech, gesture and eye-tracking as an integrated set of concurrent processes at the interface has, as its paradigm, the concurrent processes that we find in human-to-human communication (with concurrent speech processing, interpreting of gesture and eye contact). These applications promise the designer radically different forms of interaction with and manipulation of the proposed digital design model (Purcell, 1985).

Visual Information Systems (VIS) are a recent development in imaging technology which seek to do for the world of images and image retrieval what information technology has already done for on-line bibliographies, catalogues and full-text searches (Purcell and Applebaum, 1990). The professions most directly concerned are those for whom the image has primary importance (including, for example, graphic artists, designers, architects and planners) (Figures 17.6 and 17.7).

In terms of hardware, the original aim of the VIS research has been to investigate the potential of combining the optical storage media laser disc, local area networks, the campus cable system and a cluster of videographic workstations as a vehicle for a distributed image retrieval system. The primary outcome of the project is a highly interactive videographic interface, capable of connecting to different visual information systems. At this point, the VIS source images have been based almost entirely on the MIT Rotch Collection. This collection consists of over 300 000 images relating to architecture and planning, graphics, fine art, photography etc. The Rotch Collection is being progressively transferred to electronic media as a college-wide facility accessible by all students (Smith, 1987).

Electronic imaging in design

Investigation of applications of the electronic image has been an area of substantive and varied research, and is possibly the most pervasive topic of enquiry in the Media Laboratory at present. It has a bearing on the work of groups as seemingly diverse as holography, computer animation, the visible language workshop,

Figure 17.6
The VIS. The designer retrieves images from remote electronic image banks.

Figure 17.7
Details of the screen display of the designer's visual information system

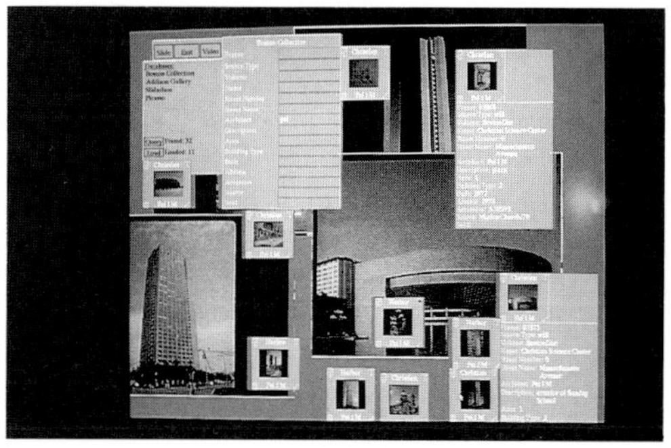

electronic publishing and advanced television (Lippman *et al.*, 1989). Imaging research is a multi faceted topic with many dimensions, addressing issues in image coding, image compression, image transmission, decoding and storage. In a complementary mode, there is a very active research programme in image analysis (in the areas of both machine and human vision).

The applications flowing from this research in digital imaging take the form of 'dial-up' movies, movies in three-dimensional (Bove, 1989), hypermedia journals and holographic video. Digital movies offer new and versatile modes of movie-making, in all its aspects, covering shooting, distribution, and broadcasting. However, the digital format will reveal its full potential as a new form of film and video only when film directors, script writers and editors conceive, script and edit in this new medium, exploiting, for example, its innovative capacity for interaction with the viewer and its multi scenario modes of operation.

The Interactive Cinema Group has a strong commitment to both the content and the innovative form of movies, which brings the insights and professional experience of film-making to this new technology (McKay and Davenport, 1989). Several projects in the Interactive Cinema Group have significant application in both the natural and the built environment: 'The New Orleans Project', an urban planning case study, and 'Elastic Charles', a hypermedia journal of a riverside community (Davenport and Brondmo, 1989).

The premise of the case study 'A City in Transition: New Orleans: 1983–1986' (Davenport, 1987) is that interactive cinema in combination with text could provide insights into the parts played by both citizens and the various professionals concerned with design and urban planning. It deals with the empowerment of people and the processes through which the participating citizenry can effect urban change. It covers many interlocking roles, involved in urban change, including those of planners, architects, developers, local government, and neighbourhood activists. It was edited for both linear presentation and interactive use. The computer-driven laser disc version has been developed as a highly interactive curriculum resource for students of urban planning and political science.

Rather than creating an inflexible scripted experience, course tutors set assignments which prompt the student's exploration of the planning case study on the interactive system. An associated database of the system carries on-demand information about many aspects of the case study. It also provides a facility for recording the student's personal text notes as he or she progresses through the case study.

'Elastic Charles' is a project with twin goals relating to both form and content. In terms of form, the project seeks to explore the concept of a multimedia 'journal' on a PC platform, configured as a Mac II PC with video disc and CD-ROM. In terms of content it deals with the life and times of the Charles River in Massachusetts, in terms of its denizens, its pollution issues, its demographics and ,not least, its physical characteristics. It runs on a 30-minute laser disc with a substantial amount of additional text.

Additionally, it is a test bed for several technical issues; for example, to explore the concept of dynamic links for temporal media. Another interest was to create a system design approach which would result in effective and smooth transitions between the 'Elastic Charles' text and associated images in the video.

A further significant technical innovation in this

Figure 17.8
Details showing MICONS on the interactive learning system screen.
(Courtesy MIT Interactive Cinema Group)

project was the invention of the Micon (movie ICON) – a computer graphic device which shows evidence of making a significant impact on the future development and operation of interactive multimedia systems (Figure 17.8). The micon is, in effect, a low-bandwidth digital motion picture icon. It represents a major advance for the use of micromovies as navigational cues in complex multimedia systems. In this context the micon operates as a four-second loop of motion of a particular scene which the user needs to remember and to return to subsequently.

Conclusion

As we enter the 1990s, it may be timely to consider the prospects of design and designing in the light of prospects for foreseen developments in media technology. The progressive growth and development of the techniques of parallel processing will lead to the application of increasingly powerful computer graphics techniques, such as interactive mapping systems (Figure 17.9), to increasingly detailed digital design of the built environment. The most dramatic of these visualization techniques will be digital holographic video.

Also, we can foresee the development of more sophisticated design systems in the area of multi-modal systems, leading to design scenarios, where the inadequacies of the qwerty keyboard and the joystick give way to human-like interaction speech, in which gesture, touch and gaze all combine to enhance the design process. In a similar vein the implementation of new graphics will offer the designer a vision of CAD 'in the round' in which the designer works within models of the proposed design in full-size virtual space.

The increasing linkage of computers and electronics with telecommunications will bring to the design computer workstation instant access to a range of information services, chief of which will be a new genre of visual information services of particular significance to all design professions.

Acknowledgements

This chapter owes much to the work of many colleagues at MIT and in particular in the MIT Media Laboratory. In terms of the development of the VIS, the contribution of Daniel Applebaum is paramount. Merrill Smith, originator of the Boston Project and erstwhile Head of the MIT Rotch Visual Collection, whose visual resources formed the basis of the visual information systems described in the chapter and whose guidance of the Boston project is bringing electronic image retrieval to the students of MIT, deserves special mention.

The author also greatly appreciates the advice and facilities provided by Muriel Cooper and associates in the MIT Visible Language Workshop. The help and advice provided by Glorianna Davenport and the Interactive Cinema Group is also highly valued, and the ideas and output from this group have made a significant contribution to the substance of this chapter.

Finally the author acknowledges the contribution of many colleagues whose work in this paper and whose spirit of community he has enjoyed since the inception of the MIT Media Laboratory. These include Nicholas Negroponte, Richard Bolt, Andrew Lippman, Walter Bender, Marvin Minsky, Michael Bove, Chris Schmandt, Seymour Papert, Stephen Benton and David Zeltzer.

Figure 17.9
Very high resolution composite electronic image with interactive mapping applications. Each frame is composed of 10 million picture elements.
(Courtesy: MIT Visible Language Workshop)

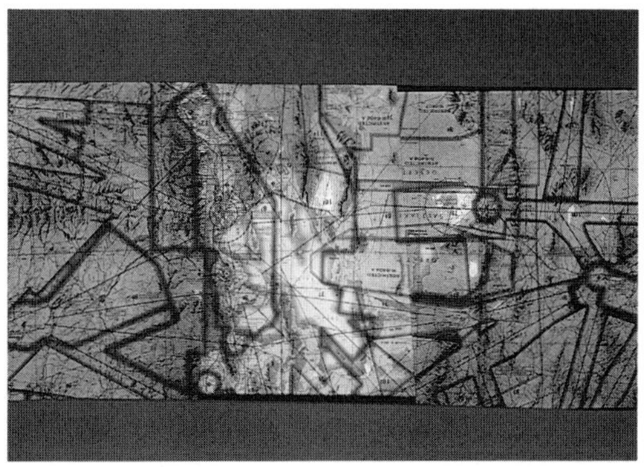

References

Benton, S.A. (1988) The principles of reflection holographic stereograms. In T.H. Jeonng (ed.), *Proceedings of the 3rd Annual Symposium on Display Holography,* Lake Forrest College, Illinois, July.

Bolt, R.A. (1987) The integrated multi-modal interface. *The Information and Communications Engineer,* 70(11), 2017–25.

Bove, B.M. (1989) Pictorial Applications for range sensing cameras. *SPIE Journal* 901.

Davenport, G. (1987) A city in transition: New Orleans 1983–1986. *Proceedings of the International Congress for Design & Planning Theory,* American Society of Mechanical Engineers, Washington, DC.

Davenport, G. and Brondmo, H.P. (1989) Creating and Viewing the Elastic Charles – a Hypermedia Journal. MIT Media Lab. Paper, Massachusetts Institute of Technology, Cambridge, MA.

Lippman, A., Girod, B. and Solomon, R.J. (1989) Extensible television: views from MIT. MIT Media Lab. Paper, Massachusetts Institute of Technology, Cambridge, MA.

McKay, W.E. and Davenport, G. (1989) Virtual video editing in interactive multi-media applications. *Communications of the ACM,* 32(7).

Negroponte, N. (1985) What is the media lab? MIT Media Lab. Paper, Massachusetts Institute of Technology, Cambridge, MA.

Purcell, P.A. (1985) Beyond the keyboard: gestural input to interactive systems. *BCS Computer Bulleting,* 1(3), 3–5.

Purcell, P.A. (1990) Interfacing to virtual reality. *Proceedings of Computer Graphics '90.* Blenheim-Online, London.

Purcell, P.A. and Applebaum, D.I. (1990) Light table: interface to visual information systems. In P.A. Purcell *et al.* (eds) *Electronic Design Studio.* MIT Press, Cambridge, MA.

Purcell, P.A. and Plesniak, W. (1988) Computer imagery in spatial imaging. *BCS Computer Bulletin,* 4(2).

Russo, M., Flowers, W., Tadros, A. and Zeltzer, D. (1990) Implementation of a three degree of freedom motor/brake hybrid force output device for virtual environment control tasks. Technical memo, Massachusetts Institute of Technology, Cambridge, MA.

Smith, M.W. (1987) The Boston Project. Internal paper, Department of Architecture, Massachusetts Institute of Technology, Cambridge, MA.

Zeltzer, D., Pieper, S. and Sturman, D. (1989) An integrated graphical simulation platform. MIT Media Lab. Paper, Massachusetts Institute of Technology, Cambridge, MA.

The Next Ten Years

Paul Richens
The Martin Centre, Department of Architecture,
University of Cambridge

Introduction

Computing for architects has become a reality within the last decade, although the seeds were sown at least ten years earlier. Useful work started in the early 1970s with the advent of the storage tube graphic display from Tektronix, and was boosted by the arrival of effective minicomputers such as the PDP-11 and the Prime 300.

During the 1970s a number of ambitious software projects were commissioned by public sector bodies. The OXSYS and HARNESS projects were concerned with hospitals and CEDAR was concerned with schools and Post Office workshops; the work done at the Edinburgh Architectural Research Unit for the Scottish Special Housing Association was concerned with 'Rat-Trad' public-sector housing. Others were concerned with schools, and RUCAPS was developed for the construction of Riyadh University.

These projects had a number of things in common. They were commissioned by public bodies who had building programmes managed by in-house architects. These bodies designed buildings for their own occupation and use. They were prepared (at least in principle) to spend more on design and construction in order to reduce cost in use. They were interested in using computers as part of a much broader programme aimed at improving the efficiency of building design, construction and use. Prefabrication, system building, dimensional co-ordination and serial tendering were all part of the programme, and considerably affected the kind of software that was written.

Some of the projects (such as OXSYS) covered a large part of the building process – including briefing, planning, evaluation of alternatives, cost planning, heating, lighting, ventilation, structural design, the detailing of a building in terms of a predetermined 'kit of parts', production documentation and on to commissioning. HARNESS was particularly concerned with the strategic planning of very complex buildings, but other projects tended to concentrate on detailing – on the realization of a design using simplified three-dimensional modelling (sometimes called two and a half dimensional, or box-geometry). With the exception of RUCAPS, none of these systems achieved very wide use, and even now, their ambitious objectives have hardly been achieved.

It is often said of the computer business that most of the progress has come from improvements in hardware, which tend to be exploited very rapidly. Software innovation is rare, and, when it does occur, seems to take 10 or 12 years to become commonplace.

One example is the relational database, first proposed by Codd in 1970 but which did not become the norm until the late 1980s. Kernighan and Ritchie published the C language specification in 1978. UNIX dates from the same period. Most significant of all was the SmallTalk project at Xerox Parc, which pioneered object-oriented programming, bit-mapped raster graphics, the mouse, windows, pop-up menus, scroll bars and the philosophy of a model-less direct-manipulation user interface. Only now is their approach becoming the standard.

This is being rather unfair to the software industry. Most of the phenomenal growth in hardware capacity and performance over the last 30 years can be attributed to improvements in the manufacturing process. The logical design of computers has hardly changed since the time of von Neumann.

The last ten years

The architectural systems of the 1970s did not pay much attention to straightforward draughting. In theory they eliminated the need for it by completely automating the production of documents. By 1980 the naivety of this approach was obvious, and systems aimed solely and simply at draughting became the norm. An example is GDS, which was designed as a successor to OXSYS and is now the most widely used 'big' system among UK architects. When it was released it was aimed purely at two-dimensional draughting; its original functionality is broadly comparable with that of ClarisCAD, released for the Macintosh nine years later – although GDS was harder to use, needed a special environment and cost at least 20 times as much. MEDUSA is another example from that time. In addition, systems from Computervision and Intergraph, originally written for other applications, began to appear in architectural offices. These draughting systems were expensive and appealed only to the more adventurous of the larger practices (over 30 people). They were also, by modern standards, very unfriendly.

Meanwhile, a dramatic revolution in hardware was taking place, leading to the establishment of a new industry supplying personal desktop micro computers. Key events in the next few years include the following.

1980 GDS launched on Prime 400 computers. Meanwhile Apple is having a field-day with the Apple II, and goes public. A project at Microsoft called QDOS (quick and dirty operating system) should have warned the world about what was coming next.

1981 IBM announces the personal computer (PC), with MS-DOS occupying 4 K of memory. The Xerox Star workstation brings the SmallTalk work to a wider audience, but does not take off.

1982 Visicorp, the proprietors of VisiCalc, the original spreadsheet program, becomes the world's largest software company. A clutch of ill-fated CP/M machines launched (Osborne 'portables', DECMates). First release of AutoCAD.

1983 PC reaches the UK. Lotus launches 1-2-3, and overtakes VisiCalc in four months. AutoCAD offers dimensioning at extra cost.

1984 Apple launches the Macintosh, embodying the user interface philosophy of SmallTalk, but without much of the underlying software engineering.

1985 Laser printers appear, and desktop publishing is born.

1986 Compaq produces a 386-based PC, and Apple introduces the Macintosh II. CAD on a desktop computer becomes realistic.

After that, the second half of the decade was quite uneventful. There was a steady stream of hardware improvements (processor speed, larger memories and discs), the Macintosh initiative was strenuously imitated (MS-Windows, X-Windows, Presentation Manager) and MS-DOS looked more and more worn-out. This triggered the OS/2 initiative from IBM, and what we may eventually come to term the 'UNIX wars' between competing groups of would-be standardizers.

The architectural draughting systems did not stay static; indeed, they all seem to follow a similar path. Over ten years, a typical sequence of development would be as follows:

- First release as a pure two-dimensional draughting system.
- Second release: improved circle construction, line-styles and snapping, but fundamental philosophy unchanged.
- Ability to combine fragments of several drawings to make one composite plot.
- User-defined non-graphical attributes, to allow schedules to be derived from drawings. Programming language so that users can write their own commands, very necessary for data collection.
- Application modules added (e.g. reinforced concrete detailing, piping and ducting).
- Simple three-dimensional forms (extruded shapes and solids of revolution), and elementary rendering programming giving hidden-line or cosine-shaded views.
- Multiple access: allows members of a team to work on the same project at the same time without conflict and with the ability to see each others' changes.
- Superior rendering using smooth shading and shadow casting.
- Solid modelling for three-dimensional work facilitates the construction of arbitrarily complex objects by combining simpler ones or using one to cut away part of another.
- Assembly modelling to handle very large numbers of three-dimensional solid objects. Connection to a remote relational database.

This history gives a reasonable indication of what you can expect to find inside a mature architecturally oriented system such as Intergraph or GDS. AutoCAD (Release 10) has reached stage 6, and most Macintosh systems are at about stage 2. The full history involves around ten years of accretion, often somewhat at cross-purposes with the original philosophy. So the older systems are relatively complete, but tend to be inconsistent and confusing to use.

The position today

According to the most recent survey (RIBA Market Research Unit, 1989) the position now is as follows: 65% of architectural offices have some sort of computer; 24% use a computer for draughting; 17% also do three-dimensional modelling or visualisation; 12% have a Macintosh; 9% use AutoCAD; 5% use a Macintosh for CAD; 1% use GDS (the leading 'big' system). But the uptake is not uniform (Figure 18.1). The largest practices are almost all equipped with some sort of computer, and two-thirds of them use CAD. The smallest firms (with one or two people) are three times as numerous, but only half have a computer and only one in ten use CAD.

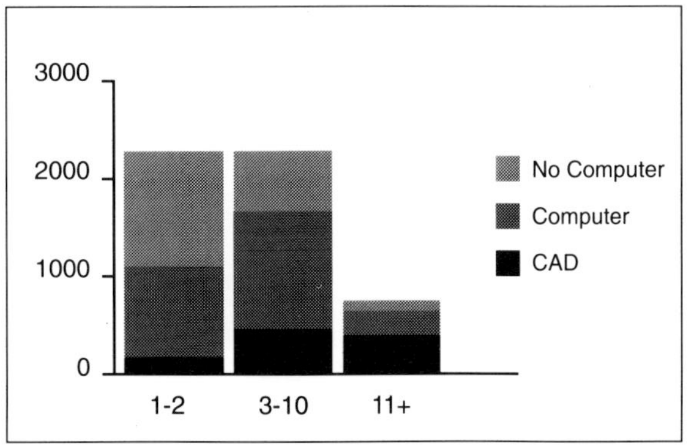

Figure 18.1
Histogram of practices by size (number of non-clerical staff), showing the proportion that uses computing

It is not quite fair to deduce from this that a 'quarter of architects use CAD'. A quarter of practices do, but this figure gives undue emphasis to the large numbers of very small practices. Figure 18.2 shows the same information but this time using 'staff employed' rather than 'number of practices' for the vertical axis.

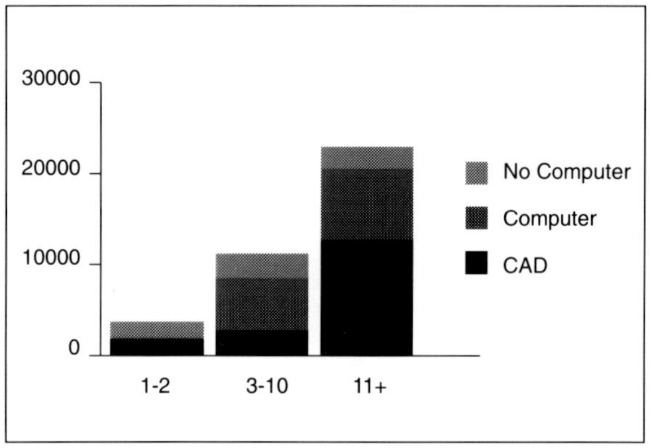

Figure 18.2
Numbers of (non-clerical) staff employed in small, medium and large practices, showing their exposure to computers

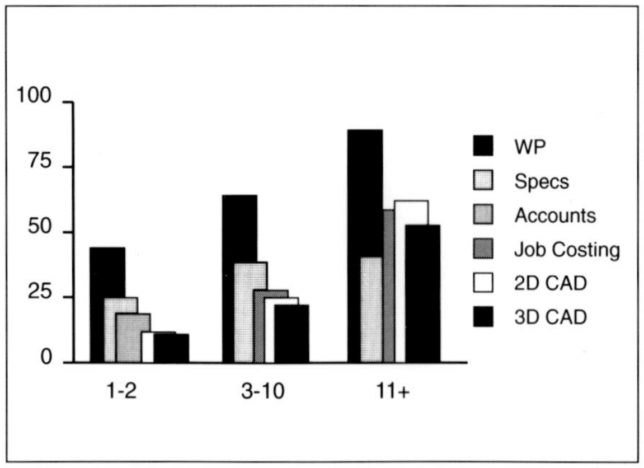

Figure 18.3
Percentages of practices (of various sizes) that make use of specific applications of computers

This figure makes it very clear that, despite the fact that over 40% of practices are very small, 60% of the people are employed in the largest practices and only 8% in the smallest. So perhaps conditions in the larger firms are more important. We can see that 45% of technical staff work for firms that use CAD. What we cannot obtain from current statistics is the number of staff who are computer literate, and the number who use CAD and other applications in their daily work.

As Figure 18.3 shows, it is a mistake to assume that CAD is the only application of computers in architecture. Specification writing and job-costing are even more popular. A very few firms (under 5%) do structural or environmental calculations on a computer. Those that do are likely to use a spreadsheet of their own devising. Many job-costing and time-sheet analysers are also based on spreadsheets.

One interesting sidelight thrown up by Figure 18.3 concerns the relative popularity of three-dimensional and two-dimensional CAD. The larger firms report a greater uptake of two-dimensional draughting than of three-dimensional, whereas the one to two person firms use three-dimensional and two-dimensional CAD equally. When we look at the software employed for CAD we see that an overwhelming 34% use AutoCAD. The next most popular (with 4% of the market) are GDS and MacDraw/MacDraft, which are at opposite ends of the scale in so far as complexity and functionality are concerned. (These figures pre-date the successful introduction of PC and Macintosh editions of Intergraph's Microstation. The dominance of AutoCAD is proving discouraging to some of the larger vendors, who are 'de-emphasizing' architecture and looking for new markets in facilities management or geographical information systems.

It would seem now that the largest practices (especially those that took up CAD in the early 1980s) are most likely to have one of the 'big' systems such as GDS, Sonata or Intergraph, running on a shared super-minicomputer for the older systems or a network of high-performance workstations for the more recent. Other firms are more likely to use a micro-system, typically AutoCAD running on a high-performance PC, with a fraction of around 5% using a Macintosh. A growing number of firms use more than one system.

The future of established CAD systems

If we compare systems at opposite ends of the scale, i.e. a big integrated system as opposed to a Macintosh with a suitable collection of programs, we find that their capabilities are largely complementary. The strengths of one are the weaknesses of the other. The Macintosh solution is cheaper, but the big system has distinctly higher performance and capacity. The Macintosh offers a diversity of software for CAD and many other functions, whereas a specialized workstation will probably run only the one CAD package and little or no 'personal productivity' software. On the other hand, the big system will offer an effective network and the ability for members of a project team to share files and access them simultaneously.

The most striking difference is in the user interface. The Macintosh offers a mouse-driven graphical direct-manipulation interface which is easy to learn by exploration. The big system (if it is of any age) will have a command language interface thinly disguised by badly behaved menus backed up by voluminous and difficult manuals, and will require training courses and specialist users. On the other hand, the command language interface will be extensively customizable – expert users or their suppliers can rearrange menus and add specialist commands, something which is rarely possible on the Macintosh. This ability is important when and graphical data are to be linked, which is necessary if the CAD system is to produce anything more than drawings. Again, this is common on the big systems but rare on the Macintosh.

The Macintosh is well organized to handle raster as well as vector, data which is unusual in the big systems. It is much better adapted for desktop publishing activities, e.g. the production of brochures, let alone multimedia presentations.

This leaves us with the core activities of draughting, modelling and rendering. Most two-dimensional needs can be met more easily on the Macintosh, unless very large drawings or multiple access are needed. Macintosh three-dimensional systems are good for 'freehand' modelling of small projects, but are rather simplistic. Good renderings of simple scenes can be obtained if you choose your software carefully—a number of popular programs are very unreliable (Richens, 1990). Precision modelling of complicated shapes, the assembly of models with thousands of elements and the rendering of huge scenes require the computational power and sophisticated functionality of a larger system.

AutoCAD is somewhere in the middle. Conceptually it is more akin to the older and larger systems, although reduced in scope to fit the smaller machines. It has a command-driven interface, supplemented by poor menus, but is readily customized and has some capability for data linkage. Its two-dimensional functionality is good, although its three-dimensional functionality is weak (but much improved in Release 11), it does not understand rasterdata and it is not geared to multiple access over a network. But it is affordable and very popular, which brings considerable advantages of its own.

The next few years will see players at each point on the spectrum develop their own strengths and attempt to rectify their weaknesses by emulating their rivals. The Macintosh community will pursue its strength in user interfaces by dealing with the problems of three-dimensional modelling and viewing, and with data linkage. There is still plenty of room for improvement in the handling of two dimensional draughting, as the release of Vellum (Newell, 1989) has shown. The 'intelligent cursor', which eliminates the switching of snap modes (and most temporary construction lines), is sure to be widely imitated (see, for example, the most recent issues of ClarisCAD and MiniCAD). Solid modelling, rendering, constraint modelling and topological modelling will become available as soon as (probably sooner than) the requisite processing power is available. Customization and user programming are perhaps most remote from the current Macintosh philosophy. HyperCard was a bold approach to the problem, but (despite a lot of early excitement) has not produced the anticipated revolution.

The vendors of big systems will adapt to rather less expensive hardware (such as UNIX workstations based on Sparc or Intel 486 chips) and will attempt to improve their user interfaces, which will not be easy.

Hardware

As in the past, improvements in hardware are much more certain than those in software, where so much of the effort goes into mutual catching-up (and adapting to new hardware) rather than into fundamental innovation.

The phenomenal rate of improvement in processors will continue unabated. The density of microcircuits doubles every year, and the cost-to-performance ratio halves every 18-24 months. A good deal of this new power will be devoted to improving user interfaces and interactivity.

Networks and file servers will come into their own in the microcomputer world. The advantages of central secure filing are too great to ignore. In fact, a number of techniques perfected in minicomputers ten or more years ago, ignored at the time of QDOS, are due to be reinvented for PCs. To someone used to UNIX or VMS, microcomputer operating systems such as DOS or the Macintosh Toolbox seem chaotically under-engineered. Lack of power is no longer an excuse, as a current PC considerably outperforms the original minicomputers. Macintoshes use the same processor chips as Suns and Apollos.

Apart from shared filing, the most important innovations are to do with multi-tasking – the running of several programs at the same time, without mutual interference. Memory protection prevents one application from corrupting another, or the operating system, and ensures that when a task is finished the memory it uses is freed. Multi-tasking allows several applications to run at the same time (not merely to be co-resident). Virtual memory allows the total size of applications to exceed the available random access memory (RAM), by swapping parts of it to the hard disc. Instead of messages saying 'Insufficient space for application' things work as they should, but a trifle more slowly. It is a major liberator of applications, as they can employ large amounts of memory without worrying about the consequences. It is particularly valuable for large-scale three-dimensional work, where hundreds of megabytes may be needed for rendering a complicated scene. Long-term storage technology is also improving by leaps and bounds. There are a number of very promising technologies, both optical and magnetic. In five years' time the upper limit for disc storage on a workstation will be around 10 gigabytes; slower storage based on digital audio tape technology could provide thousands of gigabytes in a very small volume.

When high-definition television becomes common every home will be equipped with a monitor with roughly twice the resolution of the average present-day desktop computer. The same 1000-line standard will be the inexpensive norm for computers. Higher-performance displays will achieve finer quality by improving the pixel density from around 60 to 120 dpi. Small colour liquid crystal display screens will certainly be common on portable computers, and if large-screen flat-panel displays fail to appear it will not be for want of effort in the Japanese research laboratories.

Image capture devices such as colour scanners (at over 300 dpi) and video frame-grabbers will be commonplace. So will optical character recognition programs that will be able to convert scanned print into editable (machine-readable as we say today) text files. On the output side, the norm will be for a workstation to be equipped with a 300 dpi colour printer (working on both sides of plain paper), whereas a network will commonly share a 1000 dpi device. Digital signal processing hardware will commonly be used to capture, filter and digitize images, sound and other sensory input. Synthetic speech will become as ubiquitous as Muzak.

The effect of these changes in input, display and storage will be dramatic. No longer will computers be restricted to text and crude images. It will be as natural to file a high-resolution colour image, a video clip or a sound-bite as it is now to file a typed document. They will be as easily transmissible as a fax message. Multimedia 'soft publication' will become a routine way of distributing information, first on optical media and later by satellite broadcasting. Digital photo retouching, video editing, sound editing, animation and production will be offered as consumer products.

Less likely changes

Despite many years of development, parallel processing is likely to remain restricted to specialist applications. The programming techniques needed are so different (and the inertia in software development so high), that massively parallel machines are not likely to be employed for everyday purposes. However, plug-in transputer arrays for rendering, finite-element analysis and the simulation of heat and light flow can already be seen in the laboratory, and may reach the market.

Opinions are divided on the future of man-machine interaction. It is quite possible that the mouse and qwerty keyboard driving a Mac-style direct-manipulation graphical interface represents a sort of plateau, and will become as standard as the controls of an automobile. Limited voice control is certain, but it is not likely to become the universal mode of interaction. The most likely alternative is touch input using a stylus on a pressure-sensitive screen, combining pointing with gestures (drawing symbols). Although this would seem retrograde in the West, it is a promising solution to the problem that the Japanese still face in communicating Kanji characters. By far the most intriguing possibility is that of neural networks which seem to offer a novel (and far more plausible) approach to the problems that have been baffling the artificial intelligence community for decades. However, development is at an early stage, the concept is surrounded by a nebula of hype and black magic, and it is far too soon to be certain what the potential and limitations of the approach will be.

A neural net consists of several arrays of simple processing elements (neurones), arranged in layers. The first layer is some sort of sensor—it could be the bit map representing a raster image. Each neurone on a higher layer is connected to several cells on the layer below. Each interconnection has a variable 'weighting factor' applied to it; the output of a neurone is simply some sort of weighted average of its inputs. The outputs of the uppermost layer provide the answers.

A neural network is not programmed in any conventional sense – instead it is trained to recognize patterns by showing it examples and adjusting the weights of the interconnections so that the desired output is obtained. For example, raster images of letters of the alphabet (in a variety of styles) could be placed in the input layer, and the weights adjusted so that a different cell in the output layer fires for each one. Successful training algorithms have already been developed. One of the most intriguing does not require the trainer to define the required output. The network itself learns to discriminate different inputs (pictures of different human faces, for example). A trained network has some remarkable abilities. For example, given a badly formed or incomplete letter, it can successfully classify it, and even fill in the gaps. If it is given two overlapping letters, it can provide a double output from the uppermost layer. The network itself is fault tolerant; a few dead cells will not make much difference to the outcome.

The black magic in neural networks lies partly in the training procedure, although this is becoming well understood. So far, little is known about how to design the architecture of the network – the number of layers, the patterns of interconnection, the kind of averaging function that each cell performs.

The strength of neural networks is in recognizing signals in noisy and cluttered surroundings. They can recognize different kinds of ships from sonar signals, as well as processing images. They can perform diagnostic tasks currently undertaken by expert systems, such as recognizing good and bad credit risks among would-be borrowers from a bank. The difference is that no expert is needed to formulate the rules, just sufficient historical data to train the network. The application to speech recognition is obvious.

Currently, neural networks are simulated on an ordinary computer, at least during training. For faster response, a transputer array can be used. Ultimately they will be built from special purpose circuits, giving instantaneous response. They may prove as revolutionary as the computer itself.

Architectural CAD

The typical CAD system today is a general purpose graphical system. It understands lines and circles, text, and perhaps raster images. In some cases it also understands three-dimensional forms – planes, surfaces and solids. It does not know anything about buildings or architecture; it has low intelligence but is highly flexible. The same software is equally adept at drawing a building, a landscape or a ship.

A few systems (e.g. ArchiCAD, (Bojár, 1989) work on a different level. The elements they deal with are slabs and walls, doors and windows and roofs and rooflights. This is more intelligent (to an architect), but less flexible. There will be a general purpose object intended for furniture and equipment, but how about columns, beams, rafters, pipes, ducts, pads, piles and all the hundreds of other elements that might occur in a building? In general it is harder to deal with them than in the general purpose system.

Yet another approach (which is rare in the market) would treat buildings as sculptural volumes, know about their subdivision into floors and zones, and know the location of cores and circulation. As an extra it might deal with occupants – people, plant and processes. This is a more functional model than the other two, and hard to combine with them. Yet it would be better while a building concept is being formed, and for cost planning and environmental analysis.

There is no doubt that all three approaches have some validity; the problem for the CAD system designer is how to combine them so as to achieve both flexibility and intelligence without excessive complexity. Some well-informed opinion would regard this as impossible, but we are sure to see attempts.

The most likely route is to construct a system in layers, using the principles of object oriented programming. This treats the world as composed of a hierarchy of objects, with each level being more specialized and intelligent. At the root is a general purpose object, from which ascend user interface objects such as windows, icons and menus, process objects such as commands and UNDO stacks and the familiar graphical objects of the general purpose CAD system.

Intelligent building objects (like slabs and walls), are at a higher level, and know how to represent themselves in the more primitive terms of graphical objects in two-dimensional or three-dimensions, or even as text. They also contain their own rules for intelligent behaviour, for example a window knows that it must make an appropriate opening in a wall and a wall knows that it must extend upwards to the ceiling or to the structural slab. To retain generality it will be essential that these rules be easy to formulate and change according to the needs of a project. This requires the use of non-procedural techniques derived from the theory of logic programming and intelligent knowledge-based systems.

The storage of a model constructed like this, in such a way that it is accessible to many different applications, presents a formidable problem. The familiar Macintosh techniques of clipboard, scrapbook and import and export procedures will not be adequate, and anyway cannot be used for substantial models. Current wisdom would suggest a database to isolate the data from its applications and allow for parallel access from all members of the team. However, relational databases are not a good match with the object-oriented philosophy, and something new will be needed. There is some hope that current research into entity modelling, engineering databases and object-oriented databases will converge into a post-relational solution.

If the objects in a system have variable intelligent behaviour, then the way that a designer interacts with them will be similarly variable. Thus the user interface must be customizable. The techniques pioneered in HyperCard (Atkinson, 1989) give a reasonable model of how the 'look' of a user interface might be modified, but there is still no satisfactory way of dealing with the 'feel' – the resulting behaviour of the interface and the objects it controls – other than a textual programming language.

In summary, tomorrow's CAD systems (certainly those that are under development now) will be based on object-oriented programming, rules and hypermedia. In the longer term we are likely to see a new approach to databases and a visual approach to programming.

Who is to benefit?

It is unwise to focus too closely on architecture. If we step back a little we see that the most solidly computerized people in the construction industry are the quantity surveyors. Measurement, estimating and construction planning are all major areas of computer application, at least as important as draughting and modelling. But they are all separate. So are structural design and environmental simulation.

Organizations which undertake a number of these activities, and with a few years' experience of elementary CAD, are eager to build bridges between these islands of computing. The CAD industry will respond to their demands by developing products which are easier to interconnect and to customize for the needs of a particular business. Many of the concepts pioneered in the 1970s are being resuscitated, not this time by public sector bodies that design buildings for their own use, but by private companies that integrate design with construction. This already happens on a very large scale in Japan, and there are plenty of examples nearer home.

There was a hope a few years ago that computers would revitalize the small architectural practice. The gain in 'personal productivity' would allow it to compete effectively against better resourced large practices, and the design-construct conglomerates. Indeed we can see today a two-tier CAD market comprising the small-scale systems (exemplified by the Macintosh), aimed at the individual practitioner, and the large networked systems aimed at the needs of an organization. But in the long term, the competitive advantage that information technology offers to a vertically integrated design and construction organization is so great that the isolated practitioner is going to find it difficult to survive.

References

Atkinson, B. (1989) *Hypercard.* Apple Computer Inc.

Boján, G. (1989) *ArchiCAD.* Graphisoft.

Newell, M. (1989) *Vellum.* Ashlar Inc.

RIBA Market Research Unit (1989) *Survey of Computer Usage.* RIBA, London.

Richens, P. (1990) *MicroCAD Software Evaluated.* Construction Industry Computing Association, Cambridge.